Corpus Linguistics in North America

Corpus Linguistics in North America

Selections from the 1999 Symposium

Edited by Rita C. Simpson and John M. Swales

Ann Arbor
THE UNIVERSITY OF MICHIGAN PRESS

Copyright © by the University of Michigan 2001
All rights reserved
Published in the United States of America by
The University of Michigan Press
Manufactured in the United States of America
⊗ Printed on acid-free paper
2004   2003   2002   2001   4   3   2   1

A CIP catalog record for this book is available from the British Library.

Library of Congress Cataloging-in-Publication Data

Corpus linguistics in North America : selections from the 1999
    symposium
    / edited by Rita C. Simpson and John M. Swales.
        p.   cm.
    With one exception, the chapters are revisions or expansions of
papers or workshops given at a 1999 three-day symposium held at the
University of Michigan's English Language Institute.
    Includes bibliographical references and index.
    ISBN 0-472-09762-8 (cloth : alk. paper) — ISBN 0-472-06762-1
(paper : alk. paper)
    1. Computational linguistics—Congresses. 2.
Linguistics—Methodology—Congresses. I. Simpson, Rita C. II.
Swales, John.
P98.C6378   2001
410'.285—dc21   00-12728

Contents

Introduction: North American Perspectives on Corpus Linguistics at the Millennium

Rita C. Simpson and John M. Swales
University of Michigan

Corpus linguistics is essentially a technology, but like many technologies, it may have, at least potentially, considerable consequences. After all, the telescope transformed astronomy, the X-ray machine radicalized medicine, the tape recorder impelled the advance of sociolinguistics and the study of oral discourse, the video recorder advanced the study of small-group interactions, and the spectrograph (and similar devices) consolidated the development of instrumental phonetics. Corpus linguistics technology requires a computer that can store a collection of text files (the **corpus**) and then apply software to those files to produce frequency lists, lists of key words, and, most importantly, strings of words showing which words co-occur (or **collocate**) with others. The text files in a corpus may consist entirely of written texts (as in the Helsinki Corpus of English Texts), entirely of transcriptions of speech (as in MICASE—the Michigan Corpus of Academic spoken English), or of both (as in the Bank of English).[1] These corpora are typically constructed on certain principles that lead to appropriate sampling, and they can vary greatly in size. The Bank of English corpus, an earlier stage of which underpinned the important corpus-based *COBUILD English Language Dictionary*,[2] is huge and, at the time of writing, rapidly approaching 400 million words; small specialized corpora, especially those devoted to single genres, such as research articles or university lectures, can be orders of magnitude smaller. The pros and cons of large diffuse corpora and small narrow ones is a matter of current debate.

The range of corpus-based research currently taking place is both wide and growing, and this small volume does not attempt to cover all of it; instead, we have focused here on work that is descriptive of languages (mostly English, but also French and Spanish), often with direct or indirect applied pedagogical purposes. This approach, we believe, provides a certain coherence to the collection, although at the cost of excluding certain contemporary initiatives and activities. For example, no chapters here make use of the Linguistic Data Consortium's corpora for the study of American dialects, and no contribution here utilizes the pioneering CHILDES database designed for the study of child language acquisition.[3] Also excluded here is the use of corpora in connectionist approaches to acquiring languages[4] and in natural language processing.[5]

From a more global perspective, many of the developments in corpus linguistics over the last 15 years or so are due to the work of European scholars, with particularly active groups in the United Kingdom and Scandinavia. Despite the work of Douglas Biber at Northern Arizona University, Michael Barlow at Rice University, and important corporist groups at the University of California, Santa Barbara, and the University of Pennsylvania, North America has generally lagged behind. For many years now, for example, the Europeans have had several annual or biennial conferences on corpus linguistics, under such acronyms as ICAME (International Computer Archive of Modern English) and TALC (Teaching and Language Corpora). In North America, the first national symposium devoted to this kind of linguistics was held at the University of Michigan in May 1999, and selected and revised papers from this event form the basis of the current volume.

The reasons for the current greater European interest in this area are complex and interesting. The powerful role of theoretical linguistics in the United States, under the equally powerful influence of Noam Chomsky, has privileged a certain link between language and cognition, in which the focus has been on language structure rather than language use, and for which exemplification has relied more on introspection than on attested or authentic data. On the other hand, in much of Europe, especially in northern Europe, the prime link for linguists has been that between language and social life, and in consequence there has been greater interest in usage, in the co-occurrence of certain vocabulary items with certain grammatical forms, and in an accounting for linguistic expressions that incorporates social, ideological, and emotional factors as well as purely cognitive ones. On a more practical level, the multiplicity of languages in Europe, particularly within the European Union, has given corpus linguistics an additional impetus because of the roles it can play in translation, translation studies, and comparative and contrastive linguistics. Even more practically, there has also been substantial financial backing for corpus developments in Europe, coming from major educational publishers, such as Collins, Longman, and Cambridge and Oxford University Presses. These publishing houses have been able to fund or cofund initiatives that have led to important developments in dictionaries, in the teaching of vocabulary (such as McCarthy, O'Dell, and Shaw's widely admired work for nonnative speakers of English), and for grammar, as best exemplified by the new corpus-based 1,200-page *Longman Grammar of Spoken and Written English* (1999).[6]

That said, the United States has a well-attested capacity for playing catch-up, as we saw in space in the post-*Sputnik* era, and as we have seen over the last decade in the U.S. automobile industry. We hope this collection will play its smaller part in a comparable process, working alongside other developments, such as the rapid growth in digital library services at major American universities. We see corpus linguistics as not only expanding our understanding of linguistic phenomena but also becoming an increasingly powerful pedagogical tool for both students of linguistics and learners of languages. For the latter, there are intriguing possibilities of **data-driven learning** whereby learners use **concordance programs,** such as MonoConc or Wordsmith Tools, to explore for themselves patterns in their target foreign languages, as well as more traditional utilizations by instructors and materials writers.[7]

At this juncture, we offer two brief illustrations of how corpus linguistics works. The first is pedagogical and thus follows on from the previous paragraph. It is well known that many learners of English as a second language (ESL), even those at an advanced level, have difficulty with the *to* + verb + *-ing* structure as most obviously represented by phrases like "I am looking forward to seeing you next week." This structure tends to be counterintuitive for nonnative speakers of English, who have likely only been taught the patterns "I remembered to set my alarm clock" or "I remembered setting my alarm clock" (see Hongyin Tao's "Discovering the Usual with Corpora" in part 2). The main problem for ESL instructors is coming up with examples of the *to* + verb + *-ing* structure, and here a corpus plus concordancing software can quickly come to the rescue. We ask the computer to search for all strings containing the structure "to *ing," where the asterisk stands for any letter or letters preceding *-ing*. This request will, in fact, produce items that we do not want, such as "to sing" and "to bring," but it will also produce the following usages (all taken from MICASE, with minor editing in some cases):

1. it really opened my eyes to the idea that there could be more than one *approach to doing* my job.
2. how good this is gonna taste when you *get around to eating* it
3. or if it was really an *aversion to seeing and performing* surgeries at that time
4. they have real bottlenecks when it *comes to being* dispersed
5. we are deeply *committed to supporting* the library system and the museums

The instructor now has a quickly available bank of examples from which she or he can adapt and derive teaching materials.

This applied example is relatively straightforward, but using corpora for general linguistic purposes is not. It is becoming increasingly clear, we believe, that intuitions play a major role in deciding what might be interesting, and even then there is much trial and error involved. Absent effective pragmatic **parsers** or **taggers,** the investigator has to work from small-stretch surface forms and then try to incorporate these into some bigger picture—a procedure that is the direct opposite to most approaches to text and discourse analysis. Although there have been some important corpus-based contributions to our understanding of English, such as McCarthy and Carter's 1997 article,[8] progress has been somewhat slower than anticipated.

To illustrate these complexities, we draw on an interesting observation made by Stubbs, who noted that in spoken British English, surface use of phrases like "so to speak" or, more surprisingly, of the verb *call* had a tendency to show detachment by the speaker for hedging and/or ironic purposes.[9] We began to explore the extent to which Stubbs's observation holds true for our corpus of American academic speech (MICASE). As it turned out, in an early stage of MICASE (350,000 words), we could identify a total of only 42 tokens of surface markers of detachment. Five of the most common phrases are italicized in the examples that follow:

 6. we have the luxury, *if you will,* to play with crossing boundaries
 7. in terms of the demise, *so to speak* of the Passenger Pigeon
 8. in understanding *quote* the criminal mind
 9. I need to re-fashion the *so-called* data in the direction of . . .
10. the per capita growth, the growth rate *if you like,* is constant . . .

We were somewhat surprised by these low numbers, because we thought that academic speech would be particularly rich in these verbal and terminological demurrals and prevarications. What we do not know, of course, is how completely we have covered the options, because there may be phrases that function as detachment markers that we have not had the wit to search for ("roughly speaking" might be one putative example), or detachment might be commonly signaled by the familiar quotation-mark gesture—the simultaneous bending of the first two fingers of each hand.

We then turned to the verb *call* itself and produced 225 examples of it functioning as a naming verb. It turned out that about 60 percent of these occurrences were primarily didactic rather than detached or ironic.

11. this led to what fish biologists call Fry's paradigm
12. I execute some code, called the loop body
13. with this little capital-A little-A thingy called a flag

Some of the remaining examples clearly show speaker detachment.

14. he went back to what are called primitive cultures
15. what people colloquially and popularly and inaccurately call dialects

A good number of the examples seem to fall somewhere between these endpoints; we here illustrate three of these, with brief commentary in square brackets.

16. that became the standard of what we call Spanish [Should we or should we not call it Spanish?]
17. such as the hymen, what the Victorians called the meaningful membrane [Is this statement making fun of the Victorians or providing information about their beliefs?]
18. this is essentially an atlas it's called of wintering North American

Birds [Is the speaker here providing further information about the book (i.e., it is entitled an atlas), insinuating that *atlas* is a pretty odd choice of term, or doing both?]

It seems to us that the semidetachments (or perhaps dual functions) expressed in the last three examples make a subtle but important contribution to the flavor of academic speech. We do not know, at this juncture, whether the apparent differences we have uncovered between our data and that discussed by Michael Stubbs are primarily due to the difference between academic and nonacademic speech settings or to differences between British and American speech practices, but we suspect the former.

The initiative for the 1999 symposium—and hence this volume—came from Rita Simpson's involvement as project manager for MICASE. MICASE started in late 1997 at the University of Michigan and is designed to digitally audio-record and transcribe about 1.5 million words of contemporary academic speech at that major American research university, covering speech events ranging from freshman advising to doctoral defenses to a speech by a newly announced Nobel Prize winner in physics, along with traditional university lectures and class discussions. As of early 2000, over half of the data has been collected and transcribed. Major funding for this project has been provided by the university's English Language Institute's (ELI's) Testing and Certification Division (which wishes to use the resource for test research and development), with additional support provided by the university's Digital Library Production Service, through which increasing amounts of data, accompanied by appropriate search tools, are freely accessible on their Web site. As part of the project's attempts to grapple with all the new issues that corpus building raises, Rita Simpson gave a preliminary account of MICASE at the TALC conference at Oxford University in the summer of 1998, and she returned convinced that a comparable get-together of corpus linguistics enthusiasts in North America would be an essential step toward generating further momentum.[10]

The three-day symposium in 1999 attracted over 80 people—at least twice as many as originally envisioned for what was to have been a small working group. By all accounts, the symposium exceeded everyone's expectations; both senior and junior scholars came away feeling refreshed, inspired, and connected to an important, burgeoning subcommunity of linguists in North America. Sites were chosen for at least two successive follow-up conferences, the first of which took place in Flagstaff in April 2000.

The University of Michigan's English Language Institute has historical roots that made it an especially appropriate venue for the first North American conference on corpus linguistics. As it happens, although corpus linguistics and the term *corpus* in its present-day sense are pretty much synonymous with computerized corpora and methods, this was not always the case, and earlier corpora, of course, were often not computerized. Before the advent of computers, or at least before the proliferation of personal computers, many linguists who were interested in function and use did essentially what we now call "corpus linguistics." One linguist who pioneered in the precomputer era of American corpus studies was Charles Carpenter Fries, who also became the founding director of the ELI in 1941.

A brief passage from Fries's obituary published in 1968 in *Language* gives an idea of the extent to which his research activities resembled the kinds of studies we associate today with corpus linguistics. Talking about Fries's dissertation work on *shall* and *will* in Modern English, Marquardt writes:

> Even this early work possessed certain qualities which were to characterize Fries's approach to linguistics problems throughout most of his career. It was based upon a specific corpus, carefully selected for its representative quality. . . . Although the corpus, as a body of relevant linguistic performance, has become somewhat unfashionable in certain quarters today, one cannot help admiring Fries's ingenuity in selecting the kinds of evidence that he did: drama, for his study of the periphrastic future; letters to a bureau of the federal government, for the *American English Grammar* (1940); taped telephone conversations for *The Structure of English* (1952); tapes of the 'What's My Line' television program for his analysis of English intonation patterns in questions.[11]

In the preface to *The Structure of English*, Fries himself writes about the spoken corpus that constituted the data for that book, arguing, in 1951, for the importance of studying the spoken language.

> In the meantime, however, beginning in 1946, it became possible to obtain an entirely different kind of evidence. Instead of the letters collected and studied for the *American English Grammar* I procured the means and the opportunity to record mechanically many conversations of speakers of Standard English in this North Central community of the United States. Altogether these mechanically recorded conversations amounted to something over 250,000 running words.[12]

Then, in his introduction, he goes on to highlight the book's emphasis on a descriptive approach grounded in empirical data.

> The point of view in this discussion is descriptive, not normative or legislative. The reader will find here, *not* how certain teachers or textbook writers or "authorities" think native speakers of English ought to use the language, but how certain native speakers actually do use it in natural, practical conversations carrying on the various activities of a community. The materials which furnished the linguistic evidence for the analysis and discussions of the book were primarily some fifty hours of mechanically recorded conversations on a great range of topics—conversations in which the participants were entirely unaware that their speech was being recorded. These mechanical records were transcribed for convenient study, and roughly indexed so as to facilitate reference to the original discs recording the actual speech.[13]

In a related footnote, Fries reiterates his belief in the superiority of an approach to linguistic analysis based on naturally occurring spoken data as opposed to an approach that gives priority to introspection. So it turns out to be serendipitous that this first meeting in North America on the uses of computerized corpora in linguistics was held at the University of Michigan's English Language Institute, as it preserves a long legacy of interest in language function and use that started with the ELI's first director, Charles Fries.[14]

With one exception, the twelve chapters in this volume are revisions or expansions of papers or workshops given at the 1999 symposium. The contributions are divided into two sections: the chapters in part 1 deal with corpus development and tools for accessing existing corpus resources, while the chapters in part 2 offer a sampling of current linguistic analyses using corpora.

Part 1 contains five chapters, three of which report on the status of specific corpus projects currently underway in North America. In the first of these, Charles Meyer reviews the progress of the International Corpus of English (ICE) to date, with specific reference to the development of the American component of this comparative corpus. He then shows how a software program built specifically for ICE—the ICE Corpus Utility Program (ICECUP)—can be used to analyze both **part-of-speech tagged** and fully **parsed** components of the corpus as well as simple lexical versions.

The next two chapters describe and discuss two similar specialized corpora currently being developed in the United States. Rita Simpson and Chris Powell report on the progress of the on-line Web search interface developed for MICASE. They outline the goals, scope, and current status of MICASE, and they describe the collaboration between the team of digital librarians and programmers and the MICASE team that made the on-line access possible. They discuss the functionality as well as the limitations of the Web-based search interface, as well as specific problems and challenges of handling spoken data in this environment, in contrast to written texts, which digital librarians customarily deal with. The chapter by Doug Biber, Randi Reppen, Victoria Clark, and Jenia Walter describes a similar corpus in progress called the TOEFL-2000 Spoken and Written Academic Language Corpus (T2K-SWAL Corpus), a project coordinated at Northern Arizona University and funded by the Educational Testing Service (ETS). Their chapter focuses on the spoken component of this corpus, outlining the major goals, design strategies, and methodology issues. These two chapters are useful contributions to this volume, especially because of the similarities between the T2K-SWAL Corpus and MICASE. The target size for both corpora is approximately the same, the kinds of speech events and representation across academic disciplines are comparable, and both projects are being funded by testing organizations. The first major difference is in geographical representation: while MICASE is limited to data from one large research university, the T2K-SWAL Corpus includes data from institutions in four different geographical regions. The second major difference is in the speaker demographic information available: MICASE includes four categories of variables for all speakers, while the T2K-SWAL Corpus in most cases differentiates only between students and instructors. There are also minor differences in the primary data collection methods, and there is a significant difference in the planned availability of the completed corpora, with MICASE to be freely accessible on the Web, a feature that the ETS-sponsored T2K-SWAL Corpus does not currently include. These projects are two examples of corpora that have arisen to fill the gap in medium-sized specialized and genre- or register-conscious corpora of spoken language—in this case, in the academic arena. We hope that these projects might inspire other researchers to build comparable specialized corpora in other speech domains—such as, for example, business, medical, legal, or political speech—in the near future.

   In considerable contrast, the chapter by Mark Davies outlines a method for creating multimillion-word written corpora from publicly available texts on the Web, providing step-by-step instructions for building a customized corpus of this kind. Davies refers specifically to two corpora he himself has created and used—one of Spanish and one of Portuguese texts—and provides several examples of syntactic analyses he has conducted using the large Spanish corpus, in which he traces the spread of unusual and innovative syntactic structures in both peninsular and Latin American Spanish. He specifically highlights the value of the multimillion-word corpus in supporting his claims.

The last chapter in part 1, by Susan Hockey, offers an overview of the features of some commonly used concordance programs. Though oriented toward the relatively inexperienced individual researcher, the chapter includes a concise summary of some of the more advanced technical issues to consider in choosing and using concordance programs, including the handling of various markup and annotation schemes, such as **SGML**-encoded text and part-of-speech tagging. She presents an overview of the different retrieval and sorting functions a linguist might find useful, and she discusses trends in the development of desktop tools for corpus linguistics. This chapter also offers some interesting observations on the similarities and differences between the concordancing requirements of literary versus linguistic corpus work.

Part 2 contains seven chapters on a variety of corpus-based studies, including studies of grammar and usage, studies of discourse features from spoken corpora, and studies oriented specifically toward language teaching and testing applications. Douglas Biber's chapter, which opens part 2, draws on research done for the *Longman Grammar of Spoken and Written English*. Biber discusses three case studies of English verbs revealing features that he claims are counterintuitive and that he demonstrated to be so at his workshop for the 1999 symposium. The first two cases concern the relative frequencies of common verbs and differing grammatical forms of verbs in four different registers, and the third one shows how two grammatically similar (if semantically unrelated) verbs (*stand* and *begin*) actually exhibit strikingly different patterns of use. In all three cases, the chapter argues for the importance of considering register when analyzing grammatical patterns of use.

Hongyin Tao presents here an in-depth study of a single word, *remember*, in which he argues that one of the major strengths of corpus linguistics lies in its potential to discover and illustrate the more common patterns of language use. One of the more intriguing findings of Tao's study is that postverbal complement clauses of *remember*—for example, "John remembered *to turn the faucet off*" and "John remembered *turning off the faucet*"—are actually quite infrequent in the four corpora he analyzed, despite the fact that these features have attracted the most attention from traditional grammarians and theoretical linguists. In the second part of his chapter, Tao turns to a discussion of the discourse-pragmatic functions of *remember*, making the important point that corpus linguistic tools and sociocultural linguistic analyses can—and should—be treated as complementary methodologies. He identifies two major pragmatic functions of *remember:* it functions primarily either as an epistemic indexical, indicating certainty or uncertainty, or as one of three kinds of metalinguistic devices. He then illustrates the correspondences between these two pragmatic functions (and their subcategories) and their grammatical contexts. He finds, among other things, that there is a strong tendency for the epistemic function to occur with first-person subjects, the metalinguistic function with second-person subjects.

The next two chapters in part 2 are based on the emerging MICASE. John Swales and Bonnie Malczewski focus on a set of discourse markers used either to move from monologue to dialogue (or vice-versa) or to initiate or announce the beginning of a new segment, or episode, of the discourse. Asserting that the varied and multiple tasks of academic speech necessitate much negotiation and management of the discoursal floor, they identify the range of linguistic resources used as "new episode flags" in the MICASE data and analyze the occurrence and functions of the most common ones, concluding that these markers often cluster together, as in the frequently attested combination *okay, so now.* This corpus work stands in contrast to more traditional studies that have considered discourse markers one by one. In another study using MICASE data, Anna Mauranen examines discourse practices in the academy, this time focusing on reflexive talk, or metalanguage, especially in monologic contexts. In addition to showing how reflexivity functions to construct, maintain, and reflect the social and interactional characteristics of the discourse in which it is embedded, Mauranen also points out an interesting connection between reflexivity and hedging, a connection that relates, again, to the social and interactional realities of academic speech situations; that is, many of the reflexive expressions typically co-occur with hedges. One possible explanation for this clustering is that discourse reflexivity and hedging both function largely as indicators of speaker orientation toward the ongoing dialogue.

Two of the remaining chapters are aimed explicitly at language teachers. The first of these, by Aaron Lawson, examines a corpus of spoken French to compare the spoken language of educated adult native speakers with the language prescribed by mainstream textbooks for instruction of French as a second language. Looking specifically at one grammatical feature that is emphasized in almost all French textbooks (the subjunctive) and at two grammatical constructions that are very common in the spoken corpus, he finds overwhelming discrepancies between attested usage for these features and the extent of their coverage in the texts. Perhaps his most striking finding is that the anaphoric and deictic use of the demonstrative *ça*, the second most common type of pronominal reference in the spoken data, is not covered adequately in any of the textbooks in his study. In a similar vein, Stephanie Burdine uses corpus data on expressions of disagreement in English to argue for the importance of lexical phrases as pedagogical tools for language learners, as an alternative to the dichotomy between grammar and lexis that is so prevalent in second language textbooks. She compares the kinds of disagreement phrases presented in several ESL textbooks with the phrases found in the corpus (finding, like Lawson, significant incongruities) and shows how the lexical phrase can be exploited in various task-based, data-driven language learning activities.

In the final chapter, Randi Reppen presents the results of a study investigating the writing development of children in elementary school from two different first language backgrounds. She analyzes a corpus of texts written by third- and sixth-grade students and compares the developmental progress of L1 English students with L1 Navajo students by means of a multidimensional approach that identifies the relative extent to which linguistic features cluster together. Her study finds a corpus-based approach to be advantageous in providing more generalizable information about the specific developmental changes that take place as students become increasingly literate.

The seven chapters in part 2, combined with the specific examples included in the chapters in part 1, provide a useful overview at the millennium of the range of topics currently being studied in North America under the rubric of corpus linguistics, from applications with direct implications for teaching and testing, to detailed lexico-grammatical or discourse-level analyses of specific words, word classes, or sets of related words, to developmental language studies. Though none of the chapters in this volume was necessarily prepared as a state-of-the-art piece, the volume stands as a sampling of current states of the art in this emerging subfield. We hope that the chapters herein, like the symposium in which their contents were first presented, not only provide an overview of this multifaceted area of research but also inspire further explorations along these lines by scholars in language teaching and linguistics. We anticipate that both undergraduate and graduate courses in corpus linguistics will rapidly escalate over the next few years in North America, driven by both technological advances and growing interest in the subfield. Our final hope, therefore, is that this wide-ranging volume could also provide students with reading matter that introduces them to the intriguing possibilities of corpus linguistics.

Notes

1. For more information, see <http://www.ling.upenn.edu/mideng>, <http://www.hti.umich.edu/micase>; <http://titania.cobuild.collins.co.uk/boe_info.html>.
2. J. Sinclair, ed. in chief, *Collins Cobuild English Language Dictionary* (London and Glasgow: Collins, 1987).
3. B. MacWhinney, *The CHILDES Project: Tools for Analyzing Talk*, 2d ed. (Hillsdale, NJ: Lawrence Erlbaum, 1995).
4. N. C. Ellis, "Emergentism, Connectionism, and Language Learning," *Language Learning* 48, no. 4 (1998): 631–64.
5. S. Bayer et al., "Theoretical and Computational Linguistics: Toward a Mutual Understanding," in *Using Computers in Linguistics: A Practical Guide*, ed. J. Lawler and H. Aristar-Dry (London: Routledge, 1998).
6. M. McCarthy, F. O'Dell, and E. Shaw, *Vocabulary in Use: Upper Intermediate* (Cambridge: Cambridge University Press, 1997); D. Biber, S. Johansson, G. Leech, S. Conrad, and E. Finegan, *Longman Grammar of Spoken and Written English* (London: Longman, 1999).
7. T. Johns, "Should You Be Persuaded: Two Examples of Data-Driven Learning Materials," *ELR Journal*, vol. 4 (1991): 1–16; M. Scott, *Wordsmith Tools* (Oxford: Oxford University Press, 1998); M. Barlow, *MonoConc* (Houston: Athelstan, 1998).
8. M. McCarthy and R. Carter, "Grammar, Tails, and Affect: Constructing Expressive Choices in Discourse," *Text* 17, no. 3 (1997): 405–29.
9. M. Stubbs, *Text and Corpus Analysis* (Oxford: Blackwell Publishers, 1996), 209.
10. R. Simpson, B. Lucka, and J. Ovens, "Methodological Challenges of Planning a Spoken Corpus with Pedagogical Outcomes," in *Rethinking Language Pedagogy: Papers from the Third International Conference on Teaching*

and Language Corpora, ed. L. Burnard and T. McEnery (Frankfurt: Peter Lang, 2000).

11. A. Marquardt, "Charles C. Fries," *Language* 44, no. 1 (1968): 205–10.

12. C. Fries, *The Structure of English* (New York: Harcourt, Brace, and Company, 1952), vii–viii.

13. Ibid., 3.

14. As a further note of historical interest, Peter Fries, Charles Fries's son, now a linguist at Central Michigan University, is one of the speakers in that corpus, which was recorded from the Fries's home telephone. The younger Fries reported at the May 1999 symposium that the original recordings were made on a device called a Soundscriber, and he is hopeful that at some point in the near future, these recordings—along with the transcripts—can be converted to some kind of digital format so that this small historical corpus can be resurrected.

Part 1

Corpus Building and Tools

The International Corpus of English: Progress and Prospects

Charles F. Meyer
University of Massachusetts at Boston

When Sidney Greenbaum conceptualized the creation of the International Corpus of English (ICE) in the late 1980s, he envisioned international teams of researchers collecting and computerizing similar types of speech and writing representing the national varieties of English that exist around the world, such as British English, American English, Nigerian English, and Indian English. Once computer corpora of these varieties were created, they would be fully **tagged** and **parsed.** The resultant corpora would enable not just the comparison of the various national varieties of English that have evolved around the world but the linguistic analysis of one of the lengthiest and most extensively analyzed corpora of speech and writing ever created.

Unfortunately, Sidney Greenbaum did not live to see the completion of ICE, but his dream to create computerized corpora of the many regional varieties of English that evolved around the world is currently being carried out by the 13 research teams participating in the ICE project.[1] Now that various regional components of ICE are beginning to be released, it is worthwhile to review the initial design of the corpus, particularly to illustrate the difficulties of creating a corpus in an international context; to describe the software that has been developed over the course of the project; and to illustrate the kinds of studies that can now be conducted on the various regional components of ICE.

The Initial Design of the ICE Corpus

When the structure of the ICE corpus was originally planned, it was decided that each component of ICE would be divided into 2,000-word text samples representing various kinds of spoken and written

English (see the appendix for a complete listing of the genres included in the corpus). In most cases, text fragments rather than entire texts were included so that as many different speakers and writers as possible could be represented in the corpus. Although text fragments do not permit certain kinds of discourse studies to be conducted, including 2,000-word samples follows in the tradition of earlier corpora, such as the Brown and Lancaster-Oslo-Bergen (LOB) corpora, which have stood the test of time and shown that significant linguistic information can be obtained from corpora consisting of 2,000-word samples. It was originally decided to restrict the collection of spoken and written texts to the years 1990–95. However, because many teams have fallen behind, text collection is ongoing for many components.

Extensive discussion among ICE teams took place to determine what kinds of English should be represented in ICE corpora and how many samples from each type should be included. In the end, it was decided to include a range of different text types but a greater number of samples of those types that were more common in English. This decision is particularly reflected in the spoken part of the corpus, where nearly one-third of the samples consist of spontaneous dialogues. This is the most common type of speech in which English speakers engage. Consequently, it is well represented in the corpus. Other types of speech that are represented include radio broadcasts, telephone conversations, scripted speeches, and classroom dialogues.

The written part of the corpus represents a broad spectrum of writing, such as fiction, press reportage and editorials, and popular and learned writing. In addition, three types of writing not typically found in corpora are included: personal letters, business correspondence, and student essays and exams. Notably missing from the written part of the corpus is legal English, a highly specialized type of English that was excluded on the grounds that it represented a highly fossilized type of English intended mainly for a very specialized audience.

As teams began to collect texts for their components of ICE, it soon became evident that the original text categories were overly biased toward the use of English in Western contexts and that many of the teams working with non-Western varieties of English would not be able to collect samples for all of the categories. Schmied (1996) describes his experiences collecting texts for the East African component of ICE. In Tanzania, for instance, most uses of English are restricted, Schmied observes, to "the upper part of the formal spectrum" (185), thus making it very difficult to collect spontaneous dialogues, which typically took place in the native language. In fact, notes Schmied, speaking English in many informal contexts "would be considered rude" (186), since it would exclude non-English speakers from the conversation. Other ICE teams, such as those in India and the Caribbean, had similar experiences. As a solution to this problem, ICE teams agreed that if a particular team could not collect examples in one category, the team would collect more examples in a category that was easier to fill (e.g., press reportage). The result is that each ICE team will collect one million words of speech and writing, but some ICE components will have missing categories. Although this solution is not ideal, it seemed to be the most reasonable way around the problem of text collection, short of completely redefining the text categories to be included in the ICE corpus.

A number of practical matters also complicated text collection. For instance, some of the spoken and written texts were copyrighted, and permission for their use had to be obtained before a text could be included in the corpus. It turned out that this was a difficult task for all ICE teams, but especially for the American component of ICE. To understand how truly difficult an issue this is in the United States, it is instructive to compare the British experience collecting one type of copyrighted text, broadcast English, with the American experience. ICE contains a significant number of samples of broadcast discussions, interviews, and newscasts. In Britain, most of the samples were taken from BBC radio and television broadcasts. The BBC gave permission to the British team to use any program they broadcast, but only if each person in the broadcast gave their permission. To help the British team obtain permission, the BBC agreed to contact all individuals. With only a few exceptions, everyone contacted agreed to have their speech included within the British component of ICE.

In the United States, in contrast, no one centralized organization owns the rights to radio and television programs broadcast in this country. Consequently, each station had to be contacted individually, involving an enormous amount of paperwork, particularly because many stations refused to give permission or did not respond to a written inquiry requesting permission. Even the one quasi-public broadcast network in the United States, National Public Radio, refused permission to have any of their broadcasts included in the corpus unless a fee was paid for their use. These complications forced the American team to collect far more texts than were necessary to ensure that permission was ultimately received for the requisite number of texts for a given category. In general, copyright issues were the single biggest challenge for the compilation of the American component of ICE and for many other ICE components as well.

The ICE project began in the early 1990s at the start of the Internet revolution. This had implications for the collection of texts in two respects. First, one of the ICE categories is personal correspondence. As E-mail grew in popularity, personal letters sent through "snail mail" became harder and harder to collect. It was decided not to include E-mail in this category, since it was really a genre itself (cf. Collot and Belmore 1993). Second, as publication on the World Wide Web became more common, ICE teams had to decide whether to include on-line articles in the corpus. There is a distinct advantage in collecting on-line material, since it exists in computer-readable form and avoids the inaccuracies of computerizing printed texts with an optical scanner. At the same time, including electronic texts in a corpus with traditional printed texts raises an obvious methodological issue: are we dealing here with one text type or two? Obviously, if an article appearing in an electronic journal goes through the same editorial process as an article published in a printed journal, it is not likely that the linguistic structure of the two types of articles will be different enough to constitute two separate text types. But many articles appearing on the World Wide Web are not put through any kind of editorial process. Thus, it is quite possible that this kind of article will be different from a more traditionally published article. There was no general policy among ICE teams to exclude electronic articles from the ICE corpus. For the American component, I tried to restrict articles collected electronically to those that appeared in electronic journals or magazines that put their publications through some kind of editorial review process.

The remaining problems were difficulties encountered by anyone creating a corpus and were primarily related to lack of the necessary resources to carry a given ICE component through all phases of development. Collecting and transcribing speech is a costly and time-consuming process that delayed progress on many ICE components for years.[2] Inserting **SGML-conformant markup** into a text to indicate such features as paragraph boundaries, font changes, and overlapping segments of speech is also a formidable task. As a consequence, as the ICE Project evolved, the amount of markup required for inclusion was greatly reduced to expedite the completion of the project (see Meyer 1997 for more on this point). While it was originally intended that all ICE components would be tagged and parsed, parsing spoken English, with all its dysfluencies, proved so difficult for the London team working on the British component of ICE that other ICE teams are likely to produce (at best) a tagged version of their component or (more likely) only a lexical version. But despite the difficulties that parsing speech caused, the London team was able to produce a fully tagged and parsed version of the British component of ICE (ICE-GB) and a text analysis program, ICECUP (the ICE Corpus Utility Program), that allows users to automatically retrieve grammatical information in the corpus.[3]

In addition to ICE-USA, there is one other North American component of ICE: ICE-Canada, which is directed by Nancy Belmore (Concordia University, Montreal). The collection and computerization of texts for both North American components is ongoing. All of the written texts for ICE-USA have been collected and computerized and are in the process of being edited and annotated with SGML-conformant ICE markup. The spoken part of ICE-USA is being created in conjunction with the Santa Barbara Corpus of Spoken American English (see Chafe, Du Bois, and Thompson 1991), sections of which will be included in ICE-USA. Most of the spoken texts have been collected, but not all have been transcribed. All of the written and most of the spoken ICE-USA texts will be included on a CD containing an interim release of the entire ICE Corpus, which is due to be completed some time in 2001. In addition, an ICE sampler is now in production and will include a series of CDs, each containing 20 digitized samples of speech from a given ICE component with accompanying transcriptions. Users will be able to conduct lexical searches of the transcriptions on each CD and will be able to have the search results displayed in **KWIC** (key-word-in-context) format. By clicking on each concordance line, they will also be able to hear a digitized recording of the sentence (or utterance) in which the search item occurs. The first CD will be released in 2000 and will contain a sampling of spoken texts representing such varieties as British, Australian, and American English. The other CDs of individual varieties will be released as they become available.

Software Development

Although ICECUP is the most significant piece of software to be developed in the ICE Project, other software was developed as well, particularly to facilitate the insertion of various kinds of **annotation** in

ICE corpora. All ICE components can be annotated with up to three different kinds of **tags:** structural tags (obligatory), part-of-speech tags (optional), and grammatical tags (optional).

Structural tags provide descriptions of the texts themselves. All texts contain file headers, which provide general descriptive information: for instance, a full bibliographic citation for written texts and an identification of speakers in spoken texts.[4] Each text is divided into text units, which correspond either to grammatical sentences or, in spoken texts, to coherent utterances. Some structural tags are particular to speech or writing. In spoken texts, structural tags serve, for instance, to identify speakers, mark segments of speech that overlap, and indicate two lengths of pauses. In written texts, structural tags mark such features of writing as paragraph boundaries and section headings. To assist in the insertion of structural tags, the Markup Assistant was created. This program uses WordPerfect macros to, for instance, automatically insert text unit tags after every period in a written text or manually insert speaker identification tags before a given speaker's turn. The following excerpt illustrates a text annotated by the Markup Assistant with ICE markup.

<$A><#:1>   yes that I think you told me <{_><[_>I<[/>
<$B><#:2>   <[_>and<[/><{/> none of them have been what you might call very successful in this world

Two of the tags, <$A> and <$B>, indicate who is speaking at a given time in the conversation; two other tags, <#:1> and <#:2>, set off and number two text units. Two tags, <{_> and <{/>, mark the beginning and end of a speech segment containing overlapping speech; within this lengthier segment are two sets of additional tags, <[_> and <[/>, which mark the two individual segments of speech in each speaker turn that overlap. While ICE markup is SGML-conformant, because the project began prior to the **Text Encoding Initiative** (TEI), ICE markup is not TEI-conformant.

To insert part-of-speech and grammatical tags, the TOSCA tagger and parser was extended to insert ICE-conformant markup (see Aarts, van Halteren, and Oostdijk 1998 and Oostdijk 2000 for a description of the TOSCA tagger and parser). Currently, only ICE-GB is fully tagged and parsed. For each text unit, a parse tree has been created, providing a visual representation of the part of speech of each word in the tree, the particular phrases and clauses that these words are members of, and the function that they serve (subject, object, etc.). A fully tagged and parsed corpus is only as useful as the tools that are used to analyze it. To analyze texts annotated with ICE tags, a special **text retrieval program**, ICECUP, was developed. This program can perform tasks normally associated with text analysis programs: it can do simple lexical searches as well as generate KWIC concordances. But ICECUP performs other tasks not normally associated with text analysis programs. To illustrate the capabilities of ICECUP and the kinds of analyses that can be conducted on ICE corpora, the next section describes the usage in ICE-GB of the expression "like," as in the construction "He's, like, really cool." This usage originated in American English (cf. Romaine and Lange 1991), but as the analysis in the next section illustrates, it is now common in British English as well.

A Sample Analysis

One of the major features of ICECUP is that it allows one to search not just for lexical items, as any concordancing program can do, but for all or part of a syntactically analyzed parse tree. This capability of ICE-CUP—to search for what are known as "fuzzy tree fragments," or FTFs (cf. Aarts, Nelson, and Wallis 1998)—is crucial for studying the usage of the term *like* illustrated in the preceding section. Since *like* has many forms (e.g., preposition, conjunction), a lexical search of *like* would turn up thousands of instances, which would have to be analyzed by hand to find the relevant examples, a process that would involve many hours of painstaking work. ICECUP can greatly automate this type of analysis by searching for instances of *like* that have been parsed in a particular way.

Before *like* can be searched, however, it is necessary to determine precisely how it is parsed in ICE-GB, so that an accurate FTF can be constructed. One way to do this is to do a lexical search of all instances of *like* and to scroll through the various instances of *like* until a relevant example is found. Figure 1 contains a sample KWIC concordance window for *like* from ICE-GB, with the text unit for the relevant example highlighted. For any highlighted text unit, a parse tree can be automatically displayed by clicking the right mouse button and selecting the "View spy tree" option off the pop-up window. Invoking this feature of ICECUP for the highlighted text unit in figure 1 yields the

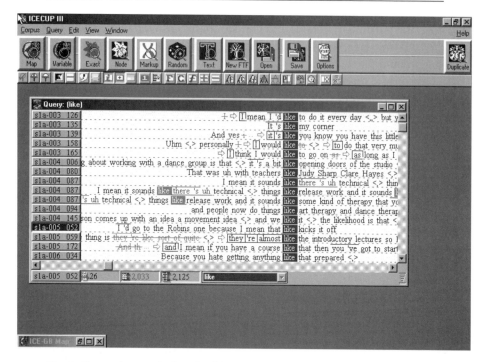

Fig. 1. Concordance window for *like*

parse tree in figure 2. As this parse tree reveals, this usage of *like* is parsed as a discourse marker (DISMK) that is a formulaic expression (FRM).

From this parse tree, an FTF can automatically be created using the FTF Wizard. The FTF Wizard contains a number of options for creating FTFs (see fig. 3). Since the search to be created is for a particular lexical item, *like*, with particular grammatical characteristics, the "Include both the tree and the text" option is selected. Otherwise, if the search is based only on the parse tree, the FTF will find all formulaic discourse markers in ICE-GB. Because only part of the tree will be searched for, the box under "Tree options" indicates that the tree nodes will be chopped at one row below the current point. The default selections for the other options are maintained, since these options are not directly relevant to the search. Running the FTF Wizard generates the FTF in figure 4. As constructed, this FTF will find all instances of *like* in ICE-GB that have been parsed as formulaic discourse markers.

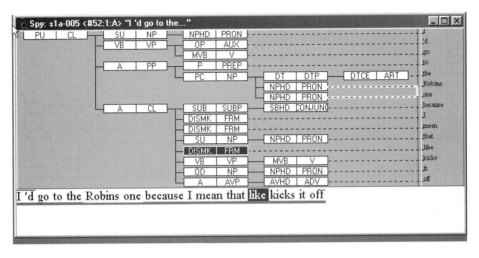

Fig. 2. Parse tree for *like*

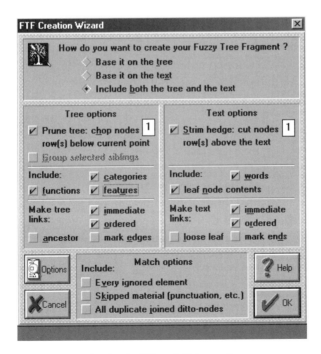

Fig. 3. FTF Wizard dialogue box

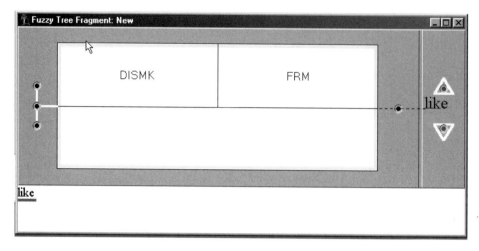

Fig. 4. FTF to find all instances of *like* as a formulaic discourse marker

Running this search yielded 156 instances of tree structures that met this structural description.

In addition to finding all instances of a particular FTF, ICECUP can restrict searches to particular sections of ICE-GB. Research on *like* as a discourse marker has noted that it tends to be used by younger speakers, particularly females. Figure 5 contains a dialogue box that allows the search for *like* to be restricted to a particular age-group. Running a search on the various age-groups listed in the dialogue box represented in figure 5 confirmed the earlier hypothesis: 93 of the 156 instances were used by the 18–25 age-group, 43 by the 26–45 age-group, and 12 by the 46–65 age-group.[5] If these figures are normalized, taking into consideration that there were fewer speakers in the 18–25 age-group than in the other age groups, the findings are even more pronounced: there were 338 instances of *like* per 1,000 speakers in the 18–25 age-group; 84 instances per 1,000 speakers in the 26–45 age-group; and 28 instances per 1,000 speakers in the 46–65 age-group.

Selecting other options in the "Socio-linguistic variable search" box allows searches to be conducted on other ethnographic variables. For instance, a search of *like* stratified by gender revealed that females accounted for 76 instances (172 per 1,000 female speakers), males for 71 instances (76 per 1,000 male speakers). If gender is combined with

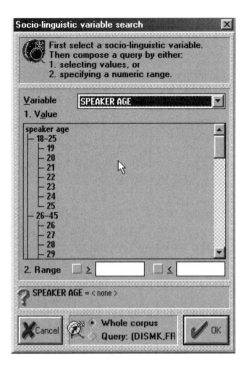

Fig. 5. Dialogue box for restricting searches to particular sociolinguistic variables

age, it turns out that 40 of the 76 instances of *like* used by females were used by females in the 18–25 age-group.

As these analyses indicate, ICECUP can quickly and efficiently yield detailed information on the usage of grammatical constructions in ICE-GB: none of the above searches took more than a couple of seconds to perform. And while ICECUP has a learning curve, I found that with a little practice, it was quite easy to use.

Conclusions

ICE-GB and ICECUP demonstrate the value of having a fully tagged and parsed corpus and a text retrieval program to analyze it. However, it is important not to underestimate the value of a simple lexical version of ICE for analyzing differences between the various regional varieties of English represented in the ICE project.

To illustrate this point, I recently conducted a study (reported in Meyer 1999) that analyzed sections of press reportage in the British, American, Jamaican, Philippine, Singaporean, and East African components of ICE to document the evolution of a grammatical construction called the "pseudo-title" (Bell 1988). Pseudo-titles are constructions, such as *linguist* in "linguist Noam Chomsky," which are intermediate between full titles and appositives: they behave like titles (e.g., *president* and *professor*) except that they are usually not capitalized, and they are very similar to appositives (cf. "the linguist Noam Chomsky") but lack a determiner. This construction is thought to have originated in *Time* magazine (Quirk et al. 1985, 276 n) and spread to British English, where its use is stigmatized and associated with tabloid journalism. I found the construction well established in the press reportage of all the newspapers in the components of ICE I investigated, with the British-influenced varieties (Jamaican, Singaporean, and East African) at times mixing the conservative British norm (e.g., "the British Prime Minister, Mr. Tony Blair") with the American norm (e.g., "British Prime Minister Tony Blair"). In addition, I discovered that in Philippine English, an innovative form of the construction was sometimes used containing a fairly complex nominal group in the pseudo-title, as in constructions such as "Salamat and Presidential Adviser on Flagship Projects in Mindanao Robert Aventajado" (ICE-Philippines). This construction was not found in the other components of ICE I investigated.

Such findings demonstrate the usefulness of components of ICE for the study of the evolution of English as a world language and will become more widespread once additional components of ICE are released.

Appendix: The Composition of the International Corpus of English

Type	Number of Texts	Length	Percentage of Spoken Corpus
Speech	300	600,000	100%
Dialogues	180	360,000	60%
Private	100	200,000	33%
Direct conversations	90	180,000	30%
Distanced conversations	10	20,000	3%

Type	Number of Texts	Length	Percentage of Spoken Corpus
Public	80	160,000	27%
Class lessons	20	40,000	7%
Broadcast discussions	20	40,000	7%
Broadcast interviews	10	20,000	3%
Parliamentary debates	10	20,000	3%
Business transactions	10	20,000	3%
Monologues	120	240,000	40%
Unscripted	70	140,000	23%
Spontaneous commentaries	20	40,000	7%
Speeches	30		
Demonstrations	10	20,000	3%
Legal presentations	10	20,000	3%
Scripted	50	100,000	17%
Broadcast news	20	40,000	7%
Broadcast talks	20	40,000	7%
Speeches (not broadcast)	10	20,000	3%
Writing	200	400,000	100%
Nonprinted	50	100,000	25%
Student untimed essays	10	20,000	5%
Student examination essays	10	20,000	5%
Social letters	15	30,000	8%
Business letters	15	30,000	8%
Printed	150	300,000	75%
Informational (learned) humanities, social sciences, natural sciences, technology	40	80,000	20%
Informational (popular) humanities, social sciences, natural sciences, technology	40	80,000	20%
Informational (reportage)	20	40,000	10%
Instructional administrative, regulatory, skills, hobbies	20	40,000	10%
Persuasive (press editorials)	10	20,000	5%
Creative (novels, stories)	20	40,000	10%

Source: Adapted from Greenbaum 1996, 29–30.

Notes

1. The countries currently active in the ICE project and whose regional variety of English will be included in the ICE corpus are Australia, Canada, the Caribbean, East Africa, Great Britain, Hong Kong, India, Ireland, New Zealand, the Philippines, Singapore, South Africa, and the United States. An overview of the project can be found on the Web site maintained by the Survey of English Usage (University College, London): <http://www.ucl.ac.uk/english-usage/ice/components.htm>.
2. See Holmes 1998 for a discussion of ways to expedite the collection of spoken texts.
3. ICECUP is supplied with ICE-GB and is available with the ICE-GB Sample Corpus for free download at <http://www.ucl.ac.uk/english-usage/ice-gb/icecup.htm>.
4. In many ICE components, information that is normally included in a file header—a series of SGML-conformant statements coming at the start of a text—is stored in a database separate from the text. Handling the information this way avoids creating huge text files in the corpus itself but still allows users access to the information. In the case of ICE-GB, ICECUP allows for automatic retrieval of bibliographic and ethnographic information, a point that will be illustrated in the next section of this chapter.
5. The figures cited here add up to 148 rather than 156, the total number of instances of *like* as a formulaic discourse marker in ICE-GB. This discrepancy reflects the fact that there is missing ethnographic data on many speakers and writers in ICE-GB.

References

Aarts, Bas, Gerald Nelson, and Sean Wallis. 1998. Using Fuzzy Tree Fragments to Explore English Grammar. *English Today* 14, no. 3:52–56.

Aarts, Jan, Hans van Halteren, and Nelleke Oostdijk. 1998. The Linguistic Annotation of Corpora: The TOSCA Analysis System. *Corpus Linguistics* 3:189–210.

Bell, Alan. 1988. The British Base and the American Connection in New Zealand Media English. *American Speech* 63:326–44.

Chafe, Wallace, John Du Bois, and Sandra Thompson. 1991. Towards a New Corpus of American English. In *English Corpus Linguistics*, ed. Karin Aijmer and Bengt Altenberg, 64–91. London: Longman.

Collot, M., and Nancy Belmore. 1993. Electronic Language: A New Variety of English. In *English Language Corpora: Design, Analysis, and Exploitation. Papers from the Thirteenth International Conference on English Language Research on Computerized Corpora, Nijmegen 1992*, ed. Jan Aarts, Peter de Haan, and Nelleke Oostdijk, 41–55. Amsterdam: Rodopi.

Greenbaum, Sidney, ed. 1996. *Comparing English Worldwide: The International Corpus of English.* Oxford: Clarendon.

Holmes, Janet. 1998. Notes on Collecting Conversations for the ICE-NZ [New Zealand] Corpus. *ICE Newsletter* 26. <http://www.cs.umb.edu/~meyer/speech.htm> (October 16, 2000).

Meyer, Charles. 1997. Minimal Markup for ICE Texts. *ICE Newsletter* 25. <http://www.cs.umb.edu/~meyer/icenews2.html> (October 16, 2000).

———. 1999. Pseudo-Titles in the Press Genre of Various Components of the International Corpus of English. Paper presented at the Twentieth Annual ICAME Conference, Freiburg, Germany, May.

Oostdijk, Nelleke. 2000. English Descriptive Linguistics at a Cross-roads. *English Studies* 80: 127–41.

Quirk, Randolph, Sidney Greenbaum, Geoffrey Leech, and Jan Svartvik. 1985. *A Comprehensive Grammar of the English Language.* London: Longman.

Romaine, Suzanne, and Deborah Lange. 1991. The Use of *Like* as a Marker of Reported Speech and Thought: A Case of Grammaticalization in Progress. *American Speech* 66:227–79.

Schmied, Josef. 1996. Second-Language Corpora. In *Comparing English Worldwide: The International Corpus of English,* ed. Sidney Greenbaum, 182–96. Oxford: Clarendon.

Collaboration between Corpus Linguists and Digital Librarians for the MICASE Web Search Interface

Christina Powell and Rita C. Simpson
University of Michigan

The seed for the Michigan Corpus of Academic Spoken English (MICASE) originated with Sarah Briggs of the Testing and Certification Division at the University of Michigan's English Language Institute (ELI). She believed that an academic spoken corpus would become a valuable resource for the division's suite of listening comprehension tests, which are used both within and outside the university. The idea was enthusiastically endorsed by the ELI director, who saw the potential contribution of a corpus to the institute's curriculum for international graduate students, as well as its important role in furthering our understanding of academic speech per se. In November 1997, with major funding from the ELI's testing division and minor funding from its teaching and publication activities, the MICASE project was officially launched. Shortly thereafter, Rita Simpson was appointed project manager. Recording and transcription got underway in February 1998 and continues to be carried out by a half-time research assistant and a rotating cadre of part-time linguistics undergraduate and graduate students under the supervision of the project manager. The goal for this first phase of the project is to compile a corpus of some 1.5 million words of academic speech, balanced across a range of academic divisions, departments, and speech event types.

The project took a second leap forward in May 1998 when another unit on campus, the Humanities Text Initiative (HTI), agreed to develop a Web-based search interface so that MICASE would be available not only to researchers at the University of Michigan but to students, teachers, and researchers around the world. The HTI is a unit of the University of Michigan's Digital Library Production Service (DLPS) that has been creating and delivering electronic texts in **SGML** (Standard Generalized Markup Language) via the World Wide Web since 1994. Much of the work of DLPS consists of making licensed full-text collections and resources (e.g., Chadwyck-Healey's English Poetry Database or the electronic version of the *Oxford English Dictionary*) available to the faculty, staff, and students of the university. The HTI creates and delivers electronic texts based on the holdings of the library, and these text creation initiatives (e.g., the American Verse Project and the Corpus of Middle English Prose and Verse) are freely available to anyone with Internet access. The HTI has also partnered with other academic groups, both at Michigan and at other institutions, to help them create and deliver electronic texts, including text collections, bibliographies, and on-line journals. The HTI was thus a natural partner for MICASE, and Chris Powell took primary responsibility for the ensuing collaborative project. The HTI staff were excited and challenged at the prospect of expanding their expertise to include work on a corpus of spoken language. This project presented a challenge because the nature of the work of transcribing, **encoding,** and delivering speech is quite different from that of converting printed texts to electronic form; in addition, the typical ways in which a spoken corpus is utilized tend to differ significantly from those of a collection of literary texts.

In May 1999, the first set of transcripts was made publicly available via the searchable interface on the World Wide Web (<http://www.hti.umich.edu/micase>).[1] This chapter focuses on the creation of the computerized transcripts for on-line delivery and the development and progress to date of the Web interface that resulted from the partnership between MICASE and the HTI. Other more general issues of corpus design and methodology are described in detail in Simpson, Lucka, and Ovens 2000.

Creating the Transcripts

Transcription Conventions

The MICASE transcription system is based on standard orthography with a limited set of common phonologically reduced pronunciations (e.g., "gonna," "wanna," "kinda," "sorta," etc.), but with no attempt made to represent dialectal or nonnative phonetic details. Representation of prosody is also kept to a minimum: commas represent one- to two-second pauses with a non-phrase-final intonation contour, and periods are used for one- to two-second pauses with a phrase-final fall; ellipses are used for slightly longer pauses—between two and four seconds; question marks indicate any utterance that functions pragmatically as a question, regardless of intonation or syntax. Pauses longer than four seconds are timed and marked with a <PAUSE> **tag.** All hesitation and filler words, backchannel cues, and transcribable exclamations are spelled out, as are all repetitions of a word, partial word, or phrase. Truncated words are marked with a hyphen at the end, and false starts ending with a whole word are marked by an underscore at the end of the word. Uncertain speech is enclosed in parentheses, while two *x*'s in parentheses indicate one or more words that are completely unintelligible. Backchannel cues and unsuccessful interruptions are embedded into the turn of the speaker who holds the floor, not shown as a separate line or paragraph. Overlapping speech segments occurring either at turn transitions or as interruptions or backchannel cues in the middle of one speaker's turn are marked with a tag. Description of nonspeech events is kept to a minimum; they are included only when the contextual event would affect comprehension of the surrounding discourse. The two most common types of events included in an <EVENT> tag are laughter and writing on the board, though a variety of other events are also noted as necessary. (For a more detailed explanation of all spelling, transcription, and markup conventions, see <http://www.lsa.umich.edu/eli/micase/transcription.html>.)

Encoding Conventions

The transcripts are created with the commercial SGML text-editing program Author Editor, using a document structure that is based on the **Text Encoding Initiative** (TEI) guidelines for speech transcription, with some changes to support local practice. The **base tag set** for the transcription of speech in the TEI is designed for use with a wide variety of spoken material, but as it was never intended to support all types of research on speech without modification, our emendations are not unexpected. The overriding concern for the MICASE transcriptions was that the **encoding scheme** would be unambiguous for student encoders to apply consistently and in accordance with the project guidelines, allowing them flexibility to transcribe a speech event as it occurred, but not permitting them to introduce tags that were available in the base tag set but not intended for use in this project. Our working **Document Type Definition** (DTD) for MICASE removes **elements** for subdividing utterances or transcriptions; for encoding features that imply or require editorial intervention in the speaker's words—such as the regularization or correction of pronunciation; for recording shifts in tempo, pitch, and loudness; for kinesic events, like gestures; and for nonlexical speech phenomena (e.g., filled pauses) that are currently transcribed but not **tagged.**

The working DTD is also modified to require elements deemed necessary in each transcription (primarily in the **header**) and to provide elements to replace TEI conventions that seemed problematic to apply consistently by a changing group of encoders working over a fairly long time span. The most notable modification involves the markup for overlapping speech. We replaced anchors requiring unique identifiers (IDs) marking the point of occurrence of overlapping words or phrases with an element (imaginatively named "OVERLAP") to surround these overlaps. This resulted in a less cluttered and more efficient way of marking overlapping speech that simplified the transcribers' tasks in this regard. It also provides the ability to revisit the decision at a later point and adopt the TEI method should we decide to do so (e.g., for reasons of compatibility with other projects).

The header of each transcript contains SGML tags with all the information about the speech event and the speakers that we wanted to include as possible **search parameters.** The speech event attributes encoded in the headers are speech event type, academic division, academic discipline, participant level, and primary discourse mode. Table 1 shows these categories and all the possible attribute values. Each speaker in the transcript is identified with an element that contains their demographic information. The speaker attributes encoded in the headers are gender, age-group, academic role, native speaker status, and first language (if other than American English). See table 2 for descriptions of and codes for these categories.

Some information that is not included in any of the searchable parameters is included in the headers of the transcripts—namely, number of speakers and number of participants in the speech event, duration of the recording, and the recording location. We also collect

Table 1. Speech Event Attributes

Category	Code	Definition/Comments
Speech Event Type		
All classroom speech events are defined externally by the university regardless of the actual speech event characteristics, except in cases where prepared student presentations constitute the majority of the speech, in which case the event type is "student presentations."		
Classroom Events		
Small Lectures	LES	Lecture class; class size = 40 or fewer students
Large Lectures	LEL	Lecture class; class size = more than 40 students
Discussion Sections	DIS	Additional section of a lecture class designed for maximum student partici-pation; may also be called recitation
Lab Sections	LAB	Lab sections of science and engineering classes; may include problem-solving sessions
Seminars	SEM	Graduate or undergraduate class defined as a seminar
Student Presentations	STP	Class, other than a seminar, in which one or more students speak in front of the class or lead discussion
Nonclassroom events		
Advising sessions	ADV	Interactions between students and acad-emic advisors
Colloquia	COL	Departmental or university-wide lec-tures, panel discussions, workshops, brown-bag lunch talks, etc.
Dissertation Defenses	DEF	Defenses of Ph.D. disserations or Mas-ter's theses
Interviews	INT	One-on-one interviews for research or media purposes
Meetings	MTG	Meetings of faculty, staff, student gov-ernment, research group meetings, not including meetings of study group
Office Hours	OFC	Held by faculty or graduate student instructors in connection with a specific class or project
Service Encounters	SVC	Interactions on the library, computer center, or language resource center
Study Groups	SGR	Informal student-led study groups
Tours	TOU	Campus, library, or museum tours
Tutorials	TUT	Individualized help between a student and tutor

Academic Division
One of four divisions defined according to the classification of departments by the Horace H. Rackham School of Graduate Studies.

Biological and Health Sciences	BS	Includes Biology, Biochemistry, Dentistry, Genetics, Immunology, Natural Resources, Neuroscience, Nursing, Pathology, Pharmacy, Physiology, Public Health
Physical Sciences and Engineering	PS	Includes Astronomy, Chemistry, Computer Science, Engineering (all), Geology, Mathematics, Physics, Statistics, Technical Communication
Social Sciences and Education	SS	Includes Anthropology, Business Administration, Communication, Economics, Education, History, Public Policy, Political Science, Psychology, Social Work, Sociology, Urban and Regional Planning
Humanities and Arts	HA	Includes Area Studies (all), Architecture, Classics, Comparative Literature, English, Fine Arts (all), Foreign Languages, History of Art, Information and Library Science, Linguistics, Philosophy, Women's Studies

Academic Discipline
Corresponds to individual university departments when applicable; otherwise assigned as miscellaneous

Participant Level
Corresponds to the level of the majority of students for classes or participants for other events.

Junior undergrad	JU	First- and second-year undergraduates
Senior undergrad	SU	Third-year and above undergraduates
Mixed undergrad	MU	Mixed undergraduates
Junior graduate	JG	First- and second-year or master's-level graduate students
Senior graduate	SG	Third-year and above Ph.D. students
Mixed graduate	MG	Mixed graduate students
Junior faculty	JF	Lecturers and assistant professors
Senior faculty	SF	Associate professors and above
Mixed faculty	MF	Mixed faculty
Staff	ST	Nonteaching university employees
Visitor/other	VO	Non-University of Michigan or nonacademic affiliates
Mixed	MX	Mixed faculty, staff, and students

Primary Discourse Mode
Refers to the predominant type of discourse characterizing the speech event

Monologic	MLG	One speaker monopolizes the floor, sometimes followed by a brief question-and-answer period
Panel	PNL	Several consecutive monologues, usually followed by multispeaker interactions
Interactive	INT	Interactional discourse involving two or more speakers
Mixed	MIX	No one discourse mode is predominant

data on the speaker's geographical origin (i.e., city, state, region, or county of longest residence) but do not include that information in the header. The decision to exclude dialect information was based on a number of factors, including the research goals of the MICASE staff and of other potential users in the areas of applied linguistics and ESL/EAP, the difficulty of collecting reliable information about dialect origins for all speakers without individually interviewing them, and the difficulty of sampling enough speakers from different dialect areas for this to become a meaningful category within a corpus of the projected size. Information on geographical origins is therefore kept only in the archived speaker information forms.

The main structural elements in the body of the transcript are utterances, marked with a <U> tag, which correspond to speaker turns. Each <U> tag contains an attribute identifying the speaker (i.e., "S1," "S2," etc.) that is referenced back to that speaker's demographic information in the header. In cases when an utterance cannot confidently be assigned to a particular speaker, the ID "SU," for "speaker unknown," is used. As mentioned earlier, pauses longer than four seconds and select contextual events are marked with <PAUSE> or <EVENT> tags. Other tags used in the body of the text include <FOREIGN> for non-English words or phrases; <SIC>, used when a speaker makes a mistake without self-correcting and the resulting error might otherwise appear to be a transcribing error; and <READING>, used to mark segments of speech that are read verbatim.

Designing and building a spoken corpus requires a number of difficult decisions and compromises, not to mention a tremendous amount of time and resources. One area we chose not to compromise

TABLE 2. Speaker Attributes

Category	Code	Definition/Comments
Gender		
Female	F	
Male	M	
Age-group		
17–23	1	
24–30	2	
31–50	3	
51 and older	4	
Academic role		
Junior undergrad	JU	First- and second-year undergraduates
Senior undergrad	SU	Third-year and above undergraduates
Junior graduate	JG	First- and second-year or master's-level graduate students
Senior graduate	SG	Third year and above Ph.D. students
Junior faculty	JF	Lecturers and assistant professors
Senior faculty	SF	Associate professors and above
Researcher	RE	Nonteaching researchers
Post-Doctoral Fellow	PD	Postdoctoral research fellows
Staff	ST	Nonteaching University employees
Visitor/Other	VO	Non-University of Michigan affiliates
Native Speaker Status		
Native Speaker	NS	Native speakers of North American English
Native Speaker Other	NSO	Native speakers of non-American English
Near Native Speaker	NRN	Nonnative speakers who consider English as their current dominant language and who appear to have nativelike fluency and grammatical proficiency.
Nonnative Speaker	NNS	Nonnative speakers of English other than near-native speakers
First Language		
Only given when first language is other than North American English		

on was the accuracy of the transcription; that is to say we decided to place a high priority on accuracy, at the expense of time and money. For this reason, our transcription process consists of three stages: for every speech event, one person transcribes it a first time, a second person listens to the recording and rechecks the entire transcript, and a third person proofreads the transcript and checks the accuracy of the header information. When possible, at least one of the first two transcribers is someone who was present at the speech event. Given this lengthy transcribing process, we are confident that errors have been kept to a minimum by the time transcripts are made publicly available on the Web. Nonetheless, problems do crop up, and one of the challenges of creating the transcripts has been maintaining consistency of tagging by a group of student transcribers. For example, which contextual events get noted and the exact wording that goes into a tag is an issue that has been revisited often, as has the less significant but no less problematic issue of editorial style conventions, such as hyphenation and capitalization.

The Web Interface

Access

The HTI makes its collections freely accessible to the general public, and the MICASE team agreed that a spoken corpus such as this one would be much more widely used if it were made easily and freely accessible. At this time, only the text transcripts are being posted on the Web server; plans for distribution of the original sound files (online or otherwise) are in the beginning stages. In addition to the technical challenges of delivering sound files, especially ones of this size, there is the added problem of the need to exclude the utterances of the speakers who have not consented to having their audio file accessible on the Web. Excluding these utterances would require editing some of the sound files—as MICASE could not deliver the archival versions—and would add the complication of maintaining multiple versions. The exclusion is more easily handled with the SGML text files, as the programs that deliver the text files via the Web look for the utterances by speakers who have withheld permission and supply a notice that an utterance is not being displayed. (See the following section on consent restrictions for more information.)

Functionality

The transcripts available on the Web are created dynamically from the SGML when they are requested by a user; the HTI does not store static versions of the texts in **HTML.** The HTI staff **indexes** the transcripts using the OpenText Corporations's search engine software and writes the programs required to work with the Web interface and the indexes of the transcripts. The program takes the information submitted on the Web page, formats it into a syntax understood by the search engine, and submits the search. It then retrieves the text found by the search engine, transforms the SGML into HTML, and sends it to the user's Web browser. The transcripts can only be retrieved through the MICASE Web interface.

MICASE staff worked with the DLPS Interface Specialist to create this interface for browsing and searching the transcripts, presenting results, and displaying the text of the transcripts. The on-line search interface was designed to be able to search for words or phrases according to any of the ten categories of speech event or speaker characteristics that are encoded in the header (see tables 1 and 2), display the results within a surrounding context line (as a **KWIC**, or keyword-in-context, concordance), and re-sort those results according to several possible options. In addition, the entire transcript (with the exception of utterances suppressed for confidentiality) can be viewed on-line or downloaded in its original SGML-encoded text format.

Structure

There are two main search modes for accessing the corpus, called "browse" and "search." Browse is a search that returns only names of transcripts contained in the current collection that meet certain user-specified criteria. For example, browse mode is used to find out which transcripts in the collection include female speakers, which include undergraduates, or which include nonnative speakers. Similarly, browse mode is used for finding transcripts of certain types of speech events, such as all lectures, all transcripts in the humanities, or all graduate-level classes or meetings. It is also possible to find all the transcripts in the collection that contain a specific word or phrase and to combine several search parameters for a narrower search. In this way, a user could find all the transcripts of lectures in the social sciences that include female speakers, all transcripts of lectures and colloquia that include the word *indeed*, and so on.[2] The results page in browse mode displays the list of transcripts meeting the specified criteria and, if a search word was specified, the number of occurrences of that word in each transcript. Links lead from the transcript name to the actual header and then to the full text of the transcript.

Search mode is a more traditional concordance-style search of the actual texts of the transcripts. The search can be conducted on the entire corpus or on a subset thereof, specified in the same manner as in browse mode. In addition to the primary search term or phrase, a context word can also be specified for the search, with the option to specify the proximity of the context word to the search word, in number of words to the left, to the right, or to the left or right (see fig. 1). At this point, the search facility is not yet programmed to include a wildcard (*) character, nor does it provide options for searching **regular expressions.**

The results of a search are displayed as concordance lines, with a certain number of words to the left and right of the search term, which is highlighted in red (see fig. 2). In addition, each key-word-in-context line includes the file number, the sequential number of that token in the search results, the speaker ID number, and the two speaker variables (gender, age-group, academic role, or native speaker status) chosen by the user when executing the search. From the results page, links lead to several different options: the file name link leads to the header information (and subsequently to the full transcript); the sequential token number link leads to the full utterance or turn in

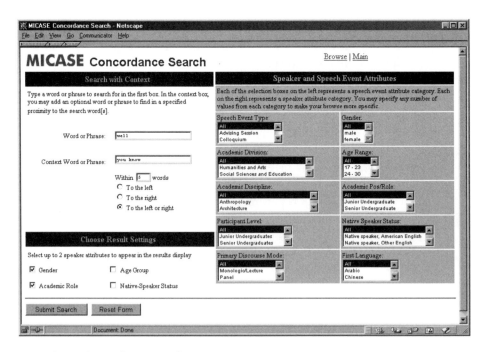

Fig. 1. Concordance search screen

MICASE Search Results

Revise Search | Browse | Main

Concordance Search Results

Sort filters 1: None   2: None   3: None   sort

File #	Key Word in Context	Sp. ID	Gender	Academic Position/Role
Total matches: 25				
COL002MX040 1	contact with saying you know well have you thought about this	S7	F	SG
COL002MX040 2	well no you're tenured now. well you know when we were	S8	F	RE
COL002MX040 3	that you could say oh well i i feel like you	S4	F	UN
COL285MX038 4	even considered it. <L> you know well just just deal with it	S1	F	SG
DEF420MX022 5	know you get the feeling well, you know a a writer	S3	M	SF
DEF420MX022 6	well, you know, there are there	S5	M	SF
DEF420MX022 7	at this and i'm thinking well you know th- there's an	S5	M	SF
DEF420MX022 8	have these long rubato introductions well late Bill Evans you know	S4	M	SF
INT175SF003 9	well	S1	M	SF
LEL115SU005 10	little bit by just saying well gosh you know i i	S1	F	JF
LEL115SU005 11	epidemiologists come in and say well you know for every thousand	S1	F	JF
LEL115SU005 12	and goes on to say well you know i've seen seven	S1	F	JF
LEL115SU005 13	that and say you know well, who'd be_ who's so stupid	S1	F	JF
LEL300SU020 14	he he says you know well she, she wanted to be	S1	M	SF

Document: Done

Fig. 2. Search results screen

which that token appears; the speaker ID link leads to the demographic information for that speaker. One helpful feature of the program is that when the user follows a link to view the full utterance or full transcript after executing a search, the search word is highlighted in red (and the context word, if any, in green) throughout the transcript. The results of a search can also be re-sorted (with up to three sorting levels) according to a number of different criteria, including the first through fifth word to the left or right, the search term itself (e.g., to separate out instances of the search word followed by a question mark), or either of the two speaker attributes chosen for display.

Consent Restrictions

One of the issues that arises in spoken corpus compilation is the protection of speakers' privacy. We inform participants that no identifying information will be used and that if participants' last (and in some cases first) names occur in a recording, they are changed to pseudonyms in the transcript, except in the case of public colloquia with large audiences. Despite our assurances of anonymity, a certain number of people are still hesitant to give their full consent, especially given the public availability of the MICASE data. Informed consent for primary speakers is obtained on a written form that provides options for speakers to restrict the use of their speech in various ways. Speakers are allowed to specify whether they consent to Web availability of the data (text and/or audio) and whether they wish to restrict citation of their speech in published materials or presentations. A small number of speakers consent to Web access but not to having their speech cited in published materials, textbooks, or conference presentations. An even smaller number of speakers do not consent to having their speech available via the Web, although they do consent to being recorded and do not specify any citation restrictions. Both of these types of consent restrictions are rare, so very few transcripts appear differently on the Web-delivered version than in the original, archival version. These restrictions (or lack thereof) are encoded in the header as an attribute in the <PERSON> element for each speaker, which indicates either that there are no restrictions, that there are citation restrictions, or that the speech is restricted from appearing on the Web. Furthermore, every transcript has a note in the availability statement of the header specifying either that there are no consent restrictions on any speakers in that transcript or that there are citation restrictions for one or more speakers.

Programming Challenges

While Web access is ideal for making MICASE available to a large number of users around the world, it presents a number of challenges in both the design of the interface and the programming of the search functionality. The nature of designing for the Web as opposed to creating a desktop application means that you have no control over which browsers, which versions of those browsers, or which computer platforms users might have. Relying on features available in one browser or browser version—XML (Extensible Markup Language) support or style sheets, for example—in the design of MICASE would mean that people without that version would have a very different experience of the corpus. While it might not be an insurmountable problem to have varying levels of functionality, it is an issue that must be considered, tested, and documented.

A further design challenge is the presentation of a great deal of detail in a relatively small space, even on a large monitor (and while statistics gathered by the Web server can present us with some information about the browsers, versions, and platforms of MICASE users, we know nothing about the sizes of their monitors). The searching and browsing interfaces needed to present the ten speaker and speech event attributes (see tables 1 and 2), as well as some information about how to choose them. The results screens were more problematic; here, it was necessary to display the search term with sufficient surrounding context. We also wanted to display the speaker ID, the two speaker attributes that the user chose on the search interface, and links to both the complete utterance (i.e., turn) in which the search term occurs and the full transcript. The largest challenge was not displaying the speech itself but displaying all of these different pieces of descriptive information about the speaker and speech event in a compact yet easily understandable manner.

For Web delivery of both the lines of search results as well as the views of the full utterances and full transcripts, several of the conventions marked with SGML tags had to be translated into HTML. Unfortunately, HTML does not offer many style options for distinguishing the difference between, for example, a place where two speakers overlap and a place where the first speaker cedes the floor to the second. The complex SGML encoding created by the MICASE staff had to be simplified into what is possible with HTML, through the use of colors or font shifts (i.e., italics or bold), in a way that is reasonably transparent to the user. Some of these style conversions were intuitive, as in the case of words marked with a <FOREIGN> tag, which are set to appear in italics. Others were not so simple; the most complex tags to convert into clear HTML were overlaps and embedded utterances, which may or may not be overlapped. In the case of embedded utterances, the SGML convention we adopted was simply to nest another "<U>" element with the appropriate speaker ID into the main speaker's utterance. In the HTML version, embedded utterances appear in orange, to contrast with the surrounding text, and are preceded by the speaker ID and surrounded by square brackets. A similar solution was applied for overlapping speech, which appears in blue. When an embedded backchannel cue or unsuccessful interruption is also overlapping, the text appears in blue, but the speaker ID and surrounding brackets are orange.

The statelessness of the Web presents another challenge; each search is a onetime transaction between the browser and the server. Unlike a **concordance program** that may be installed on a particular computer, all the Web server knows about a user is what is submitted at the time of a particular search, not what has been previously submitted or even if anything has been previously submitted by this user. "Cookies" are a common way around this for many Web sites, but because of privacy concerns, they have not been used by the HTI in any other collections, so this is not an approach that was taken for MICASE. To provide the ability to re-sort results by different criteria, the search engine needs to be reminded what the user did before and what needs to be done now that is different. The programs written by the DLPS Information Retrieval Programmer carry this information along, since the Web browser does not.

Future Developments

In addition to adding new transcripts as they become available and fixing bugs identified by MICASE staff or users, there are some areas of the Web interface that could use some attention. One desirable improvement for users of MICASE would be to assure that the token numbers get reassigned when a search is re-sorted. In the present implementation, the token numbers from the original search results are carried over into the re-sort results screen, making it problematic to easily count the number of tokens for each sort category. Another improvement would be the addition of capabilities for searching with wildcard characters and regular expressions. There are also a number of improvements that would be solely for the benefit of MICASE and HTI staff. Currently, we have no automated means for MICASE staff to add new transcripts, so this process requires a great deal of manual intervention by DLPS programming staff. Since another collection of the HTI does have an automated updating process, there is a possible solution to that problem. This would not, however, minimize the need for informed testers—generally MICASE staff—to ensure that rules for HTML delivery apply to the new material and that differences are the result of new features in the transcript, not inconsistent application of tagging. The decision to post a small set of transcripts last year and continue adding transcripts until the corpus is complete was a beneficial one in this respect, as it has given the MICASE staff an opportunity to test the interface before the corpus is complete, and as it has led to continued collaboration between MICASE and the HTI in the process of working out bugs.

At present, we are just over two-thirds of the way through our data collection and are encouraged to hear that teachers and researchers around the world are already making use of the data we have made available so far. We expect the rest of the data collection and transcribing to be completed by the summer of 2001, with some additional time for finalizing and editing the remaining transcripts. At that time we will move on to the second phase of the project and reassess prospects for further markup, tagging, or other development of the corpus.

Notes

1. At the time of writing, the corpus is over halfway done, with over 110 hours of speech recorded and over 900,000 words transcribed, although only a subset of this total is currently available on the Web. New sets of transcripts will continue to be posted periodically as they are finalized.
2. Many of these search parameters are not extremely useful at this point, because of the small number of transcripts currently available on-line. However, the interface was designed with the full corpus of 1.5 million words in mind, and the five speech event attributes and five speaker attributes constitute the primary social or contextual factors believed to be of greatest potential research interest once the corpus is complete.

Reference

Simpson, R., B. Lucka, and J. Ovens. 2000. Methodological Challenges of Planning a Spoken Corpus with Pedagogical Outcomes. In *Rethinking Language Pedagogy from a Corpus Perspective: Papers from the Third International Conference on Teaching and Language Corpora,* ed. L. Burnard and T. McEnery. Frankfurt: Peter Lang.

Representing Spoken Language in University Settings: The Design and Construction of the Spoken Component of the T2K-SWAL Corpus

Douglas Biber, Randi Reppen, Victoria Clark, and Jenia Walter
Northern Arizona University

It is widely agreed that second language exams should assess competencies in the actual registers that students interact with on a regular basis. Similarly, teaching materials should accurately reflect the patterns of language use in those registers. At the university level, these varieties include a range of spoken registers (e.g., lectures, classroom discussions, student study groups, campus-related service encounters) and written registers (e.g., textbooks, course syllabi, assignments, university catalogs).

However, researchers at present know relatively little about the patterns of language use that are typical of academic registers, especially spoken academic registers. For the most part, previous studies have analyzed a few linguistic features in only a few texts from selected registers. While the multi-dimensional approach (Biber 1986, 1988) has been used for generalizable studies of written academic registers (e.g., Grabe 1987; Biber and Finegan 1994, 1997; Conrad 1996; Atkinson 1999), there have been fewer large-scale empirical investigations using other approaches, and there have been virtually no such investigations of spoken academic registers.

One reason for this gap is that there are no readily available representative text collections from academic registers that can be used for research studies, for materials development, or to construct items for second language tests. Most available corpora are designed as collections of general English registers, such as conversation, newspaper language, fiction, and academic journals and trade books. Corpora of this type include the Brown, LOB (Lancaster-Oslo-Bergen), London-Lund, BNC (British National Corpus), COBUILD's Bank of English, and ACL/DCI (see Biber, Conrad, and Reppen 1998, app. I). Many of these corpora represent British rather than American English, and none of them is designed to represent the spoken and written registers used in student academic life. This gap is especially acute for spoken academic registers.

The TOEFL 2000 Spoken and Written Academic Language Corpus (T2K-SWAL Corpus) was designed to help fill this gap, representing the range of spoken and written registers encountered in student academic life. The project was supported by a contract from the Educational Testing Service, with the goal of providing a more representative basis for test construction and validation (although we anticipate that the corpus will have a wide range of research uses beyond that). In the present chapter, we focus on the spoken component of that corpus. We describe the research goals of the corpus, discuss the overall design and methodology used in its construction, and briefly summarize the final composition of the corpus.

The Research Goals of the Corpus

The T2K-SWAL Corpus is designed to be used for two major purposes.

1. To study the patterns of language use found in academic registers
2. To develop procedures for assuring that the language used in TOEFL Exam tasks is representative of real-life language use

Related to the first purpose, analyses based on the corpus can investigate a wide range of research issues relating to the linguistic characteristics of academic texts; these include vocabulary distributions, the use of collocations and idioms, grammatical characteristics, syntactic complexity, informational density, and patterns of rhetorical organization. In all cases, the design of the corpus will allow research to be undertaken from a register perspective; that is, each register (e.g., textbooks, course syllabi, lectures, or service encounters) can be studied in relation to the full range of other academic spoken and written registers. In addition to text studies, the corpus will be used to develop diagnostic tools to ensure that test stimuli represent the same range of variation and linguistic (lexical and grammatical) complexity that students encounter regularly in academic life.

There are at least four major advantages to adopting a corpus-based approach for these research purposes.

1. The adequate representation of naturally occurring discourse, including representative text samples from a range of academic registers. Corpus-based analyses can be based on long passages from each text, multiple texts from each register, and a full range of spoken and written registers.
2. The (semi-)automatic linguistic processing of texts using computers, enabling analyses of much wider scope than otherwise feasible. With computational processing, it is possible to undertake a comprehensive linguistic characterization of a text, analyzing a wide range of linguistic features. Further, once the software tools are developed for this type of analysis, it is possible to process all available on-line texts.
3. Much greater reliability and accuracy for quantitative analyses of linguistic features. Computers do not become bored or tired—they will count a linguistic feature in the same way every time it is encountered.
4. The possibility of cumulative results and accountability. Subsequent studies can be based on the same corpus of texts, or additional corpora can be analyzed using the same computational techniques.

Design and Methodology

The two most important considerations in the design of corpora are (1) the representation of the full range of register diversity within the target discourse domain and (2) the size of the sample from each register (number of texts and number of words per text). At the same time, these considerations must be balanced by practical considerations relating to the amount of time and resources available for corpus construction.

We designed the T2K-SWAL Corpus to be relatively large (minimally 2 million words for the spoken and written components combined) and representative of the range of the academic registers that students must listen to or read. We aimed to represent five major situational parameters in the design and construction of the T2K-SWAL corpus: register, level, discipline, subdiscipline, and interactiveness (for class sessions).

The register categories chosen for the corpus are sampled from across the full range of spoken and written activities associated with academic life. However, given the constraints of time and budget, it was not feasible to attempt a comprehensive sampling of all distinctions (e.g., including language from all disciplines, sampled from the full range of American universities). Instead, we have focused on a finite number of registers from five selected disciplines (natural science, humanities, business, engineering, and social science) representing the range of variability that students will encounter in academic life. The relative weight given to each register category reflects our assessment of its relative availability and importance. We evaluated this balance during corpus construction, adjusting it as we determined that particular categories were more or less important than expected.

The sampling of all register categories is split evenly between undergraduate- and graduate-level texts. Further, we collected texts at four academic sites (Northern Arizona University, Iowa State University, California State University at Sacramento, and Georgia State University). We did not attempt to achieve exact equivalence of sampling from the academic sites. Our goal was rather to avoid marked skewing that might result from texts being sampled from a single university setting, although we did not anticipate any systematic differences across universities.

Data collection has focused on capturing naturally occurring discourse. One major obstacle that we needed to address was that the presence of research assistants in spoken settings is intrusive and likely to result in somewhat artificial discourse. As a result, we employed target participants to carry tape recorders and record academic speech as it occurred spontaneously. We have obtained high-quality, natural interactions using this approach; the major disadvantage is that we have not observed the interactions firsthand and thus have not been able to obtain detailed information about the setting and participants.

In general, we used students as our primary participants, recruiting them to record class sessions, study groups, and other academic conversations. We also recruited faculty members to help with the recording of office hours and university staff for recording service encounters. Participants were evenly distributed across the five disciplines (natural science, humanities, business, engineering, social science) and three levels of education (lower-division undergraduate, upper-division undergraduate, graduate). We also targeted specific subdisciplines (e.g., chemistry, philosophy, psychology) to enable register comparisons at a more specific level. Student participants recorded the class sessions and study groups that they were involved in during a two-week period, keeping a log of speech events and participants to the extent that it was practical. University staff members were recruited from offices and areas that regularly interact with students (e.g., the office of the registrar, the book store, the library).

In the design of the corpus, we have tried to balance four desirable criteria (see Biber 1990, 1993a, 1993b; Biber, Conrad, and Reppen 1994, 1996, 1998).

1. The corpus must be as large as possible.
2. The corpus must be as representative as possible (of registers, disciplines, levels of education, universities, teaching styles, etc.).
3. The corpus must be collected, transcribed/scanned, edited, tagged, and tag-edited within a two-year period.
4. The corpus should be constructed in a cost-efficient manner.

Unfortunately, these criteria can conflict with one another, so that the resulting design is a compromise among the four. With respect to size, the T2K-SWAL Corpus is designed to meet the million-word standard used in the Brown, LOB, and ICE corpus projects. (Much larger corpora, such as the BNC and COBUILD Bank of English, have been constructed recently, but these grew out of much larger projects and were not developed for specialized domains.) The T2K-SWAL corpus will be more than adequate for analyses of major grammatical features, since Biber 1990 shows that the distribution of common grammatical features is stable across text samples as small as 1,000 words. The corpus will also be large enough for analyses of common vocabulary patterns, although it would need to be extended for collocational studies of less common words.

With respect to the representation of diversity, our design is intended to sample the range of differences found in academic language use. Although there are gaps not included in the corpus (e.g., aspects of regional or demographic variation), we intend the corpus to represent the various types of spoken academic language that students can expect to encounter on virtually any American university campus.

These design goals and sampling methods obviously do not allow a full representation of demographic variation (regional, ethnic, social, or other) in the United States. For example, there are 18 major speech areas in the eastern United States alone, each associated with a different regional dialect. In addition, it is possible to identify numerous urban dialects within the country, as well as several well-defined social and ethnic dialects within most of those urban centers. Attempting even a minimal representation of these dialect patterns would require a project many times larger than the present one. Similarly, we have not attempted a full representation of the kinds of academic institutions found in the United States, since this also would have required a much larger project.

While we have not achieved full demographic/institutional representativeness, we have avoided obvious skewing for these factors. Further, we believe that we have face validity in relation to these factors, recognizing and including at least some of the major differences. The corpus materials have been collected from four major regions in the United States: the West Coast, the Rocky Mountain region, the Midwest, and the Deep South. Further, we collected materials from several different types of academic institutions: a teacher's college (California State University, Sacramento), a midsize regional university (Northern Arizona University), an urban research university (Georgia State University), and a Research 1 university with a national reputation in agriculture and engineering (Iowa State University). Although this design does not represent the full range of demographic or institutional variation in the U.S., it is also not skewed toward any particular regions or types of institution.

All texts in the corpus were coded with a header to identify content area and register. Spoken texts have been transcribed using a consistent transcription convention (see Edwards and Lampert 1993). To the extent possible, speakers were distinguished and some demographic information (e.g., status as instructor vs. student) is supplied in the header for each speaker.

All texts were edited to ensure accuracy in transcribing. Then, all texts were grammatically annotated using an automatic grammatical "tagger" (developed and revised over a 10-year period by Biber). The grammatical tags are subsequently edited using an interactive grammar-checker ("fixtag"), to assure a high degree of accuracy for the final annotated corpus (see Biber, Conrad, and Reppen 1998).

The Current State of the Spoken Component of the Corpus

Construction of the T2K-SWAL Corpus began in fall 1998. As of June 30, 2000, we had collected (on tape), transcribed, and "fixtagged" over 1.6 million words. Tables 1 and 2 summarize the breakdown of texts in the spoken component across disciplines, levels, and registers.

We have not segmented recordings into subtexts, since we believe that would compromise the integrity of the text. Instead, we classify each file (representing a single recording session) according to the predominant kind of language represented (e.g., lecture vs. in-class group work, high-interaction vs. low-interaction class session). Secondary kinds of discourse represented in the transcript are identified in the header of the file. At the same time, it is important to note that most recordings are not "pure" instances of a category. For example, class sessions shift from lecture mode to group work, and lecturers shift from a high-interactive style to monologue.

Class-management discussion stands out here, with only 39,255 words. When it occurs at all, speech from this register takes place only at the beginning and end of class sessions and typically takes only one to two minutes. Apart from this category, all "texts" in the corpus are intact, representing the complex interweaving of tasks found in normal spoken discourse. However, we copied the class-management

TABLE 1. Overview of the Spoken Component of the T2K-SWAL Corpus

Categories	No. of Tapes Collected	No. of Tapes Transcribed and "Fixtagged"	No. of Words Transcribed and "Fixtagged"
University class sessions	510	176	1,248,811
In-class group work	17	17	88,234
Classroom management	(62)	(40)	39,255
Study groups	25	25	141,140
Office hours	15	11	50,412
Service encounters	31	22	97,664
Total	598	251	1,665,516

[a]Classroom management is extracted from class session tapes, so it is not included in the total tape counts.

TABLE 2. Breakdown of University Class Sessions by Levels for the Spoken Component of the T2K-SWAL Corpus

Categories	No. of tapes collected	No. of tapes transcribed and "fixtagged"	No. of words transcribed and "fixtagged"
Lower level	19	8	44,418
Upper level	43	20	126,026
Graduate	33	8	66,010
Total business	95	36	236,454
Lower level	4	4	26,237
Upper level	11	4	25,871
Graduate	19	8	85,135
Total education	34	16	137,243
Lower level	8	8	45,864
Upper level	44	14	72,165
Graduate	12	8	53,156
Total engineering	64	30	171,185
Lower level	48	10	65,948
Upper level	41	12	91,732
Graduate	22	9	90,946
Total humanities	111	31	248,626
Lower level	36	9	48,616
Upper level	33	7	40,447
Graduate	16	9	71,810
Total natural science	85	25	160,873
Lower level	52	15	124,435
Upper level	52	15	107,283
Graduate	19	8	62,712
Total social science	123	38	294,430
Total class sessions	512	176	1,248,811

talk found in class sessions into separate "subtexts," to study this register in more detail.

During construction of the corpus, we added several subcategories to better represent the patterns of language use that we observed. For example:

a. We have made a two-way distinction between class sessions and in-class group work.
b. In-class group work (including lab sessions) rarely constitutes an entire class session. The texts classified in this category are predominantly students interacting with other students.

c. Class sessions are classified as high interaction, medium interaction, or low interaction. These are subjective classifications, based on the extent to which both instructors and students participate.
d. We added education as a sixth major discipline, since many international students come to the United States to study in this area.
e. We attempted to track two to three specific subdisciplines within each of the six major disciplines across levels, rather than opting for an unprincipled assembly of recordings that confounds level and subdiscipline.
f. Under study groups, we classified texts according to whether the interactions involved pairs (two students studying together) or groups (more than two students).

Conclusion

The present chapter has highlighted the major research goals, design considerations, and construction of the spoken component of the TOEFL 2000 spoken and Written Academic Language Corpus. The major goal of the corpus is to provide a more representative basis for test construction and validation. We also plan to analyze the corpus to uncover the major patterns of language use that characterize each academic register. These research goals include detailed lexical and grammatical analyses of each register, together with a multi-dimensional analysis (see Biber 1988) of the underlying patterns of register variation.

References

Atkinson, D. 1999. *Scientific Discourse in Sociohistorical Context.* Mahwah, NJ: Lawrence Erlbaum.

Biber, D. 1986. Spoken and Written Textual Dimensions in English: Resolving the Contradictory Findings. *Language* 62:384–414.

———. 1988. *Variation across Speech and Writing.* Cambridge: Cambridge University Press.

———. 1990. Methodological Issues regarding Corpus-Based Analyses of Linguistic Variation. *Literary and Linguistic Computing* 5:257–69.

———. 1993a. Representativeness in Corpus Design. *Literary and Linguistic Computing* 8:243–57.

———. 1993b. Using Register-Diversified Corpora for General Language Studies. *Computational Linguistics* 19:219–41.

Biber, D., S. Conrad, and R. Reppen. 1994. Corpus-Based Approaches to Issues in Applied Linguistics. *Applied Linguistics* 15:169–89.

———. 1996. Corpus-Based Investigations of Language Use. *Annual Review of Applied Linguistics* 16:115–36.

———. 1998. *Corpus Linguistics: Investigating Language Structure and Use.* Cambridge: Cambridge University Press.

Biber, D., and E. Finegan. 1994. Intra-textual Variation within Medical Research Articles. In *Corpus-Based Research into Language,* ed. N. Oostdijk and P. de Haan, 201–22. Amsterdam: Rodopi.

———. 1997. Diachronic Relations among Speech-Based and Written Registers in English. In *To Explain the Present: Studies in the Changing English Language in Honour of Matti Rissanen,* ed. T. Nevalainen and L. Kahlas-Tarkka, 253–75. Helsinki: Societe Neophilologique.

Conrad, S. 1996. Investigating Academic Texts with Corpus-Based Techniques: An Example from Biology. *Linguistics and Education* 8, no. 3:299–326.

Edwards, J. A., and M. D. Lampert, eds. 1993. *Talking Data: Transcription and Coding in Discourse Research.* Hillsdale, NJ: Lawrence Erlbaum.

Grabe, W. 1987. Contrastive Rhetoric and Text Type Research. In *Writing across Languages: Analysis of L2 Text,* ed. U. Connor and R. B. Kaplan, 115–35. Reading, MA: Addison-Wesley.

Creating and Using Multimillion-Word Corpora from Web-Based Newspapers

Mark Davies
Illinois State University

With the dramatic increase in the past few years of newspapers and magazines that are available on the Web, it has now become feasible for researchers to create multimillion-word corpora for their research. This chapter will first discuss two large corpora that I have created for Spanish and Portuguese (35 million and 26 million words, respectively) and how they complement other corpora that I have created for these two languages. I will then discuss—in a fairly practical and step-by-step fashion—the process by which researchers can create their own corpora, as well as some of the challenges they might face. Finally, I will discuss how large multimillion-word corpora can be used to complement more traditional corpora, specifically in the sense of studying newly emerging syntactic constructions in a particular language.

Two Multimillion-Word Web-Based Corpora

I have created a 35-million-word corpus of Modern Spanish and a 26-million-word corpus of Modern Portuguese. The Spanish corpus is composed of 20 million words from newspapers in Latin America and contains a total of 1 million words from at least two newspapers in each of the twenty Spanish-speaking countries. It also contains 15 million words from eight newspapers in Spain. (A list of the newspapers included in the Spanish corpus can be found in my appendix.) The Portuguese corpus is composed of 26 million words, including 15 million words from twelve newspapers in Brazil (representing the different geographical regions of the country), as well as 10 million words from eight newspapers in Portugal. One of the unique aspects of the Portuguese corpus is that there is an additional 1 million words of text from interviews extracted from these newspapers, including 625,000 words from five newspapers in Brazil and 390,000 words from five newspapers in Portugal. In summary, these corpora constitute some of the largest and most comprehensive corpora of Spanish and Portuguese in existence.

These corpora supplement a number of other, nonnewspaper Spanish and Portuguese corpora that I have created, which are summarized in tables 1 and 2 (more details are available at <http://mdavies.for.ilstu.edu/personal/texts.htm>). In table 1, I have divided the corpora into spoken and written texts. The distinction here is between those texts that are the transcripts of actual conversations (spoken), on the one hand, and, on the other, novels, short stories, and newspapers (written), which, although they may attempt

TABLE 1. Modern Spanish Corpora

Country	Corpus	Number of texts/ conversations	Number of words
Spoken			
Latin America	*Habla Culta* (Bogotá, Buenos Aires, Caracas, Havana, La Paz, Lima, Mexico City, San Jose [Costa Rica], San Juan [P.R.], Santiago [Chile])	385	2,193,000
Spain	*Habla Culta* (Madrid, Sevilla)	72	328,000
Spain	*Corpus oral de referencia de la lengua española contemporanea*	498	948,000
Written			
Latin America/ Spain	Novels	15	1,327,000
Latin America/ Spain	Short stories (same countries as those in the *Habla Culta* corpus)	356	1,054,000
Argentina	*Corpus lingüistico de referencia de la lengua española—Argentina*	22	1,913,400
Total		1350	7,763,000

TABLE 2. Modern Portuguese Corpora

County	Corpus	Number of texts/ conversations	Number of words
Brazil	*Linguagem Falada* (Recife, São Paulo, Rio de Janeiro, Salvador)	85 conversations	570,800
Brazil	Borba-Ramsey Corpus (essay, novel, journal, technical, drama)	102 blocks	1,670,300
Brazil	Short stories	26 authors	75,100
Portugal	Novels	11 novels	239,000
Total		224	2,555,200

to model the author's perception of native speech, are in fact inventions of the author.

Looking at the lists of corpora in tables 1 and 2, one can see that although the nonnewspaper corpora are fairly large (10 million words in both spoken and written texts between the two languages), the 60 million words from the Web-based newspapers represent much larger corpora and can thus provide some useful insight into certain syntactic constructions, a point that I will return to in the final section of this chapter.

Creating Multimillion-Word Web-Based Corpora

In what follows, I will discuss—step-by-step—some of the more important procedures in creating large multimillion-word corpora from Web-based newspapers and magazines. Although the discussion may appear a bit rudimentary at times, my purpose is to guide others through the process and hopefully help them to deal with some of the technical challenges that I faced when creating my two corpora.

Finding Newspapers

As most people who have spent much time on the Web are aware, there has recently been a virtual explosion in the number (and quality) of newspapers on the Web. While researchers of English have had access to large multimillion-word corpora for a number of years, these

Web-based newspapers constitute an important resource for those working in other languages or perhaps specialized varieties of English, such as obituaries, law reports, and editorials. In compiling my corpus of Spanish newspapers, it was encouraging to find that even small, less-developed countries, such as El Salvador and Paraguay, have three or four newspapers on-line. There are a number of excellent lists of international newspapers on-line, and a partial list of these lists can be found at <http://dir.yahoo.com/News>.

Evaluating Newspapers

As might be expected, there are differences between the various on-line newspapers in terms of how easily they can be incorporated into a corpus. One issue is the thematic content of the newspaper. While some have extensive sections for national and international news and for society, sports, and finance news, other newspapers are monothematic, focusing on one topic, such as sports or finance. For researchers wanting a wider range of styles and registers, newspapers with many different thematic sections are of course preferable. A second issue is the server on which the newspaper is located and the speed at which articles can be downloaded, especially when corpus creation involves downloading hundreds of thousands of articles.

A more important issue concerns the archives of past editions. Many newspapers (including some of the best ones) only provide links to the editions for the past week, which makes it difficult to create a multimillion-word corpus, unless one revisits the site over a number of weeks. Other newspapers, however, provide an archive of issues for the entire past month, and some provide every issue for the past two or three years.

The final issue, and perhaps the most important one, deals with the amount of redundancy in articles from day to day. If the same article appears two or three days in a row, automated downloading of the contents for those days means that tokens from that article will appear multiple times in the corpus, which is of course problematic. The best solution is to avoid newspapers with a high degree of redundancy, but another solution (if the newspaper has extensive archives) is to download just one day a week for the past two or three years and hope that there is little overlap. One final possibility is to take care of matters at the level of text retrieval, using a program or algorithm to account for redundancy at that point.

Locating Past Editions

The next stage is to develop a sense of the structure of the Web site, so that the individual articles can be downloaded as efficiently as possible. Let us suppose that the "home page" for a particular issue has the address <http://www.excelsior.com.mx/9807/980704/>; after the domain (www.excelsior.com.mx) is the date, with the format */yymm/yymmdd/*. In our word processor, we can copy this address, or URL, for as many days as we want to download, then use macros to modify the "base" URL for all of the particular dates that we want to download (e.g., /9710/971005/ [October 5, 1997], /9805/980522/ [May 22, 1998]). Finally, we can save this list of links in **HTML** format (<A HREF="<link>"><title></A>).

Employing Automated Downloading

It would of course be impractical to manually download tens and hundreds of thousands of articles. Fortunately, there is software that will do this for us. Using an **off-line browser,** such as Grab-A-Site (<http://www.bluesquirrel.com/products/grabasite/grabasite.html>; see the related software at <http://tucows.pdnt.com/offline95. html>), we indicate the starting URL and how many levels down we want to "crawl." For example, the Web page containing the list of URLs (from the previous section) would be level 1. The links to the home pages for the different issues of the newspaper would be level 2. The links on those home pages to the various sections (national news, society news, sports news, etc.) would be level 3. The actual articles would be level 4, so we would set the "crawling" level to "4." With such programs as Grab-A-Site, we can also direct the crawler to limit downloads to the Web site for the newspaper (rather than following links to ads or URLs for companies mentioned in the articles), as well as limiting downloads to just Web pages (HTML files) rather than graphics and other multimedia. If we have a fairly fast network connection, it is possible to configure the "crawler" for downloads and then return in the morning with several thousand articles from a particular newspaper.

Working with Directories and Files

Most "crawler" software allows us to mirror the directory structure of the Web site, so that all of the articles for a particular date will be in the same directory. After scanning through the file names, we can delete files that are clearly redundant (e.g., Web pages with subscription information) or not useful (e.g., stock quotes, where there is little usable text), and we can delete these files recursively in child directories with just one command. In some cases, simple **batch files** may help to automate the process.

In cases where the directories on the Web site organize articles by date, all of the articles for the same date will be together, and we can use a simple command (e.g., "copy *.html 0502.htm" for articles in the May 2 directory) to concatenate all of the separate files for one day into just one file, which is easier to use in subsequent stages. There is a problem, however, when different articles for a particular date are spread among different directories (e.g., /sports/1998/0502,/finance/1998/0502). In such cases, we sometimes have to resort to fairly complex batch files to get all of the files for one date into the same directory, so that we can concatenate them into one file.

Converting from HTML Files to Text

At this stage, the Web pages will usually still be in HTML format, with all of the style and formatting tags that entails. If we want simple text files for the corpus, we will need to convert all of the tens of thousands of files, and it would of course be impractical to do this manually. The process can be automated using a program, such as HTMASC32 (<http://www.bitenbyte.com/htmasc.htm>). This particular software can very quickly convert to text tens of thousands of HTML files, and it can also handle files as large as 10 to 20 megabytes, for those cases in which we have created large concatenated files.

Using Macros to Clean Up Texts

Most newspaper articles contain redundant information that we probably do not want as part of the corpus, such as headers or footers containing links to other articles, subscription information, and links to ads. Using macros in our word processor, we can strip out as much of this information as we would like. For example, we can create a macro to search for certain text that indicates the beginning of the footer on the Web pages. We then block the material between that text and the title of the following article (to eliminate the header from that article). The macro then deletes all of the blocked material, eliminating the headers and footers. However, to determine which textual elements we will want to delete on every page, we need to obtain some sense of the layout of the pages for a particular newspaper.

Assuming we have a fairly powerful computer, we can have the macro run on hundreds of files (e.g., one for each day's issue) and strip out this text from hundreds or thousands of articles in each file. I offer one caveat, however—the faster the word processor, the better. When dealing with hundreds of thousands of articles, we do not want a complicated word processor that is overloaded with features or has an overly complex graphical interface. In my work, I have used Word-Perfect 5.1 (DOS) or TextPad (<http://www.textpad.com>), both of which are quick, allow macros, and have worked quite well.

Locating and Extracting Special Kinds of Texts

In some cases, we might want to select certain types of articles (based on thematic or subgenre characteristics) and create a special subcorpus of these materials. For example, I was aware that my 25-million-word Portuguese corpus contained over a thousand transcripts from oral interviews, and I wanted to create a special "spoken" corpus of just these materials. Again, using macros, this should be feasible. We first find the textual markers that reoccur in all of the articles that interest us. For example, all of the interviews in one of the Brazilian newspapers had a hard return and then the word *Estado* (the name of the newspaper) and a hyphen at the beginning of the interviewer's comments. Once we know what these markers are, we can write a simple macro to search for that marker, then block the entire article and place it in a separate file that contains the specialized corpus. By running the macro iteratively on multiple files, we can easily and quickly extract all of the desired articles.

Using a Text Retrieval and Analysis Program

The final stage in creating the corpus is to do whatever processing is necessary to get the files in a form that can be used by our concordance or text retrieval and analysis program. In my research dealing with dialectal and historical variation in Spanish syntax, I have used WordCruncher (DOS). Once I have the text files, I simply insert markers to identify newspaper, date, and article name, then the Word-Cruncher indexing program can create an every-word index for the corpus. Although I do not use tagged corpora, in WordCruncher I can create and save part-of-speech lists (e.g., all infinitives, prepositions, or pronouns) that can be retrieved and used time after time. For example, in looking in the corpus of Latin American Newspapers for cases of the newly emerging construction "lexical subject of infinitive" (e.g., "es difícil **para él hacer**lo" [it's hard **for him to do** it]), I can search for a preposition (2,400,000+ tokens), followed by a personal pronoun (26,000+ tokens), followed by an infinitive (540,000+ tokens). Once the search has been set up, it takes fewer than two seconds to find the 80 to 90 tokens, and it would still take fewer than three seconds even if there were 5,000 to 10,000 tokens.

Using Multimillion-Word Web-Based Corpora in Research

With a few exceptions, most of the corpora currently available from works of literature or transcripts of conversations are much smaller than the Web-based corpora that I have discussed to this point; they are often in the range of 100,000–5,000,000 words. As Biber notes (1990, 1993), these smaller corpora are usually sufficient for most kinds of linguistic research. However, with emerging constructions that are still quite rare, the sheer size of the corpora of Web-based newspapers makes them a welcome addition to more traditional corpora by providing data on constructions that will appear in sufficient numbers only in very large corpora. In the sections that follow, I will focus on just my Spanish corpus and discuss how the 35-million-word corpus of Web-based newspapers has helped to complement the other corpora of Modern Spanish that I have created (see table 1) and how it has helped to provide important insight into the nature of syntactic variation and change.

Before examining cases in which a large Web-based corpus has been of value in examining emerging syntactic constructions, let us briefly consider three kinds of limitations that even corpora of this size have. Each limitation will be illustrated here by examples.

First, it may not make much sense to use very large corpora to study some phenomena, such as two alternate constructions that appear very frequently in the language, since these are sufficiently represented in much smaller corpora. Davies 1995a, a study of clitic climbing in Modern Spanish, shows that climbing (the movement of the unstressed object pronoun to a position in front of the main verb) is dependent on the particular verb. The data, based on more than 15,000 tokens, show that clitic climbing is more common with simple verbs, such as *querer*, "to want" (47 percent of cases with climbing in the spoken register, 15 percent in the written register), than with semantically more complex verbs, such as *desear*, "to desire" (20 percent and 4 percent, respectively), or *esperar*, "to hope" (0 percent in both registers). For an explanation of the parentheses in examples 1–3, see <http://www.mdavies.for.ilstu.edu/personal/texts.htm>.

1. a. *y qué me quiere decir* (Bogotá M14:186)
      "and what he wants to tell me"
   b. *y qué día lo desea realizar* (ARG Cartas: Carta 855)
      "and when he wants to achieve it"
   c. *porque no esperaba encontrarlo allí* (Gazapo 41)
      "because he didn't expect to find it there"

Since there are already many thousands of tokens for these constructions in the smaller, traditional corpora, there is little to be gained from the larger Web-based corpora. In the Latin American and Spanish newspapers from the Web, the frequency of clitic climbing was not significantly different with the various verbs than it was in the other corpora; it was 22 percent with *querer*, 6 percent with *desear*, and 2 percent with *esperar* (based on 8,400 tokens with these three verbs, as opposed to 1,320 tokens in the original corpus).

Second, in cases where smaller corpora already provide evidence for emerging constructions, an increased number of examples from larger corpora are not particularly insightful. Davies 1992, 1995b, and 1996 discuss the evolution of causative constructions in Spanish and Portuguese and show that there has been a shift toward "biclausal" constructions. One piece of evidence for the newer structure is the fact that with many causative verbs and verbs of perception, it is now possible to have "reflexive" embedded verbs, whereas this was not attested in older stages of the language.

2. a. *cuando lo vio balancearse por primera vez* (Hombres 75:1)
      "when she saw him rock back and forth the first time"
   b. *Oliveira lo dejó irse* (Rayuela 377:1)
      "O. let her go away"

However, one verb with which the reflexive verbs are still quite uncommon in Modern Spanish is the prototypical causative *hacer*, "to make." Although Finneman 1982 reports that some speakers allow reflexives with *hacer*, there are no cases in the 600,000-word corpus in Davies 1992. In the expanded 7,700,000-word corpus of Modern Spanish (see table 1), however, there are more than 40 examples from both written and spoken Spanish.

3. a. *acaba uno el examen y lo hacen retirarse* (Bogotá M12:165)
   "you take the test and then they make you leave"
   b. *lo hace . . . despreocuparse de lo que está diciendo* (Santiago M41:231)
   "it makes you not pay attention to what you're saying"

Not surprisingly, in the larger 35-million-word corpus of Web-based Latin American and Spanish newspapers, there are even more tokens—46 from Latin America and 39 from Spain. In this case, then, the critical increase in corpus size was not from 7,700,000 to 35 million words (and from 40 to 85 tokens) but from 600,000 to 7,700,000 words (and from 0 to 40 tokens).

Third, even large corpora are unable to provide examples of certain emerging linguistic phenomena. There are cases where (based on historical trends) one might expect certain constructions to appear in larger corpora, yet they are still unattested. Although Davies 1995a and 1998 show that there is a definite shift toward clitic climbing in Modern Spanish, there are still no cases of clitic climbing with certain verbs, such as *hay que*, "one has to" (480 tokens), *soñar con*, "to dream of" (just one token), and *insistir en*, "to insist on" (6 tokens); in all cases, clitic placement follows the infinitive.

4. a. *¡hay que abrirla!* (Cuba: *CubaNet*)
   "you've got to open it!"
   b. *soñaba con conocerlo personalmente* (Costa Rica: *Prensa Libre*)
   "she dreamed of meeting him in person"
   c. *sus detractores insisten en acusarlo* (El Salvador: *Diario*)
   "his detractors insist on accusing him"

In the Web-based corpora, however, there are still no cases of clitic climbing with these verbs (1,375 tokens with *hay que*, 16 with *soñar con*, and 28 with *insistir en*). In consequence, although there is a historical shift toward clitic climbing, it is apparently still unacceptable with certain verbs, and even the larger Web-based corpora do not (yet) show evidence of a shift.

In the examples just considered, the larger corpus of Web-based newspapers simply confirmed what might have already been proven in the smaller corpora—regarding the relative frequency of constructions, the fact that they have now become an established part of the grammar, or (conversely) the fact that certain constructions are still unacceptable. In the examples that follow, however, we will see that sometimes a larger corpus does in fact provide the crucial evidence for emerging constructions in a language—data that is unavailable in smaller corpora. In each of these examples, we will be comparing the smaller 7,700,000-word corpus of spoken and written Spanish (see table 1) with the larger 35-million-word corpus of Web-based Spanish newspapers.

Let us take as the first example the object-to-subject raising (OSR) in Modern Spanish. One difference between Spanish and English is that in Spanish, there is a much more restricted range of adjectives that allow the construction. While Spanish allows OSR with many of the synonyms of *fácil* and *difícil* ("easy" and "hard") and with the adjectives *posible* and *imposible,* the common view is that OSR in Spanish does not occur with adjectives meaning "nice," "fun," "important," and "interesting" (Reider 1993).

5. a. **ese coche es **divertido de manejar***
     "that car is fun to drive"
   b. **es una película **interesante de mirar***
     "it's an interesting movie to watch"

There are no cases of OSR with these adjectives in the 5,300,000-word corpus of historical Spanish texts, and there are likewise no cases of OSR with these adjectives in the smaller 7,700,000-word corpus of spoken and written Modern Spanish. In the larger corpus of Web-based newspapers, however, there are cases with each of these adjectives (*importante,* 4 in Latin America; *agradable,* "nice," 2 in Spain, 1 in Latin America; *divertido,* "fun," 1 in Spain; and *interesante,* 1 in Latin America), which may suggest that the range of adjectives permitting OSR in Spanish is increasing.

6. a. *lo promuevan como un destino **importante de visitar*** (Nicaragua: *Prensa*)
     "they promote it as an important place to visit"
   b. *un espacio distendido . . . [que] resulte **agradable de ver*** (Spain: *El Mundo de Baleares*)
     "a stretch of land that is nice to look at"

c. *[el libro] resulta ameno y **divertido de leer*** (Spain/Barcelona: *Van-guardia*)
"the book is nice and fun to read"

d. *cuyos efectos sin duda serían muy **interesantes de estudiar*** (Guatemala: *Prensa Libre*)
"whose effects would without doubt be very interesting to study"

In addition to the fact that OSR can occur with a wider range of adjectives than previously thought, there is also some evidence that there is a semantic reanalysis of the construction taking place, in which the fronted NP is coreferenced in some way with the subject position of the embedded clause. Evidence for this from the larger corpus is the fact that there are scattered cases of OSR involving passives, agentive phrases, and the "reflexive" marker *se*.

7. a. *las propiedades eran difíciles de **ser estudiadas** experimentalmente* (Madrid: *País*)
"the properties were hard to study experimentally" (passive)

b. *servicios que son imposibles de disfrutar **por la mayoría de la gente*** (Cuba: *CubaNet*)
"services that are impossible for most people to enjoy" (agentive)

c. *un desorden institucional difícil de **solucionarse*** (Venezuela: *Universal*)
"an institutional mess [that is] hard to fix" (reflexive)

While each of these constructions is either nonexistent or occurs just once in the smaller corpus of written and spoken Spanish, there are somewhat more examples from the Web-based corpus. For example, the reflexive *se* construction is not found in the smaller corpus but appears nine times in the newspaper corpus. In summary, the large corpus of Web-based materials provides crucial evidence for several aspects of the Modern Spanish OSR construction, evidence that is not available in any of the smaller corpora.

In papers dealing with the subject-to-subject raising (SSR) in both historical Spanish and Modern Spanish (Davies 1997a, 1997b), I briefly discuss an aspect of the construction that had previously not been studied. These are the cases of partial raising. In nonraised structures, the subject of the embedded clause stays within the lower clause (see example 8a). In full raising, the subject of the embedded clause raises to the main clause and triggers agreement only in that clause (see example 8c). In partial raising, the embedded subject raises to the main clause (and triggers agreement there) but also leaves some type of "trace" in the embedded clause, which triggers agreement in the embedded clause as well (see example 8b).

8. a. __ *parece [que saben la respuesta]* No Raising
   "it seems that they know the answer"
   b. *ellos parecen [que __ saben la respuesta]*Partial Raising
   "they seem as if they know the answer"
   c. *ellos parecen [__ saber la respuesta]* Full Raising
   "they seem like they know the answer"

I have hypothesized that partial raising was an important construction in the historical development of subject raising in Spanish. In Old Spanish, the subject of the embedded clause could not raise to the main clause (as in example 8a). In Modern Spanish, full raising (as in example 8c) is quite common, but partial raising (as in example 8b) is rather uncommon. During the 1400s–1600s, at the very moment that raising was becoming possible in Spanish, partial raising was quite common, but then it decreased sharply once full raising became common in the 1700s (Davies 1997b). I have suggested that the language moved from no raising to full raising via intermediate partial raising (active in the 1400s–1600s) and that once this construction had "played its part" (so to speak), it then died out.

The one complication, however, is that there are still a handful of cases of partial raising in the smaller corpus of Modern Spanish.

9. a. *me parecen que no eran los correctos* (La Paz M22:229)
   "they seem to me like they're not the right ones"
   b. *qué problemas te parecen que son los más import*antes (Sevilla Popular M7:176)
   "which problems seem to you like they're the most important ones"

It is difficult to explain the fact that eight of nine cases are in the corpus of spoken Spanish, even though nearly all of the more than 100 native speakers who were asked about this construction in a survey quickly rejected it. I have hypothesized that the few cases of the construction in spoken Spanish might be due to some kind of "garden path" phenomena, in which the speakers start into the SSR construction (thus the fronted NP) but then, for a number of functional reasons, "backtrack" into the nonraised construction (Davies 1997a). Since this is due to production constraints, it nearly always occurs in the spoken language. Unfortunately, the data from the larger corpus of Web-based newspapers does not allow any such "processing" or "performance" explanation. There are eight additional cases of the construction (6 from Latin America and 2 from Spain), and they are all from the written register; none of these tokens are taken from interviews or reported speech.

10. a. *me **parecen que** no **conducen** a nada* (Mexico: *Yucatán*)
    "it seems to me like they don't lead anywhere"
    b. *hasta la que **parecen que** se van de home run* (Panama: *Siglo*)
    "until they look like they're making a home run"
    c. ***parecen que** no lo **son** tanto* (Spain/Oviedo: *Comercio*)
    "it looks like they aren't that way as much"

This, then, is an example of a construction that was assumed to have more or less died out by Modern Spanish (judging again by the universal rejection of the construction by native speakers), at least in the written register, where speakers have the time to carefully craft the sentences. Therefore, the cases of partial raising in journalistic prose of the Web-based newspapers raises some questions that will need to be addressed in future research.

Perhaps the clearest example of the value of the multimillion-word corpus of Web-based newspapers concerns the construction "lexical subject of infinitive." While English easily allows subjects of nonfinite verbs (e.g., "after Bill's leaving", "it's nice for you to say that"), these are quite uncommon in Spanish. Nearly all researchers to date have commented that these constructions are restricted to the Caribbean dialects and that they are mainly a feature of informal, colloquial spoken Spanish (Suñer 1986; Lipski 1991). DeMello 1995 shows, however, that the construction has now spread to the spoken register in a number of cities of Latin America and Spain, and this is verified in my collection of texts from the *Habla Culta* project, which contains transcripts of conversations with native speakers from ten different countries.

11. a. *por el hecho de él haber sido eliminado de la presidencia* (Santiago
      M49:395)
      "by reason of his having been eliminated from the presidency"
    b. *es la consecuencia de yo haberme parado trescientas veces* (Madrid
       M13:219)
       "it's the result of my having stopped three hundred times"

In my 4,300,000-word corpus of written Spanish, however, the construction occurs in written Spanish only four times, and all of these
cases are from the Caribbean dialects.

12. a. *había tierra fértil antes de yo nacer* (Puerto Rico 1:243)
       "there was a lot of fertile land before I was born"
    b. *cualquiera es buena para tú encontrarme* (Venezuela 1:179)
       "any of them are fine for you to get [them] for me"

Therefore, there is still no evidence from the smaller corpus that this
emerging construction has now spread to written texts from other
countries beyond the Caribbean zone. In the larger corpus of Web-
based newspapers, however, there is clear evidence that the construction has in fact spread throughout Latin America (22 examples) and
even to Spain (16 examples).

13. a. **Para yo hablar** *de política tengo que estar en Colombia* (Ecuador:
       Vistazo)
       "for me to talk about politics I have to be in Colombia"
    b. *que se vaya Siles* **para él habilitarse** *como candidato* (Bolivia:
       ERBOL)
       "for S. to go away so he can get in shape as a candidate"
    c. *sería mejor* **para ella salir** *de Washington* (Barcelona: *Periódico*)
       "it would be better for her to leave Washington"
    d. **para ellos subcontratar** *y sacar su beneficio* (Oviedo: *Comercio*)
       "for them to subcontract things out and get the benefit"

The spread of this construction to the written Spanish of nearly all
of Latin America and Spain is not a trivial matter. Lexical subjects of
infinitives should not occur at all in Spanish due to several supposedly universal syntactic constraints, and its appearance in spoken
Caribbean Spanish is supposedly due to related morphological and
syntactic features of this dialect and register (see Suñer 1986; Lipski

1991). The evidence from the 35-million-word corpus of Web-based newspapers, however, shows that the theory will somehow need to be modified to allow for the numerous cases in this corpus, which have not appeared in smaller, less comprehensive corpora.

Appendix: List of Newspapers in the Spanish Corpus

The following 51 newspapers comprise my 35-million-word corpus of Spanish-language Web-based newspapers. There are 15 million words from the seven newspapers in Spain and 1 million words from each of the Spanish-speaking countries in the Americas (for a total of 20 million words in this corpus). All of the URLs in parentheses are correct as of October 1999; those in square brackets were no longer functioning as of this date, and no functioning URL could be found.

Argentina
La Nueva Provincia (www.lanueva.com.ar)
InterVoz (www.intervoz.com.ar)

Bolivia
Los Tiempos (www.lostiempos.com)
Agencia de Noticias ERBOL (jaguar.pg.cc.md.us/diario.html)

Chile
El Mercurio (www.mercurio.cl)
Hoy [www.hoy.web.cl]

Colombia
El Espectador (www.elespectador.com)
La Semana (www.semana.com.co)

Costa Rica
La Nación (www.nacion.co.cr)
Prensa Libre (www.prensalibre.co.cr/plibre.html)

Cuba
CubaNet [www.netpoint.net/~cubanet]
Trabajadores (www.trabajadores.cubaweb.cu)
Granma [206.130.183.236]

Ecuador
Estadio [www.telconet.net/estadio]
El Vistazo (www4.vistazo.com.ec)
Universo (www.eluniverso.com)

El Salvador
El Diario (www.elsalvador.com)
La Prensa Grafica (www.laprensa.com.sv)

Guatemala
Prensa Libre (www.prensalibre.com.gt)
La Gerencia (www.nortropic.com/gerencia)
La Hora (www.lahora.com.gt)

Honduras
La Tribuna (www.latribuna.hn)
La Prensa (www.laprensahn.com)

Mexico
Excelsior (www.excelsior.com.mx)
Diario Yucatán (www.yucatan.com.mx)

Nicaragua
La Tribuna [www.latribuna.com.ni]
La Prensa [www.sgc.com.ni/laprensa]

Panama
El Siglo (www.elsiglo.com)
La Prensa (www.prensa.com)

Paraguay
ABC (www.una.py/sitios/abc)
Diario Noticias Online (www.diarionoticias.com.py)

Perú
Caretas (www.caretas.com.pe)
El Tiempo (www.eltiempo.com.pe)

Puerto Rico
Noticentro (noticentro.coqui.net/pp.htm)
El Nuevo Día (www.endi.com)

República Dominicana
Ultima Hora (www.ultimahora.com.do)
Listin Digital (www.listin.com.do)

Spain
ABC (abc.es)
El Pais (www.elpais.es)
Diario AS (www.diario- as.es)
El Periodico (www.elperiodico.es)
La Vanguardia (www.vanguardia.es)
El Mundo de Baleares (www.el-mundo.es)
Diario Sur (www.diariosur.es)
El Comercio (www7.uniovi.es/noticias)

United States
Miama Herald (www.elherald.com)
Diaro de las Americas (www.diariolasamericas.com)

Uruguay
Diario El Pais (www.diarioelpais.com)
Brecha [www.chasque.apc.org/brecha]

Venezuela
El Universal (Digital (www.eud.com))
El Carabobeno (www.el-carabobeno.com)

References

Biber, Douglas. 1990. Methodological Issues regarding Corpus-Based Analyses of Linguistic Variation. *Literary and Linguistic Computing* 5:257–69.
———. 1993. Representativeness in Corpus Design. *Literary and Linguistic Computing* 8:243–57.
Davies, Mark. 1992. The Diachronic Evolution of Causative Constructions in Spanish and Portuguese. Ph.D. diss., University of Texas at Austin.
———. 1995a. Analyzing Syntactic Variation with Computer-Based Corpora: The Case of Modern Spanish Clitic Climbing. *Hispania* 78:370–80.
———. 1995b. The Evolution of the Spanish Causative Construction. *Hispanic Review* 63:57–77.
———. 1996. The Diachronic Evolution of the Causative Construction in Portuguese. *Journal of Hispanic Philology* 17:261–92.
———. 1997a. A Corpus-Based Analysis of Spanish Subject Raising in Modern Spanish. *Hispanic Linguistics* 9:33–63.
———. 1997b. The Evolution of Subject Raising in Spanish. *Bulletin of Hispanic Studies* (Liverpool) 74:399–411.
———. 1998. The Evolution of Spanish Clitic Climbing: A Corpus-Based Approach. *Studia Neophilologica* 69:251–63.
DeMello, George. 1995. Preposicion + sujeto + infinitivo: "Para yo hacerlo." *Hispania* 78:825–36.
Finnemann, David. 1982. Aspects of the Spanish Causative Construction. Ph.D. diss., University of Minnesota.
Lipski, John M. 1991. In Search of the Spanish Personal Infinitive. In *New Analyses in Romance Linguistics,* ed. Dieter Wanner et al., 201–20. Amsterdam: Benjamins.
Reider, Michael. 1993. On Tough Movement in Spanish. *Hispania* 76:160–70.
Suñer, Margarita. 1986. Lexical Subjects of Infinitives in Caribbean Spanish. In *Studies in Romance Linguistics,* ed. Osvaldo Jaeggli et al., 189–203. Dordrecht: Foris.

Concordance Programs for Corpus Linguistics

Susan Hockey
University College, London

A concordance program is an essential tool for corpus linguistics, since it generates the searches and analyses on which corpus linguists base their work. This chapter attempts to assess the functions and operations provided by concordance programs for corpus linguistics and to highlight some desirable features, while also noting some traps for the unwary. Its focus is more toward the requirements of the individual researcher in linguistics rather than toward those of the research group that has access to large-scale computational resources and special-purpose software. The discussion of functionality is presented mostly with reference to some PC programs that I happen to know best. These are by no means the only programs available, but fewer programs currently exist for the Macintosh computer. I do not claim to have comprehensive knowledge of these particular programs: the features highlighted are usually ones that I have explored and found useful. In practice, many corpus linguists use more than one tool, as I do, choosing the one that is most appropriate for each analysis.

Obviously, the better the program is, the more effective it can be, but "better" and "effective" mean different things to different people. The choice of program must depend on the nature of the application for which the program will be used, but ultimately the program will be judged on how well and how fast it helps researchers achieve their intellectual goals. As anyone who has reviewed computer programs knows, evaluating software can be very difficult: it takes considerable time to really understand the functionality of a program, which might then change as new versions are released. Reading software reviews can therefore help only a little. Often, queries posted to Internet discussion groups can produce more useful information, but in the end, a decision must be made and software tried out. Fortunately, today's desktop programs are affordable, even for individuals.

Existing Concordance Programs

A concordance program very aptly fits Burnard's 1992 description of a computer as "essentially a machine for identifying, classifying and counting symbols" (6). The program identifies sets of symbols and classifies them as "words" according to some predefined specifications. It can also count all instances of the same set of symbols and sort the sets into alphabetical or some other order. It thus produces a word list, in which words are presented in alphabetical or frequency order together with a number giving their frequency. In a further extension of this procedure, a concordance presents words within some surrounding context. There are two basic types of concordance programs. A **batch concordance program** operates on the **raw text** for every analysis that it carries out. This offers a good deal of flexibility, allowing the user, for example, (1) to determine for each analysis whether hyphenated words are to be treated as one word or two or (2) to search for punctuation characters to investigate forms that occur at the ends of sentences. But a batch concordance program is not feasible for very large corpora because of the processing time required to sort the words. An **interactive text analysis program** works in a different way by **querying** an **index** that has been built previously using a special program module. With an interactive program, some of the functions discussed later in this chapter are needed at the index-building stage, while others are required at the query stage. It is important, therefore, to consider carefully the decisions that must be made at the index-building stage.

Basic concordance functions have been in use for many years. Much previous discussion concentrates on literary applications, but this discussion can be useful for the corpus linguist, who also needs to work on complex material and thus requires a range of different functions that can be generalized to other applications. Typical computer-based literary research concentrates on examining the style of particular authors, on authorship attribution, or on themes and imagery, as well as on preparing new scholarly editions of texts that include commentary on unusual usages of words. All these applications rely on concordance programs to locate and count occurrences of vocabulary items. Many of these studies are comparative, and researchers soon recognized the need to identify the exact location of each occurrence of each word to determine whether a word occurs more often in any particular text or section of text. Researchers also soon identified other problem areas, including hyphenated words, embedded quotations, proper names, abbreviations, and homographs (words that are spelled the same but have different meanings), as well as the need to analyze linguistic units rather than sequences of letters. Many of the issues raised for the humanities in Burton 1981a, 1981b, 1981c, and 1982 are still current and just as relevant for corpus linguists. Howard-Hill 1979 gives some historical background and discusses functionality in light of the requirements for his concordances of the old spelling of Shakespeare. Further elaboration can be found in Sinclair's 1991 monograph, *Corpus, Concordance, Collocation,* which explains the three words in his title with reference to his own work discussing specific words and phrases. In Hockey 1998, using examples created with Micro-OCP (Oxford University Computing Service 1988), I attempt to show how concordance functionality developed for humanities applications can be just as useful for corpus linguistics. Barnbrook 1996 also discusses some concordance work from the perspective of language analysis.

TACT (Text Analysis Computing Tools, <http://www.chass.utoronto.ca/cch/TACT/ tact0.html>), developed at the University of Toronto in the late 1980s and early 1990s, is a DOS-based interactive text analysis program with a range of functions (Bradley 1991; Lancashire et al. 1996). Much of the design input to TACT came from literary scholars, but it can be used for many types of text. TACT is in fact a collection of programs, some of which allow the user to build up and manipulate a dictionary of words or terms. The Oxford Concordance Program (OCP: see Hockey and Marriott 1979–80; Hockey and Martin 1987) is a batch program developed to provide a general-purpose text analysis tool for British universities. Part of the funding for OCP development was directed to research on user needs, and the resulting program tried to incorporate as many different functions as possible. It was implemented on a range of mainframe computers, and the DOS version, Micro-OCP, was published by Oxford University Press in 1988 (Oxford University Computing Service 1988). Neither TACT nor OCP have been updated for a long time, and their interfaces are outdated, but their functionality is very good. Micro-

OCP runs easily in a DOS window. TACT often requires changes to the internal memory settings on the computer, and these have been known to cause unpredictable side effects.

TUSTEP (Tuebingen System of Text Processing Programs, <http://www.uni-tuebingen.de/zdv/tustep/tdv_eng.html>) is another suite of programs that have been under development almost continuously since the late 1960s (Ott 1988, 1992). The programs have been used for the preparation of many complex critical editions, most notably Gabler's *Ulysses,* but they have other applications, including concordances, which can be a useful tool in scholarly editing work. TUSTEP is a truly **modular system** where the programs can be interlinked in whatever sequence is necessary to produce the desired results. The entire system is controlled by a **command language,** which was designed by the developers. This language is used both to describe the data and to select options for processing the data. OCP, TACT, and TUSTEP offer more options than by any of the newer Windows-based programs discussed in this chapter, but it takes some time to learn the older programs, particularly if the researcher is only familiar with a graphical user interface, such as Windows, and has never used a command-driven program. However, because of the need to understand the sequences of instructions, command-driven programs encourage the researcher to think more carefully about the analyses that are to be carried out.

WordCruncher (see Lancashire 1991, 438, for a description), another DOS-based program, works in a similar manner to TACT but with rather less functionality. A Windows version has been reported to be available, but I have not been able to investigate it. For those who read Italian, the PiSystem, incorporating DBT (Data Base Testuale, <http://www.ilc.pi.cnr.it/pesystem/first.htm>), developed at the Institute for Computational Linguistics in Pisa, offers an excellent range of functions for textual, lexical, and linguistic research. This system is used both for corpus and computational linguistics and for literary computing.

Three Windows concordance programs have appeared more recently. Two of these, MonoConc (<http://www.athel.com>) and WordSmith Tools (<http://www.liv.ac.uk/~ms2928/index.htm>) were developed initially for corpus linguistics work. The third, Concordance (<http://www.rjcw.freeserve.co.uk>), derived from the developer's interest in creating Web concordances for teaching English literature and is suited to both linguistic and literary applications.

All run easily on Windows desktop machines, although Concordance, being new in 1999, requires rather more hardware power.

Markup and Text Formats

Different programs can work with different text formats, although all can handle plain **ASCII** files. It is also useful to be able to work with some word-processor files or with **HTML,** since so much electronic text is readily available in these formats. However, **markup** or **encoding** inserted into the text makes explicit for computer processing things that are implicit for the human reader. Because of the complexity of the material being studied, there has been a long tradition of markup development in literary computing, and this is now being taken up by linguistic projects. Markup can be used to identify complete texts when several texts are being analyzed or to identify chapters, pages, lines, verses, utterances, speakers, or any other structural unit within each text. It thus makes it possible to note the exact location of concordance entries within the entire text and also to search only within certain structural units. Markup can also be used to provide information about the source of the text and other **metadata** elements, such as situational details for spoken text.

Various methods have been developed for encoding structural information, one of which, called COCOA (Word Count and Concordance for Atlas) after the 1960s program that first used it, is used by Concordance, TACT, and OCP. COCOA-type references are simple and work fairly well when structural references are important. They consist of a single letter identifying the particular element or structural unit (called a reference category in the COCOA scheme)—for example, page, chapter, act, scene, speaker, and so on—followed by the particular instance: for example, <S child1> identifies an utterance by child 1. All text following this reference is assumed to be part of this particular utterance by child 1 until another instance of an <S> reference occurs. A text may contain several different reference categories, and these may overlap. TACT extends the COCOA scheme by allowing reference categories consisting of more than one letter. Both TACT and OCP require the user to specify only the delimiters for the reference category encoding and can then retain and operate with the references automatically as they analyze the text. Concordance offers less flexibility, because it requires the user to declare all the reference categories that are present in the text and uses all these categories to identify the concordance entries. The COCOA markup scheme is really intended only for structural information. It works well in many cases, but it cannot easily be used to encode small units of information within a text, such as quotations, names, foreign words, and so on.

A simpler method adopted by the Brown and LOB (Lancaster-Oslo-Bergen) corpora is to provide reference elements in fixed positions at the beginning of each line of text. This is repetitive and thus wasteful of space within the computer, but it is very easy to write programs to work with this format of references. OCP, TACT, and Concordance can also handle this format. WordCruncher uses a simpler form of encoding for references, since it assumes that each text has a three-level hierarchic structure, like books, chapters, and verses in the Bible. The data description facilities in TUSTEP's command language can be used to transform almost any markup scheme, which enables the program to work with many different schemes. However, no matter what markup scheme is used, any markup not recognized as such by the program is normally treated as "words," which appear as such in the results. The ability to recognize textual markup is therefore an important feature for a concordance program.

General dissatisfaction with encoding schemes and the need to make electronic texts independent of particular software programs led to the development of **SGML** (Standard Generalized Markup Language), which became an international standard in 1986 (International Organization for Standards 1986; Goldfarb 1990; Cover 1994–). SGML and XML (Extensible Markup Language), its successor for the Web, are not encoding schemes but metalanguages or mechanisms within which encoding schemes can be defined. An SGML **DTD** (document type definition) is a formal specification of the structure of a document that is defined as an ordered set of hierarchic or nested elements. An SGML processing program uses the DTD and can thus "know" what markup to expect as it passes through a document. In theory at least, any SGML-based text analysis program ought to be able to search and manipulate any SGML element or the contents of any element, allowing also for that element's position in the document hierarchy. For example, the program could search for examples of a specific form within utterances only if those utterances were within BBC broadcasts within all radio broadcasts.

Any SGML project must begin by defining the actual structure of the texts to be analyzed or compiled and creating an appropriate

DTD. This process, known as document analysis, can be lengthy and time-consuming. Typically it involves going over samples of documents, deciding what features are important in those documents, and defining the relationships between the features. Fortunately, several DTDs already exist and can be downloaded from the Internet. The most important one for corpus linguists is the **TEI** (Text Encoding Initiative, <http://www.uic.edu/orgs/tei> and <http://www.tei-c .org>), which has created a modular DTD for electronic texts in the humanities and language industries (Sperberg-McQueen and Burnard 1994). The SGML **tag set** used for the BNC (British National Corpus, <http://info.ox.ac.uk/bnc>) is derived from the TEI, as is the Corpus Encoding Standard (<http://www.cs.vassar.edu/CES/ CES1.html>).

Because of the DTD mechanism, SGML software can easily be generalized, but sometimes it is specific to one particular application or set of tags. For example, the SARA (SGML-Aware Retrieval Application) program only works with the BNC tag set (Aston and Burnard 1998). Special-purpose SGML editors are often used to create SGML-encoded documents. These editors can provide a template document, and they also use the DTD to offer the user only the SGML tags that are permitted at any particular point in the text. They ensure that the document is created with valid SGML and eliminate various encoding errors. The software used to create SGML documents, however, does not perform text analysis functions. Unfortunately, at the time of writing, there is no easy-to-use and affordable general-purpose desktop SGML/XML text analysis software. Corpus linguists who work with SGML usually write their own programs, often based on the SGML/XML library of routines developed at the Edinburgh Language Technology Group (<http://www.ltg.ed.ac.uk/software/xml/index.html>), which require knowledge of programming in the C language. (There is an ongoing lively debate as to whether linguists should write their own programs or not. Writing one's own program gives flexibility and the ability to deal with very specific details, but at a cost of time investment and the possibility of error.) Nothing exists for the desktop user, who is forced to try to use existing tools with SGML, often by attempting to treat SGML elements as if they were "pseudowords." Of the programs mentioned earlier, TUSTEP handles text encoded in SGML by means of its command language, which, as far as I am aware, maps the SGML elements onto the TUSTEP internal representation of the text. WordSmith has some facilities for handling SGML-like tags, and

MonoConc Pro can also use tags defined by the user to mark concordance entries, but they are not true SGML tags and do not provide the markup validation offered by true SGML software.

An electronic text obtained from elsewhere (e.g., an HTML document) may require some markup conversion before it can be used. Word processors are particularly bad at these kinds of repetitive and conditional changes. Text editors are better, and anything can be done with a computer programming language provided that the researcher has the skills to use the language. Some concordance programs provide tools for text conversion. Concordance includes a simple file editor to navigate around the text file and make changes to it, and this program also has a tool to convert UNIX files to a form suitable for use with Windows. WordSmith has a file conversion tool, which is essentially an enhanced search-and-replace tool that takes instructions from a "text converter conversion file" and allows batch renaming and batch tag reformatting. Some OCR (optical character recognition) programs offer file conversion facilities when the text is exported, but these are only able to operate on the typographic markup that the OCR program has been able to detect.

Identifying and Sorting Words

For a word list, the ideal program should be able to sort the words into alphabetical order or frequency order, with the most frequent or least frequent first. In a frequency sort, all the words occurring once, twice, and so on are themselves sorted into alphabetical order. For some kinds of applications, especially studies of inflectional endings, a reverse sort where words are alphabetized on their endings is very useful. Some programs can also sort the words according to their length. Concordance has a particularly good way of presenting the word list, displaying it in a window on the left side of the screen. The first column in this screen contains the headwords, and the user may choose whether to have frequencies or percentages or both shown in one or two additional columns. A click on the column heading will immediately change the sorting option, cycling through all the options, which are also available on a pull-down menu. WordSmith offers alphabetical and frequency lists in separate windows, also with percentage frequencies. MonoConc Pro gives a word list in descending frequency order or in alphabetical order, in both cases with percentages.

The headwords may be displayed all in uppercase, with the first letter only in uppercase, or all in lowercase. These options are offered by WordSmith and Concordance, but none of them is entirely satisfactory. Words in all uppercase are difficult to read. Using all lowercase gives rise to some peculiar forms, such as *i* and *london*. Initial capitalization may be the best option, but this can also sometimes be misleading unless the concordance entries are viewed. OCP normally displays as the headword the form that has sorted to the top in its internal sorting procedure, although the user can choose other options. This causes, for example, the form *Brown* to be displayed if every occurrence of the term *brown* is capitalized, thus reducing but not eliminating entirely the occurrences of the term *brown* meaning color when the name *Brown* is required.

Character sets and the display and treatment of nonstandard characters can lead to much angst and confusion. It is important to understand that the function and the display of characters are separate issues, both of which must be accurate. MonoConc Pro offers a whole range of Windows-supported options for European languages. WordSmith offers a range of DOS and Windows character sets, including character maps from which the user can select individual characters. Concordance includes a "Language Control" facility that brings together languages, character sets, fonts, and keyboard layouts.

As I have already indicated in my discussion of headword display, uppercase and lowercase letters need to be treated as equal for sorting purposes in most analyses. A more flexible program generalizes this to permit any letters to be treated as equal and also to allow the user to define exactly what letters make up words, the alphabetical order for sorting words, and what characters function as word separators. Thus, for Spanish, it would be possible to treat *ch, ll,* and *rr* as separate letters and to include these "letters" within the alphabet definition so that *ch* comes after *c* and so on. Hyphens and apostrophes are especially problematic, and here again the best programs allow the user to choose how these characters should be treated.

One of OCP's major strengths is in letter definitions. It allows the user to define five different kinds of letters, under the definitions "alphabet," "diacritics," "padding," "punctuation," and "ignore." Each letter can consist of up to eight keyboard characters. The "alphabet" function gives the letters of the alphabet in the order that they are to be sorted. The alphabet is likely also to include the numerals, which are perhaps better placed at the end to avoid a word list beginning with many numbers. "Diacritics" are secondary sort keys, such as accented letters, and most usually the hyphen and the apostrophe, allowing *I'll* and *ill* or *élève* and *élevé* to be separate forms but listed one after the other. "Padding" letters have no effect on the sorting. If the apostrophe is defined as a padding letter, *I'll* and *ill* are treated as if they were the same word. "Punctuation" letters are word separators. If the apostrophe is defined as a word separator, *I'll* is treated as two words, *I* and *ll*. Any letters defined as "ignore" are simply removed from the text for that particular analysis and do not appear at all in the results. Thus, it is possible to ignore certain markup tags if they are defined as letters of no more than eight characters, and it is possible to examine sequences of words at the ends of sentences by treating the normal punctuation characters as letters occurring at the ends of words and searching for words ending in these letters. OCP also allows the user to control the display of letters so that they can be displayed in another form or not displayed at all even though they have been used in the sorting. Since OCP is a batch program, the letter definitions can be respecified for each analysis.

Interactive text analysis programs require the alphabet and other letter definitions to be specified at the time when the index is built. These are then fixed and cannot easily be altered unless the index is rebuilt with different options selected. It is not normally possible to control them in the retrieval program except by rather clumsy means. For the individual researcher working on his or her own corpus, this is not so much of a problem. For a large-scale project that is creating a corpus and associated set of tools to be distributed on CD-ROM or over the Internet to a wide range of users, it means making decisions early on that affect the kinds of searches that users can carry out. Corpora such as the BNC that have word-level markup and their own retrieval software can get around some of these problems by using specific tags, for example, for genitives and contractions.

All concordance programs allow various pattern facilities to be used to search for words and phrases. Usually, these allow searching for any number of letters, including none, any single letter, and one or more letters. MonoConc Pro and WordSmith offer all these options. Concordance offers rather simpler facilities in the search pattern, but it does allow the user to scroll down the word list in the left window, as shown in figure 1, or, by starting to type a word, to jump straight to the place where that word occurs and select it for immediate display of concordance entries. UNIX-style **regular expressions** are used by

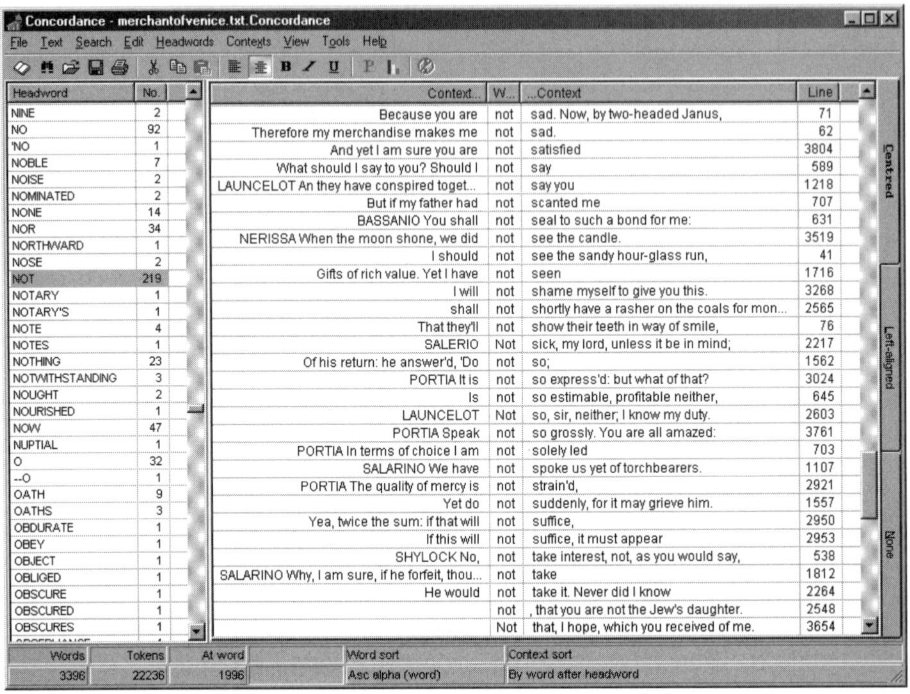

Fig. 1. Concordance of the word *not* in *The Merchant of Venice,* generated by the program Concordance

MonoConc Pro, by TACT, and by SARA for the BNC. These are more flexible and include the possibility of searching for any one of a set of characters (e.g., *b[aeiou]d* for *bad, bed, bid, bod* and *bud*) and for repeated characters. Words can also be selected by their frequencies (e.g., to find all the once-occurring words) or sometimes by random numbers to obtain a sample of the words.

Another function offered by most concordance programs is the ability to sort the concordance entries for each word in several different ways. Normally, the default sort would be the order in which words occur in the text. However, it is also useful to sort concordances according to what comes to the right or left of the keyword, since this easily shows where the keyword occurs as part of a phrase or frequently occurring sequence of words. Such a right-sorted concordance would bring together, for example, all places where a verb is followed by the same particle. Some programs give the option of including or not including any punctuation when the sorting program is comparing the concordance entries. When the entries are sorted according to what is to the left of the keyword, it is not always obvious whether the words to the left are being compared in a forward direction or backward by their endings. Most programs offer some context sorting facilities. With OCP and Concordance, it is also possible to sort concordance entries by their reference categories (i.e., by the structural markup), thus bringing together all instances of the same word uttered by the same speaker or in the same type of text. Figure 2 shows the results of this kind of sort generated by OCP.

Additional Functions

If a complex search is being carried out on several corpora, it is convenient to be able to store the search request so that it can be accessed over and over again and also possibly modified without having to

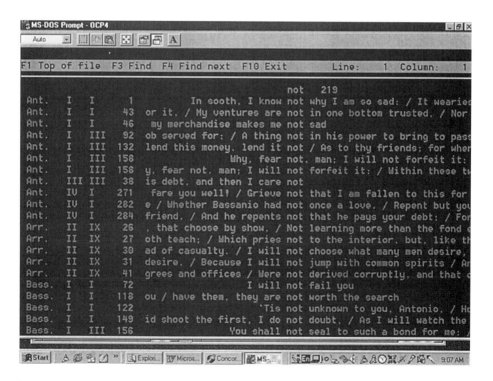

Fig. 2. Concordance of the word *not* in *The Merchant of Venice* sorted by reference categories, generated by the Oxford Concordance Program

start from scratch. Some interactive text analysis programs allow the user to build up and store more complex search patterns by using logical operators ("AND," "OR," "NOT") with existing patterns. These could also be lists of synonyms or other terms for specific categories or groups. TACT provides some useful options for this, making it possible to create, for example, a group of terms denoting "fire" or "water" or a group of words that demonstrate a particular linguistic function. McCarty 1991 and Siemens 1996 provide useful discussions of these TACT facilities.

The importance of **collocations** (pairs of words or phrases occurring close together) is now widely recognized for lexical and other studies. Most programs offer some functions for examining collocations, but these may be specified in rather different ways. One option is to find all the collocates within a certain number of words to the left or right of the search word. MonoConc Pro displays these in a table, shown in figure 3, with columns for one word and two words to the left and one word and two words to the right, with an option to extend this further to the left and right. Concordance does something similar, although it is only able to look within the bounds of the context units defined when the concordance was created. WordSmith has more options, including specifying a minimum frequency as a collocate on the grounds that once-occurring or low-frequency collocates may not be interesting. It can also display collocation clusters of a specified number of words, as shown in figure 4. Another useful possibility is to define a list of common words to be excluded from the collocate search in order to concentrate only on meaningful words. Collocations can thus be used to help distinguish between meanings of different words that are spelled the same. For example, such words as *money, account,* and *financial* are more likely to collocate with *money bank* than with *river bank.*

The significance of collocates can also be ascertained using various statistical procedures (Berry-Rogghe 1973; Church et al. 1991), but few desktop programs offer such functions. TACT can compute the z-score of collocates, which measures the frequency as a collocate against the overall frequency of the word in the text. The COBUILD Direct Collocation Sampler (<http://titania.cobuild.collins.co.uk/form.html>) gives a free demonstration using both *t*-scores and mutual information on 50 million words. The ideal program for collocations ought to be able to offer both lists of collocates

| MonoConc Pro - [Frequency Statistics - [not]] |
| File   Concordance   Frequency   Display   Window   Info |

2-Left	1-Left	1-Right	2-Right
37 I	15 will	7 that	13 me
13 you	13 would	7 the	12 I
6 You	12 is	7 a	10 the
5 it	11 you	6 in	7 you
5 he	10 do	6 to	7 my
4 do	8 are	6 for	6 to
3 they	7 me	5 be	5 it
3 Thou	6 it	5 so	4 for
3 Nor	6 shall	4 with	4 have
3 so	5 am	4 one	3 so
3 we	5 have	4 I	3 his
2 He	5 had	4 have	3 with
2 But	4 No	4 me	3 But
2 the	4 we	3 deny	2 thee
2 thou	4 know	3 yet	2 such
2 world	3 Hath	3 '	2 This
2 doth	3 I'll	3 know	2 will
2 And	2 LAUNCELOT	3 ANTONIO	2 on
2 PORTIA	2 be	3 take	2 us
2 know	2 could	2 as	2 a
2 love	2 was	2 you	2 letter
2 It	2 Let	2 see	2 if

| 22,362 words | 12.49 PM |

Fig. 3. Left and right collocates of the word *not* in *The Merchant of Venice*, generated by MonoConc Pro

according to distance from the node and several different methods of examining significant collocates.

There are many other useful tools for frequency and statistical analysis. The type/token ratio, a measure of the spread of vocabulary in a text, is commonly provided. Others include a frequency profile giving cumulative counts and percentages of words and vocabulary items. Distributions by word and sentence length can also easily be calculated, provided of course that the definition of what constitutes a sentence is clear. Windows programs can display sentence lengths in color charts, as Concordance does for word lengths. Some programs are able to provide more advanced tools for statistical analysis and comparison. Others, such as OCP, prefer not to predetermine what kinds of statistical analysis users might want to carry out, but these programs make it easy to store the frequencies and load them into

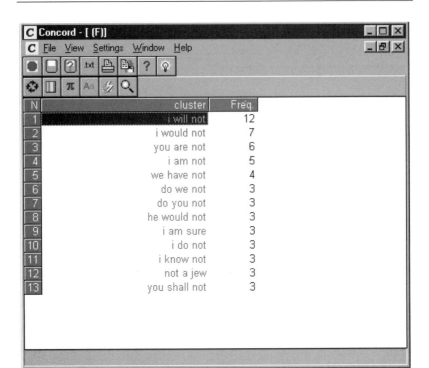

Fig. 4. Collocation clusters with the word *not* in *The Merchant of Venice*, generated by WordSmith Tools

other statistical analysis software. WordSmith can perform a keyword comparison, which compares a word list derived from one text with an existing list from a reference text to indicate what words "characterize" the text being studied. MonoConc provides a rather nicely designed chart of the distribution of the search word within the corpus, illustrated in figure 5. WordSmith can also produce a simple plot of the relative frequencies and distribution of the search word within the source files (see fig. 6), and TACT can chart distributions by reference category.

Many corpora, such as Brown, LOB, and the BNC, now include part-of-speech tagging. The SARA program, which was written especially for the BNC, provides many options for searching the BNC tag set, but it cannot easily be used with other tag sets. However, in most desktop concordance programs, the alphabet and word definitions can be manipulated to search part-of-speech markup. In the LOB cor-

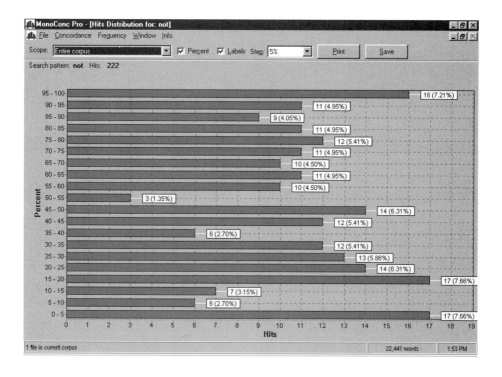

Fig. 5. Distribution chart for the word _not_ in _The Merchant of Venice,_ generated by MonoConc Pro

pus, word class tags preceded by an underscore are attached to the end of each word.

> ^ the_ATI ingenuity_NN of_IN the_ATI theories_NNS is_BEZ impressive_JJ and_CC is_BEZ the_ATI best_JJT argument_NN against_IN them_PP3OS ._. .... (Sample D01, line 40)

To find all singular nouns, the program can look for all words tagged "_NN"; to find all nouns, the search would be for all words tagged "_NN" followed by any combination of "$", "P", and "S". See Johansson and Hofland 1989 for further details of the LOB tag set.

The final sets of functions to be considered concern the display and saving of results. Windows programs can make excellent use of color to highlight features in the display, but these may also need to be mapped onto black and white for print publication. WordSmith allows the user to choose colors for a variety of features in the display.

N	File	Words	Hits	per 1,000	Plot
1	def500~1.sgm	11,628	96	8.26	
2	dis115~1.sgm	7,869	60	7.62	
3	lel115~1.sgm	11,381	82	7.20	
4	les495~1.sgm	14,807	101	6.82	
5	dis495~1.sgm	6,899	47	6.81	
6	lel220~2.sgm	9,155	61	6.66	
7	sem340~1.sgm	24,099	151	6.27	
8	sem495~1.sgm	18,432	110	5.97	
9	stp545~1.sgm	12,297	72	5.86	
10	ofc115~1.sgm	28,980	167	5.76	
11	lel115~2.sgm	11,205	62	5.53	
12	dis315~1.sgm	15,756	87	5.52	
13	lel500~1.sgm	7,417	40	5.39	
14	col285~1.sgm	8,766	46	5.25	
15	lel220~1.sgm	9,365	47	5.02	
16	lel185~1.sgm	13,337	65	4.87	
17	lel565~1.sgm	11,667	53	4.54	
18	dis280~1.sgm	8,499	35	4.12	
19	lab500~1.sgm	12,981	47	3.62	
20	col605~1.sgm	9,861	35	3.55	
21	les500~1.sgm	7,922	28	3.53	
22	ofc280~1.sgm	12,808	45	3.51	
23	stp285~1.sgm	12,346	37	3.00	
24	col385~1.sgm	7,241	18	2.49	
25	lel280~1.sgm	7,865	9	1.14	

Fig. 6. Distribution plot of the word *not* in selected files from the Michigan Corpus of Academic Speech in English, generated by WordSmith Tools

Charts and graphs (e.g., WordSmith's "plot" function) often illustrate a point much better than tables of words and numbers, and the desktop programs I have looked at could perhaps offer more options here. But reading from a screen is never easy, so the results may need to be saved either for future use or for loading into another program. The format of the saved material then becomes important. If it was originally tabular in format, as most word lists and concordance results are, the tabular format needs to be retained even if the results are changed into a different typeface. This is a particular problem with DOS-based programs. Because they assume fixed-width characters, layout can be lost if they are presented in variable-width characters. But output from the DOS programs consists of ASCII files that can easily be loaded into other programs. Both WordSmith and Concordance allow the user to select and edit items, and MonoConc has an option to select part of the results and copy them to a clipboard for further processing. The results may need to be loaded into a word processor, a spreadsheet, or a database (thus requiring column and row delimiters) or saved as plain text for analysis by other programs.

One very nice feature of Concordance is the Web concordance. Concordance can create an HTML version of the concordance and load it into a Web browser for testing. The normal layout has four frames. The word list is displayed in a frame on the left. A frame along the top has buttons for each letter of the alphabet, enabling the user to jump to a point in the word list. Frames for the concordance entries and for the text occupy the main part of the screen. Clicking on the reference for any concordance entry causes the text frame to scroll so that the entry can be seen within a wider context. See <http://www .dundee.ac.uk/english/wics/wics.htm> for an example of Web concordances of works of some Romantic poets.

The Future

There are a number of functions that current software does not provide. Perhaps the most important is the ability to manipulate the alphabet in the way that, for example, OCP can. Although they can work with other languages, the current Windows programs are most suitable for working with Modern English text. Opinions vary about whether text analysis software should provide more statistical functions. These can be useful, but they can make it very easy for users who do not fully understand the statistics to apply the wrong statistics to the results or to interpret the results incorrectly. Perhaps a better approach is to provide an easy means of storing the results and loading them into a spreadsheet or another statistical analysis program. A much bigger issue is the ability to process SGML-encoded text. This requires much more complex processing, particularly if all the SGML elements are indexed and thus accessible in the analysis.

As the Internet develops, the nature of desktop computing will change. Two trends are emerging. The first is the link with network-based, digital library electronic text projects, where many users can access the same corpus (Price-Wilkin 1994; see also Powell and Simpson in this volume). Many of these projects use a TEI-based SGML DTD and some version of the OpenText Pat search engine to search collections of text and display the results as Web pages. They can search very large amounts of text, but they work with prebuilt indexes and thus cannot provide much flexibility in terms of how words are defined or how concordance entries can be sorted further or otherwise manipulated. Normally, they display lines of context in which the search term occurs, and the user can then click on a line to display more surrounding text. The focus is thus very much on using the electronic text as a reference tool rather than as a source for the analysis and manipulation of linguistic features. The Women Writers Project at Brown University (<http://www.wwwp.brown.edu>) has built some useful concordance functions on top of INSO's DynaText/DynaWeb search engine, but, at least in its experimental version, this engine is slow to work with, especially for high-frequency words. Moreover, the INSO model of the text is rather too "booklike" for many text analysis functions. It is really intended as a hypertext system where the user can click on a word and go to an annotation or image, rather than as an analysis system where the primary aim is to bring together all occurrences of the same form.

The second trend is a growing recognition, at least in the humanities computing community, of the need for more sophisticated modular tools that can handle SGML- and XML-encoded material in a true and flexible fashion. In a session at the June 1999 joint annual conference of the Association for Computers and the Humanities and the Association for Literary and Linguistic Computing, Bradley and Horton presented some ideas for a new set of tools. These would be based on a modular and open architecture, enabling other people to contribute programs. They not only would carry out traditional text analysis functions but would also provide more generalized data transformations useful for many other applications (Bradley and Horton 1999). The tools would be primarily word-oriented, but the element-based approach of XML would also make it easier to examine text in units of more than one word. Bradley and Horton proposed that these tools should be based on the Document Object Model (DOM), which is an object-oriented model of an XML document. With such a tool set, experienced users would be able to mix and match the tools to suit their needs, while beginners might prefer to use a packaged set of them "out of the box." Bradley 1998 provides more background information, including the history of events leading up to current activities, before making wide-ranging proposals for the characteristics and architecture of such a new system. Organizing and carrying out a project like this on an international basis is no mean task, but enough of an impetus now exists to make this happen. To provide a strong user base, it would need to involve researchers in humanities computing, corpus linguistics, and digital libraries. Such a project would entail research on both user needs and system architectures and could take some considerable time to come to fruition.

The center of computing has now moved to the Internet, and one can begin to imagine what more powerful Internet technology based on XML might be able to offer. XML will make it possible to carry out more of the processing on the client computer rather than on the server computer. It will be possible to download a marked-up text and perform some analysis locally, going out to the Internet to retrieve more information if necessary. But markup does not solve all the problems of concordance analysis. To save time and costs, there is a need for part-of-speech and other **annotation** to be carried out automatically. In the early 1990s, research in computational linguistics concentrated on developing large-scale lexical databases or linguistic resources that could be used as tools or resources for a linguistic analysis program. These resources could be generally available on the Internet, possibly customizable for specific domains or types of language, and they could be used as an aid in a more sophisticated analysis. These lexical databases were originally created from electronic representations of print dictionaries, but these focus on unusual usages and are weaker for usual usages that the computer is most likely to encounter as it processes text. More recent research in computational linguistics has moved in the direction of corpus analysis and concordances, with the main purpose of augmenting linguistic resources with data derived from real text. It seems that over a long period, a full circle has been made from literary computing to corpus linguistics, and one can only hope that this will lead to more collaboration between literary computing specialists and corpus and computational linguists in the future.

References

Aston, Guy, and Lou Burnard. 1998. *The BNC Handbook: Exploring the British National Corpus with SARA.* Edinburgh: Edinburgh University Press.

Barnbrook, Geoff. 1996. *Language and Computers: A Practical Introduction to the Computer Analysis of Language.* Edinburgh: Edinburgh University Press.

Berry-Rogghe, Godelieve L. M. 1973. The Computation of Collocations and Their Relevance in Lexical Studies. In *The Computer and Literary Studies,* ed. A. J. Aitken, R. Bailey, and N. Hamilton-Smith, 103–12. Edinburgh: Edinburgh University Press.

Bradley, John. 1991. TACT Design. In *A TACT Exemplar,* ed T. Russon Wooldridge, 7–14. Toronto: Centre for Computing in the Humanities.

————. 1998. New TA Software: Some Characteristics and a Proposed Architecture. <http//pigeon.cc.kcl.ac.uk/ta-dev/notes/design.htm> (August 27, 1999).

Bradley, John, and Tom Horton. 1999. A New Computing Architecture to Support Text Analysis. In *ACHALLC '99 Conference Proceedings,* Amy Sexton ed., 135–37. Charlottesville: University of Virginia. Also available at <http//www.iath.virginia.edu/ach-allc.99/proceedings/short2.html> (August 27, 1999).

Burnard, Lou. 1992. Tools and Techniques for Computer-Assisted Text Processing. In *Computers and Written Texts,* ed. Christopher S. Butler, 1–28. Oxford: Blackwell.

Burton, Dolores. 1981a. Automated Concordances and Word Indexes: Fifties. *Computers and the Humanities* 15:11–14.

————. 1981b. Automated Concordances and Word Indexes: The Early Sixties and the Early Centres. *Computers and the Humanities* 15:83–100.

————. 1981c. Automated Concordances and Word Indexes: The Process, the Programs, and the Products. *Computers and the Humanities* 15:139–54.

————. 1982. Automated Concordances and Word Indexes: Machine Decisions and Editorial Revisions. *Computers and the Humanities* 16:195–218.

Church, K., W. Gale, P. W. Hanks, and D. Hindle. 1991. Using Statistics in Lexical Analysis. In *Lexical Acquisition: Using On-Line Resources to Build a Lexicon,* ed. U. Zernik, 115–64. Englewood Cliffs, NJ: Lawrence Erlbaum.

Cover, Robin, ed. 1994–. *The XML Cover Pages.* <http//www.oasis-open.org/cover/> (January 15, 2000).

Goldfarb, Charles F. 1990. *The SGML Handbook.* Oxford: Oxford University Press.

Hockey, Susan. 1998. Textual Databases. In *Using Computers in Linguistics: A Practical Guide,* ed. John Lawler and Helen Aristar Dry, 101–33. London: Routledge.

Hockey, Susan, and Ian Marriott. 1979–80. The Oxford Concordance Project (OCP), Parts 1–4. *Literary and Linguistic Computing* 7:35–43, 155–64, 268–75; 8:28–35.

Hockey, Susan, and Jeremy Martin. 1987. The Oxford Concordance Program Version 2. *Literary and Linguistic Computing* 2:125–31.

Howard-Hill, T. H. 1979. *Literary Concordances: A Complete Handbook to the Preparation of Manual and Computer Concordances.* Oxford: Pergamon.

International Organization for Standards. 1986. *Information Processing—Text and Office Systems—Standard Generalized Markup Language (SGML).* Geneva: International Organization for Standards.

Johannson, Stig, and Knut Hofland, eds. 1989. *Frequency Analysis of English Vocabulary and Grammar Based on the LOB Corpus.* 2 vols. Oxford: Clarendon.

Lancashire, Ian, ed. 1991. *The Humanities Computing Yearbook, 1989–90.* Oxford: Oxford University Press.

Lancashire, Ian, John Bradley, Willard McCarty, Michael Stairs, and T. R. Wooldridge. 1996. *Using TACT with Electronic Texts.* New York: Modern Language Association of America.

McCarty, Willard. 1991. Finding Implicit Patterns in Ovid's *Metamorphoses* with TACT. In *A TACT Exemplar,* ed. T. Russon Wooldridge, 37–75. Toronto: Centre for Computing in the Humanities.

Ott, Wilhelm. 1988. Software Requirements for Computer-Aided Critical Editing. In *Editing, Publishing, and Computer Technology: Papers Given at the Twentieth Annual Conference on Editorial Problems,* ed. Sharon Butler and William P. Stoneman, 81–103. New York: AMS Press.

———. 1992. Computers and Textual Editing. In *Computers and Written Texts,* ed. Christopher S. Butler, 205–26. Oxford: Blackwell.

Oxford University Computing Service. 1988. *Micro-OCP User Manual.* Oxford: Oxford University Press.

Price-Wilkin, John. 1994. Using the World Wide Web to Deliver Complex Electronic Documents: Implications for Libraries. *The Public-Access Computer Systems Review* 5:5–21. Also available at <http//jpwilkin.hti.umich.edu/pubs/yale.html> (August 27, 1999).

Siemens, R. G. 1996. Lemmatising and Parsing With TACT Preprocessing Programs. *Computing in the Humanities Working Papers,* A.1. <http//www.kcl.ac.uk/humanities/cch/chwp/siemens2/index.html> (August 26, 1999).

Sinclair, John. 1991. *Corpus, Concordance, Collocation.* Oxford: Oxford University Press.

Sperberg-McQueen, C. Michael, and Lou Burnard, eds. 1994. *Guidelines for the Encoding and Interchange of Electronic Texts.* 2 vols. Chicago and Oxford: Association for Computers and the Humanities, Association for Computational Linguistics, Association for Literary and Linguistic Computing.

Part 2

Corpus-Based Analyses and Applications

Using Corpus-Based Methods to Investigate Grammar and Use: Some Case Studies on the Use of Verbs in English

Douglas Biber
Northern Arizona University

The development of materials for language instruction and assessment requires repeated judgments about language use, as authors make decisions about the words and linguistic features to include. These decisions have usually been based on the author's gut-level impressions and anecdotal evidence of how speakers and writers use language. These impressions usually operate below the level of consciousness and are often regarded as accepted truths. For example, I have observed (in a series of lectures and workshops in recent years) that the vast majority of practicing TESL professionals are confident in their belief that progressive verbs (e.g., "She was running to the store") are more common in conversation than are verbs in simple aspect (e.g., "She ran to the store"). A second example is the belief that modal verbs are considerably more common in academic writing than in conversation.

Beliefs about language use are fundamentally important for materials development: these intuitions provide the baseline for authors as they develop the texts in textbooks, exams, and other materials. Unfortunately, linguists' intuitions about language use are often wrong. As a result, teaching and assessment materials often fail to provide an accurate reflection of the language actually used by speakers and writers in natural situations.

Empirical analyses of representative corpora provide a much more solid foundation for descriptions of language use, and the results of these analyses are often surprising to TESL professionals.

For example, it turns out that verbs in simple aspect are more than 20 times as common as progressive verbs in conversation (Biber et al. 1999, 461; see also the case study in the present chapter); this is in marked contrast to the predominant use of progressive verbs in many ESL conversation textbooks. The actual use of modal verbs is similarly surprising to most TESL professionals: Overall, modal verbs are almost twice as common in conversation as in academic prose. Only one modal verb—*may*—is much more common in academic prose and therefore especially characteristic of that register (Biber et al. 1999, 486–90).

The present chapter illustrates the kinds of unexpected findings about language use that result from corpus-based investigations. Based on research done for the *Longman Grammar of Spoken and Written English* (Biber et al. 1999), the chapter focuses on the use of verbs. Three case studies are presented: one focusing on the use of words (i.e., the most common verbs in English); the second focusing on the use and distribution of grammatical forms (i.e., the relative frequency of simple, progressive, and perfect aspect in English); and the third describing how lexis and grammatical structure can interact in complex ways (i.e., showing how verbs with the same valency patterns can have strikingly different preferences for particular valencies). The first section following introduces the corpus-based approach to grammar and use, and the next three sections present the three case studies.

Corpus-Based Investigations of Grammar and Use

There have been numerous studies of grammar and use over the last two decades, as researchers have come to realize that the description of grammatical function is as important as structural analysis. In most cases, these studies focus on grammatical features that have two or more structural or semantic variants. By studying these features in naturally occurring discourse, researchers have been able to identify systematic differences in the functional use of each variant.

Research of this type became popular in the late 1970s and 1980s. For example, Prince (1978) compared the discourse functions of *Wh*-clefts and *it*-clefts; Thompson investigated word order variation with detached participial clauses (1983) and adverbial purpose clauses (1985); Schiffrin studied the discourse factors influencing grammatical variation in verb tense (1981), causal sequences (1985b), and discourse markers (1985a, 1987). Other, more recent studies of this type include Thompson and Mulac 1991a and 1991b on the discourse conditions associated with the omission of the complementizer *that;* Fox and Thompson 1990 on relative clauses; and Myhill 1995 and 1997 on the discourse functions of modal verbs.

At one level, these studies might be regarded as early corpus-based investigations: they are all empirical studies based on analysis of grammatical features in actual texts. In addition, most of these studies have used both quantitative and qualitative analysis; that is, quantitative techniques are used to determine the distribution of grammatical variants across contexts, while detailed analyses of text extracts are used to interpret the distributional patterns in functional terms.

Despite these characteristics, there has often been relatively little concern with the generalizability of the database of texts used for analysis. Many of these studies have used a "convenience" sample, a collection of texts that was readily available to the researcher. The implicit assumption underlying this methodological decision seems to have been that any body of naturally occurring discourse will illustrate the same patterns of use. However, these text samples have often been small, and more importantly for the present purposes, there has often been no systematic control for register. Some studies are based on a single register; others are based on discourse examples with disregard to register; still others incorporate a comparison of use across registers.

More recently, researchers on discourse and grammar have begun to use the tools and techniques available from corpus linguistics. This field of study places greater emphasis on the representativeness of the database and provides computational tools for investigating distributional patterns in large text collections (see Biber, Conrad, and Reppen 1998 for an introduction to this analytical approach). There have been numerous research papers using corpus-based techniques to study English grammar and discourse. The edited volumes by Aarts and Meyer (1995), Aijmer and Altenberg (1991), and Johansson and Stenström (1991) provide good introductions to work of this type. There are also a number of book-length treatments reporting corpus-based investigations of grammar and discourse: for example, Tottie 1991 on negation, Collins 1991 on clefts, Granger 1983 on passives, Mair 1990 on infinitival complement clauses, Meyer 1992 on apposition, and several books on nominal structures (e.g., de Haan 1989; Geisler 1995; Johansson 1995; Varantola 1984).

In most cases, corpora are designed to represent some register differences, and thus many grammatical studies based on corpora have a register component. For example, Tottie 1991 and Geisler 1995 report differences for speech versus writing; Johansson 1995 distinguishes among press, fiction, and academic prose for some analyses; and Granger 1983 distinguishes among several different spoken registers (including conversation, oration, commentary, interviews). At the same time, other corpus-based studies disregard register distinctions in their studies of grammar and discourse, focusing exclusively on a detailed analysis of contextual factors (e.g., Mair 1990; de Haan 1989; Sinclair 1991).

In my own previous research, I take a strong position on the importance of register for studies of grammar and use, arguing that most functional descriptions of a grammatical feature will not be valid for the language as a whole. Rather, characteristics of the textual environment interact with register differences, so that strong patterns of use in one register often represent only weak patterns in other registers. Thus, a complete functional analysis must consider the patterns of use in several registers.

In the following sections, I illustrate the interaction of grammar, use, and register with corpus-based analyses adapted from the *Longman Grammar of Spoken and Written English* (Biber et al. 1999). The analyses are based on texts from four registers: conversation, fiction, newspaper language, and academic prose. Although these are general registers, they differ in important ways from one another (e.g., with respect to mode, interactiveness, production circumstances, purpose, and target audience). The analyses were carried out on the Longman Spoken and Written English (LSWE) Corpus, which contains about 40 million words of text overall, with about 4 to 5 million words from each of these four registers (see table 1). All frequency counts reported in this chapter have been normalized to a common basis (a count per million words of text), so that they are directly comparable across registers.

The Most Common Lexical Verbs across Registers

There are literally dozens of common lexical verbs in English. For example, nearly 400 different verb forms occur over 20 times per million words in the LSWE Corpus (see Biber et al. 1999, 370–71). These include many everyday verbs, such as *pull, throw, choose,* and *fall.*

TABLE 1. Composition of the Subcorpus Used in the Analyses (taken from the LSWE Corpus)

	Number of Texts	Number of Words
Conversation (British English)	3,436	3,929,500
Fiction (American English and British English)	139	4,980,000
News (British English)	20,395	5,432,800
Academic prose (American English and British English)	408	5,331,800

Given this large inventory of relatively common verbs, it might be easy to assume that no individual verbs stand out as being particularly frequent. However, this is not at all the case: only 63 lexical verbs occur more than 500 times per million words in a register, and only 12 verbs occur more than 1,000 times per million words in the LSWE Corpus (Biber et al. 1999, 367–78). These 12 most common verbs are *say, get, go, know, think, see, make, come, take, want, give,* and *mean*.

To give an indication of the importance of these 12 verbs, figure 1 plots their combined frequency compared to the overall frequency of all other verbs. Taken as a group, these 12 verbs are especially important in conversation, where they account for almost 45 percent of the occurrences of all lexical verbs. Obviously, any conversational primer that did not include extensive practice of these words would be short-changing students.

It further turns out that there are large frequency differences among these 12 verbs, overall and in their register distributions. For example, figures 2 and 3 plot the frequency of each verb in conversation and in newspaper language. The verb *say* is listed first in these figures because it is common in both spoken and written registers and thus has the highest frequency overall. This is not surprising, given the ubiquitous need to report the speech of others; it turns out that both speakers and writers rely heavily on the single verb *say* for this purpose, usually in the past tense expressing either a direct or indirect quote.

"No use sitting about," he *said*. (Fiction)
You *said* you didn't have it. (Conversation)

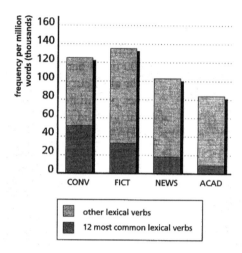

**Fig. 1. Distribution of the most common lexical verbs versus other verbs.
(From D. Biber, S. Johansson, G. Leech, S. Conrad, and E. Finegan, *Longman
Grammar of Spoken and Written English* [London: Longman, 1999].)**

The extremely high frequency of the verb *get* in conversation is
more surprising. This verb goes largely unnoticed, yet in conversation
it is by far the single most common lexical verb in any one register.
The main reason that *get* is so common is that it is extremely versatile,
being used with a wide range of meanings.

Obtaining something:
See if they can *get* some of that beer. (Conversation)

Possession:
They've *got* a big house. (Conversation)

Moving to or away from something:
Get in the car. (Conversation)

Causing something to move or happen:
Jessie *get* your big bum here. (Conversation)
It *gets* people talking again, right? (Conversation)

Understanding something:
Do you *get* it? (Conversation)

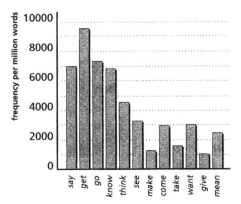

Fig. 2. Frequencies of the most common lexical verbs—conversation. (From D. Biber, S. Johansson, G. Leech, S. Conrad, and E. Finegan, *Longman Grammar of Spoken and Written English* [London: Longman, 1999].)

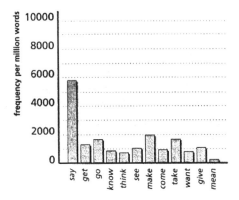

Fig. 3. Frequencies of the most common lexical verbs—news. (From D. Biber, S. Johansson, G. Leech, S. Conrad, and E. Finegan, *Longman Grammar of Spoken and Written English* [London: Longman, 1999].)

Changing to a new state:
So I'm *getting* that way now. (Conversation)

Other verbs that are extremely common in conversation are *go, know,* and, to a lesser extent, *think, see, come, want,* and *mean.* News shows a quite different pattern, with only the verb *say* being extremely frequent. However, it should be noted that all 12 of these verbs are notably common in both registers in comparison to most verbs in English. For example, as I noted already, such verbs as *pull, throw, choose,* and *fall* occur only about 50 to 100 times per million words. Countless other verbs have even lower frequencies. In contrast, the majority of the 12 most common verbs occur over 1,000 times per million words in both conversation and news.

Thus, there is a cline in the use of verbs: a few verbs occur with extremely high frequencies; several verbs occur with moderately high frequencies; most verbs occur with relatively low frequencies. In addition, different registers show strikingly different preferences for particular verbs. For example, the verbs *get, go, know,* and *think* are much more frequent in conversation than in news (see figs. 2 and 3). In contrast, such verbs as *add, spend, claim,* and *continue* are much more common in news than in conversation.

Simple, Progressive, and Perfect Aspect across Registers

One of the most widely held intuitions about language use among TESL professionals is the belief that progressive aspect is the unmarked choice in conversation. This belief is sometimes reflected in the overly frequent use of progressive verbs in made-up dialogues (e.g., those found in ESL/EFL textbooks teaching conversation skills).

Conversation from *As I was Saying: Conversation Tactics* (Richards and Hull 1987)

Doctor: Hello Mrs. Thomas. What can I do for you?
Patient: Well, I've *been having* bad stomach pains lately, doctor.
Doctor: Oh I'm sorry to hear that. How long have you *been having* them?
Patient: Just in the last few weeks. I get a very sharp pain about an hour after I've eaten.
[. . .]
Doctor: Well, I don't think it's anything serious. Maybe you eat too quickly. You don't give yourself time to digest your food.
Patient: My husband *is always telling* me that.

As figure 4 shows, the generalization that progressive aspect is more common in conversation than in other registers is correct. The contrast with academic prose is especially noteworthy: progressive aspect is rare in academic prose but common in conversation. How-

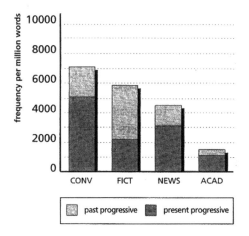

Fig. 4. Frequency of past progressive and present progressive across registers. (From D. Biber, S. Johansson, G. Leech, S. Conrad, and E. Finegan, *Longman Grammar of Spoken and Written English* [London: Longman, 1999].)

ever, the overall register distribution is surprising in that progressive verb phrases are nearly as common in fiction as in conversation and are relatively common in news as well.

Further, as figure 5 shows, it is not at all correct to conclude that progressive aspect is the unmarked choice in conversation. Rather, simple aspect is clearly the unmarked choice. In fact, in conversation, simple aspect verb phrases are more than 20 times as common as progressives aspect verb phrases. The following excerpt illustrates this extreme reliance on simple aspect in natural conversation.

B: — What *do* you *do* at Dudley Allen then?
A: What the school?
B: Yeah. *Do* you —
A: No I*'m*, I*'m* only on the PTA.
B: You*'re* just on the PTA?
A: That*'s* it.
B: You *do*n't actually *work*?
A: I *work* at the erm —
B: I *know* you *work* at Crown Hills, *do*n't you?
A: Yeah.

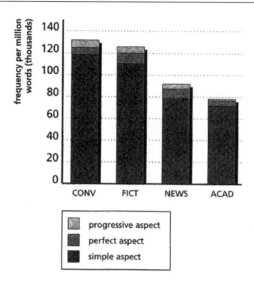

Fig. 5. Frequency of simple, perfect, and progressive aspect across registers. (From D. Biber, S. Johansson, G. Leech, S. Conrad, and E. Finegan, *Longman Grammar of Spoken and Written English* [London: Longman, 1999].)

In contrast, the progressive aspect is used for special effect, usually focusing on the fact that an event is in progress or about to take place.

> What's she doing? (Conversation)
> But she's *coming* back tomorrow. (Conversation)

With nondynamic verbs, the progressive can refer to a temporary state that exists over a period of time.

> I *was looking* at that one just now. (Conversation)
> You *should be wondering* why. (Conversation)
> We *were waiting* for the train. (Conversation)

A few lexical verbs actually occur most of the time with the progressive aspect in conversation. These include *bleeding, chasing, shopping, starving, joking, kidding,* and *moaning*. However, the norm—even in conversation—is to express verbs with the simple aspect. In marked contrast to the expectations created by some popular conversational materials, verb phrases such as "I've been having" and "is always telling" are the exception rather than the rule.

Lexico-Grammatical and Register Factors Influencing the Use of Valency Patterns

The preceding sections have illustrated the unexpected patterns of use for words and grammatical features that can be uncovered by corpus-based research. It further turns out that there are often complex interactions between word sets and grammatical variation. Such lexico-grammatical associations usually operate well below the level of conscious awareness, yet they are highly systematic and important patterns of use. In the present section, I illustrate these associations through a comparison of the valency patterns for *stand* and *begin* (see also Biber et al. 1999, 380–92).

Many verbs take only a single valency pattern. For example, *wait, happen,* and *exist* occur only as intransitive verbs, while verbs such as *bring, carry, suggest,* and *find* occur only as transitive verbs. However, many other verbs can occur with multiple valency patterns—for example, *eat, try, watch, help,* and *change.*

The verbs *stand* and *begin* have exactly the same potential for occurring with multiple valency patterns: Both verbs can occur with four different patterns.

Simple intransitive (SV):
> For a while he *stood* and watched. (Fiction)
> A number of adults and children have left the compound since the siege *began.* (News)

Intransitive with an optional adverbial (SV + A):
> I just *stood* there. (Conversation)
> This effort *began* in January of 1981. (Academic Prose)

Transitive with a noun phrase as direct object (SVO-NP):
> My mom couldn't *stand* it in the end. (Conversation)
> Mr Hawke's government has *begun* its controversial plan to compensate the three main domestic airlines. (News)

Transitive with a complement clause as direct object (SVO-Comp. Cls.):
> Carrie *stood* shivering in the cold hall. (Fiction)
> He *began* to scratch slowly in the armpit of his alpaca jacket. (Fiction)

A traditional description would note these four patterns and conclude that the two verbs have the same valencies. However, corpus-based analysis opens up the possibility of a use perspective on such points of grammar. The two preceding sections of this chapter have shown how the use of words and grammatical features is conditioned by register; the present section shows how the use of grammatical patterns is conditioned by individual words (which are in turn conditioned by register).

In fact, it turns out that the verbs *stand* and *begin* have strikingly different preferred valency patterns, despite their identical valency potentials. As table 2 shows, these two verbs typically occur with very different valency patterns: *stand* usually occurs as an intransitive verb, often with an optional adverbial, while *begin* more commonly occurs with a following complement clause. Further, there are important register differences; for example, the pattern *begin* + complement clause is especially characteristic of conversation, while intransitive *begin* is more likely to occur in news and academic prose. The predominant use of *stand* as an intransitive verb corresponds to its typical meaning marking a physical state.

> I just sort of have to *stand* there while you two stand there laughing at me. (Conversation)
> He *stood* beside her for a time. (Fiction)
> He *stood* alone in the empty hall. (Fiction)

In contrast, *begin* is more commonly used in a nonphysical sense, marking an aspectual process of "beginning" relative to some other physical activity, event, or process, which is described in the following complement clause.

> As you get older I think you *begin* to notice it more. (Conversation)
> And then it *began* to get a bit darker. (Conversation)
> Some of the crowd *began* to sing. (Fiction)
> I *began* to cry. (Fiction)

Similarly, strong use patterns are found for other verbs with the same valency potential. For example, the verb *try* has an even stronger preference for a following complement clause than does *begin*. In con-

TABLE 2. Percentage of Verb Tokens Occurring with Intransitive and Monotransitive Valency Patterns

	SV	SV + A	SVO-NP	SVO-Comp. Cls.
Stand				
Conversation	***	****	**	—
Fiction	***	****	*	**
News	***	****	**	*
Academic prose	***	****	*	*
Begin				
Conversation	**	*	*	*****
Fiction	**	*	*	****
News	***	***	**	***
Academic prose	**	***	**	***

Source: Based on Biber et al. 1999, 385, table 5.5.
Note: The analysis of valency patterns was carried out on a random sample of 800 occurrences for each verb, 200 occurrences from each register. The random samples were obtained automatically by a computer program, and the valency patterns were subsequently coded with an interactive software tool.
* Pattern is attested but occurs less than 10 percent of the time
** Pattern occurs 10–25 percent of the time
*** Pattern occurs 25–50 percent of the time
**** Pattern occurs 50–75 percent of the time
***** Pattern occurs over 75 percent of the time
— Pattern is not attested

trast, the verb *meet* has a very strong preference for a following noun phrase as direct object, while the intransitive patterns and the pattern with a following complement clause are relatively rare.

In sum, corpus analysis here allows us to understand the different ways in which verbs are actually used. Although verbs often have the same potential of occurrence with different valency patterns, corpus analysis makes it clear that our actual use of such verbs is highly systematic, with each verb having its own preferred patterns, depending on its typical meanings and functions.

Conclusion

The present chapter has illustrated the kinds of highly systematic patterns that structure our everyday use of linguistic features in speech and writing. Similarly strong patterns are found in analyses of the linguistic co-occurrence patterns that comprise the dimensions of variation among spoken and written registers (e.g., Biber 1988, 1995). Both kinds of patterns operate below the level of conscious awareness and are usually not accessible to native intuitions. However, as the preceding analyses illustrate, these patterns are extremely powerful and correspond to major differences among grammatical variants, lexico-grammatical associations, and registers.

Awareness of these patterns of use is obviously important for both educators and students. This is not to say that frequency information can be mechanically translated into materials for instruction and assessment. An additional consideration, for example, is the ease/difficulty of learning for particular features. However, we can no longer afford to ignore the typical patterns of use identified by quantitative corpus analysis. Instead, we can look forward to important gains for students as we begin to develop materials that reflect the actual patterns of use in particular registers.

References

Aarts, B., and C. Meyer, eds. 1995. *The Verb in Contemporary English: Theory and Description.* Cambridge: Cambridge University Press.

Aijmer, K., and B. Altenberg, eds. 1991. *English Corpus Linguistics.* London: Longman.

Biber, D. 1988. *Variation across Speech and Writing.* Cambridge: Cambridge University Press.

————. 1995. *Dimensions of Register Variation: A Cross-Linguistic Perspective.* Cambridge: Cambridge University Press.

Biber, D., S. Conrad, and R. Reppen. 1998. *Corpus Linguistics: Investigating Language Structure and Use.* Cambridge: Cambridge University Press.

Biber, D., S. Johansson, G. Leech, S. Conrad, and E. Finegan. 1999. *Longman Grammar of Spoken and Written English.* London: Longman.

Collins, P. 1991. *Cleft and Pseudo-Cleft Constructions in English.* London: Routledge.

de Haan, P. 1989. *Postmodifying Clauses in the English Noun Phrase: A Corpus-Based Study.* Amsterdam: Rodopi.

Fox, B. A., and S. A. Thompson. 1990. A Discourse Explanation of the Grammar of Relative Clauses in English Conversation. *Language* 66:297–316.

Geisler, C. 1995. *Relative Infinitives in English.* Uppsala: Uppsala University.

Granger, S. 1983. *The "Be" + Past Participle Construction in Spoken English with Special Emphasis on the Passive.* Amsterdam: Elsevier Science Publishers.

Johansson, C. 1995. *The Relativizers "Whose" and "of Which" in Present-Day English: Description and Theory.* Uppsala: Uppsala University.

Johansson, S., and A.-B. Stenström, eds. 1991. *English Computer Corpora: Selected Papers and Research Guide.* Berlin: Mouton.

Mair, C. 1990. *Infinitival Complement Clauses in English.* New York: Cambridge University Press.

Meyer, C. 1992. *Apposition in Contemporary English.* Cambridge: Cambridge University Press.

Myhill, J. 1995. Change and Continuity in the Functions of the American English Modals. *Linguistics* 33:157–211.

———. 1997. *Should* and *Ought:* The Rise of Individually Oriented Modality in American English. *English Language and Linguistics* 1:3–23.

Prince, E. F. 1978. A Comparison of *Wh*-clefts and *It*-clefts in Discourse. *Language* 54:883–906.

Richards, J., and J. Hull. 1987. *As I was saying: conversation tactics.* Tokyo; Reading, Mass.: Addison-Wesley Publishers, Japan Ltd.

Schiffrin, D. 1981. Tense Variation in Narrative. *Language* 57:45–62.

———. 1985a. Conversational Coherence: The Role of *Well. Language* 61:640–67.

———. 1985b. Multiple Constraints on Discourse Options: A Quantitative Analysis of Causal Sequences. *Discourse Processes* 8:281–303.

———. 1987. *Discourse Markers.* Cambridge: Cambridge University Press.

Sinclair, J. 1991. *Corpus, Concordance, and Collocation.* Oxford: Oxford University Press.

Thompson, S. A. 1983. Grammar and Discourse: The English Detached Participial Clause. In *Discourse Perspectives on Syntax,* ed. F. Klein-Andreu, 43–65. New York: Academic Press.

———. 1985. Grammar and Written Discourse: Initial vs. Final Purpose Clauses in English. *Text* 5:55–84.

Thompson, S. A., and A. Mulac. 1991a. The Discourse Conditions for the Use of the Complementizer *That* in Conversational English. *Journal of Pragmatics* 15:237–51.

———. 1991b. A Quantitative Perspective on the Grammaticization of Epistemic Parentheticals in English. In *Approaches to Grammaticalization,* ed. E. C. Traugott and B. Heine, 2:313–29. Amsterdam: John Benjamins.

Tottie, G. 1991. *Negation in English Speech and Writing: A Study in Variation.* San Diego: Academic Press.

Varantola, K. 1984. *On Noun Phrase Structures in Engineering English.* Turku: University of Turku.

Discovering the Usual with Corpora: The Case of *Remember*

Hongyin Tao
Cornell University

In current linguistics and applied linguistics, the popular practice is to focus, whether consciously or unconsciously, on the rare and unusual properties of lexical items and grammatical structures. Linguists' tendency to pay more attention to extreme, rare, and novel cases may be a reflection of the nature of human psychology, where unusual forms are easier to spot and thus contrast more readily in perception than more mundane forms. Sometimes, however, the choice of using unusual forms is a conscious decision, not an oversight. For example, in generative-style syntactic theories, it has always been the tendency to base theory constructions on very rare sentences. The extreme form of this tendency is the pervasive use of starred (*) sentences in linguistic discussions. This is obviously due to a philosophical commitment to language and linguistics (Lakoff 1991), not simply to overlooking linguistic "fact."

In this chapter, I wish to highlight one of the major contributions corpus linguistics can make to the study of language, namely, its potential to make explicit the more common patterns of language use. I will apply this methodology to the analysis of the verb *remember*. In the course of the discussion, I will also try to make the point that patterns of language use as revealed by corpus linguistics methodology are best examined from a sociocultural linguistic perspective. With an integrated approach comprising both corpus linguistic tools and sociocultural linguistic insights, we will be in a better position to understand what speakers routinely do in discourse and why grammars behave the way they do.

The English verb *remember* has been under intense linguistic investigation, as it has both interesting semantic and syntactic properties. Semantically, it represents a kind of mental process, so it is often treated as belonging to a class called "private verbs" (Quirk et al. 1985; Biber 1988), or verbs of cognition, psychology, retrospection (Fanego 1996), or thinking (Ogura 1986). Syntactically, it can take a variety of complement clauses: the gerund (-*ing*) form, the infinitive (*to*-clause), and *that*-clauses. The different complement clauses are said to correlate with different tense forms in the main verb, with accompanying differences in meaning (e.g., "remembered doing something"; vs. "remember to do something"; see Bolinger 1977; Jorgensen 1990; Wu 1997). Thus, the verb *remember* is often treated as complement-taking. Because of the complexity in complement-taking in this verb, English descriptive grammars (Quirk et al. 1985; COBUILD 1996) and language pedagogy and assessment practices (e.g., in the Test of English as a Foreign Language) often concentrate on this feature of the verb and some similar verbs.

Theoretical linguists have also been much attracted to the behavior of *remember* and verbs like it. The most comprehensive syntactic theoretical treatment of the verb *remember* in English can be found in Van Valin and Wilkins 1993, which is based on the framework of Role and Reference Grammar. Van Valin and Wilkins use the verb *remember* as a case to illustrate a theoretical conviction of Role and Reference Grammar, namely, that syntactic properties of a predicate can be predicted from its semantics and that the types and forms of the complements that a predicate takes can be deducted directly from the (decomposed) semantic representation of the verb. There is no room here for us to review all details of their study. Simply put, Van Valin and Wilkins analyze the semantic component of *remember* as having three different semantic interpretations: something the agent (1) intends, (2) perceives, or (3) knows/believes to be in the mind. From these interpretations, they postulate some rules about interclausal (i.e., occurring between the main clause and the complement clause) semantic linkage and some categories for the linkage of syntactic clauses to account for the three types of complement clauses that *remember* takes.

Since Van Valin and Wilkins's arguments depend to a large extent on the overall sentential environment in which *remember* is used (as by itself *remember* cannot be interpreted to possess all these different meaning interpretations), an analysis of the kinds of sentences they give may help us understand both their theoretical orientations and the discourse data that I will present in this chapter. For the Psych-Action type (which basically means that the verb *remember* is used to denote a psychological action), which Van Valin and Wilkins take to be the basis on which the infinitive (*to*-clause) is derived, they give the illustration

1. John remembered to turn the faucet off.

For the Perception type, from which the *-ing* type of complement clause is derived, they give

2. I remember turning off the faucet.

Finally, for the Cognition/Propositional Attitude type, from which the complement *that*-clause is derived, they give

3. John remembered that he had left the faucet on.

A quick glance at the examples given by Van Valin and Wilkins reveals some interesting characteristics. First, two of the three subject forms in the examples they give (those in examples 1 and 2) are third-person NPs (proper names). Second, both of the sentences containing these subject forms are in the past tense. Third, none of the example sentences Van Valin and Wilkins give takes any modals or modal auxiliaries, nor are any of them in negative, interrogative, or imperative forms. Overall, Van Valin and Wilkins's examples show that their intuition is mostly focused on (speculations of) a third person reporting past events; grammatically, it is verb predicate–centered and focuses exclusively on postverbal complements. Methodologically, as with many other syntactic theoretical analyses, their approach is non-empirical and based on introspection only, and the sentences are out of context. As I will show in the sections that follow, these characteristics do not correlate well with the discourse data I examined, and the discrepancy has significant theoretical consequences.

It is important to note here that I am not so much characterizing a problem with the work of Van Valin and Wilkins but rather taking their study as representative of theoretical syntactic analyses. Through comparison, I wish to demonstrate that a discourse-based study equipped with corpus linguistics tools can yield more satisfactory results. In this chapter, then, I investigate the use of *remember* in corpora of actual language use and attempt to explore the following questions: First, how is the verb *remember* actually used in discourse as revealed by our corpus data? Second, what are the implications of the corpus-based findings for language research in general?

The Corpora

Three spoken corpora and one written corpus were used in this study. Information about the databases is summarized in table 1. The CUP-CU Corpus is a spoken North American English corpus jointly sponsored by Cambridge University Press and Cornell University (Tao and Waugh 1998). For this project, I used the first 34,000 words available from the pilot project. The language of the data in this pilot project can be characterized as highly interactive, since all of the transcripts are based on multiparty informal conversations, typically among family members and/or friends. The Corpus of Spoken American English (CSAE) is a corpus built at the University of California, Santa Barbara (Chafe, Du Bois, and Thompson 1991). I used the 170,000-word sample that was available.[1] The majority of the transcripts in this corpus are based on daily conversations. There are also some transcripts based on university lectures, religious sermons, and business meetings, which make up about 20 percent of the data. The language of this corpus can therefore be characterized as mainly interactive but not as interactive as the CUP-CU Corpus. The Corpus of Spoken Professional American English (CSPAE) is constructed from a selection of existing transcripts of interactions in professional settings, including White House press briefings (Barlow 1998). For this study, I used only the corpus's academic discourse portion (drawn from committee meetings), which contains about 1,204,000 words. In terms of interactivity and conversational involvement among participants (Chafe and Danielewicz 1987; Tannen 1982), the language represented by this corpus should be regarded as the least involved compared with the other two corpora.

The only written corpus used for this study is the Brown Corpus (Francis and Kucera 1964). This corpus, with about one million words, contains a wide variety of written genres, such as news reportage, press editorials, fiction, religious texts, and memoirs. I used this corpus only for comparison with the spoken corpora, as the main goal of this chapter is to document the use of *remember* in spoken discourse.

TABLE 1. The Corpora

Corpora	Number of Words
Spoken	
CUP-CU Corpus	34,000
CSAE (UCSB)	170,000
CSPE (academic portions)	1,000,000
Total spoken	1,204,000
Written	
Brown Corpus	1,000,000

The Frequency Distribution of *Remember* across Registers

Before I discuss the usage patterns of *remember,* it is necessary to examine the overall token distribution of *remember* across discourse registers (Biber 1988) as represented by the corpora. Table 2 considers both the raw frequency and the normalized frequency (tabulation of occurrences with a fixed unit size across samples). Two general tendencies appear to be evident in the data. First, *remember* is used more frequently in spoken than in written English. In the spoken corpora, the average normalized frequency is .33 per thousand words, while in the written corpus it is only .25 per thousand. Second, within the spoken data set, the frequency of *remember* tends to increase as the level of interactivity increases. Recall that among the three spoken corpora, while the CUP-CU Corpus is most interactive, the professional academic corpus (CSPAE) is the least interactive, with the Santa Barbara corpus (CSAE) standing in the middle; the frequency of *remember* corresponds positively to the interactivity of the language represented by these three corpora. In particular, note that in the most interactive corpus, the CUP-CU Corpus, the use of *remember* is almost twice as frequent as the written (Brown) corpus. Since written language can be thought of as the least interactive of all, the frequencies across the spoken and written corpora and within the spoken group actually point to one common tendency—namely, that the use of *remember* is correlated to degrees of participant interaction or conversational involvement. This seems to be a feature of not only *remember* but also many other "private" verbs, such as *think,* according to Biber (1988, 105).

TABLE 2.   Frequency Distribution of *Remember* in Spoken and Written Corpora

Corpora	Number of Words	Raw Frequency	Normalized Frequency (per thousand words)
Spoken			
CUP-CU Corpus	34,000	15	0.44
CSAE (UCSB)	170,000	73	0.42
CSPE (academic portions)	1,000,000	311	0.31
Total spoken	1,204,000	399	0.33
Written			
Brown Corpus	~1,000,000	251	0.25

In summary, results from our mixed genre database show that it is more likely for us to find the use of *remember* in more direct, more interactive discourse contexts than in less direct and less involved discourse contexts. From a theoretical point of view, this suggests that the best starting point to study the behavior of such verbs as *remember* is the highly interactive conversation genre. Thus, in the sections to follow, I focus my investigation of the use of *remember* exclusively on the three spoken corpora.

Grammatical Characteristics of *Remember* in Spoken Discourse

In this section, I intend to profile the grammatical characteristics of *remember* by looking at the entire environment in which *remember* is used. While previous studies tended only to examine the kinds of complement clauses *remember* takes, I also describe preverbal and postverbal elements, the predicate complex involving *remember*, and the verb's prosodic correlates. The results reported in the following subsections indicate that *remember* and its associated utterances in spoken discourse can be characterized by two features: (1) skewed grammatical structures (in terms of heavy concentration on certain types of subject, tense, person, utterance type, and modal word) and (2) smallness, simplicity, and flexibility. This pattern is radically different from the complement-taking *remember* that many grammarians have described. Further, the grammatical profile presented here seems to suggest that utterances involving *remember* are an independent, highly mobile unit of some sort.

Subjects

The corpus data reveals that subjects of *remember* in spoken language are overwhelmingly first and second persons, rarely third. Furthermore, a significant subject form found in the spoken corpora is the null subject, or zero form, which has almost entirely escaped the attention of previous researchers. When zero forms are used, they are typically understood as referring to the addressee or to both the speaker and the addressee.

4. *JF: Remember,*[2]
   JL: .. @@@
   JF: .. you're gonna spend the rest of your life with m=e. (CSAE)

There are also some cases where *to remember* is preceded by a dummy *it* subject plus an adjectival construction (i.e., an evaluative adjectival construction).

5. *LP:* And I think *it's just important to remember* from a classroom perspective that any time we do any kind of assessment, it does directly impact instruction. (CSPAE)

The distribution of the subject forms is represented in table 3. As the numbers indicate, the dominance of first and second persons is indeed striking. This sharply contrasts with the artificially constructed sentences represented in the three examples from Van Valin and Wilkins cited earlier, where two out of the three examples contain a third-person full NP. In other words, the spoken data shows that *remember* utterances are not about a third-person event; they are instead primarily concerned with the speaker and the addressee present in the interactional setting. This is not a trivial phenomenon; rather, as I will show later, the heavy concentration on and main opposition between first person and second (rather than the third) person are important, and a whole range of grammatical and pragmatic properties can be shown to be closely associated with this concentration and distinction.

TABLE 3. Subject Forms of *Remember* in Spoken Discourse

Subject	N	Percentage
First person		
Singular	196	49%
Plural	23	6%
Second Person		
Singular	53	13%
Plural	5	1%
Third person		
Singular	6	2%
Plural	5	1%
Null	97	24%
Dummy + *to Remember*	14	4%
Total	399	100%

Verb Tense

In looking at the tenses used for the verb *remember*, we overwhelmingly find the use of the simple present over any other forms (see table 4). Again, this is in sharp contrast to what is presented in the artificially constructed sentences based on intuition; for instance, in Van Valin and Wilkins' examples, two out of three uses are in the past tense. In terms of what *remember* utterances do, then, this would again suggest that they are not about past events, as implied by intuition-based data; rather, they are more related to direct interaction between participants in conversation. Numerous studies (Chafe and Danielewicz 1987; Biber 1988; Thompson and Mulac 1991) have shown that high degrees of conversational involvement (hence high degrees of interactivity) tend to cluster with both first and second persons as well as with the present tense. These grammatical forms contribute to a sense of directness (see my discussion section later in this chapter).

Utterance Types

Another interesting grammatical feature revealed in the data is the large number of negative statements, imperatives, and interrogative utterances associated with the verb *remember*. Here interrogatives

TABLE 4.   Tense of the Verb Predicate Involving *Remember*

Tense	N	Percentage
Simple present	395	99%
Nonsimple present	4	1%
Total	399	100%

include expressions with a question intonation, an interrogative inversion structure (e.g., "do you remember"), or both. Taken together, these three types of utterances make up over 50 percent of the data, with imperatives alone totaling 26 percent and negatives totaling 18 percent. None of these facts is captured by intuition.

An example of the negative statements associated with *remember* is

6. I *can't remember* what test it was we were working on, but . . . (CSPAE)

An example of the imperatives is

7. The other point I wanted to make is the other reminder about the meeting norm. *Remember,* we talked about once an idea is out there that it's common property. (CSPAE)

Interestingly, as may be inferred from the examples given here, these utterance forms are distributed unevenly across persons; and as indicated earlier, they mainly cluster around the opposition between the first and second persons. Here second persons refer to both overt marking ("you," "you all," etc.) and bare verb forms understood to be addressed to the immediate addressee (as in examples 4 and 7).

The results of my analysis are shown in table 5. From this table, we can see that negative statements overwhelmingly (89 percent) converge on first persons; by contrast, imperatives are overwhelmingly (87 percent) associated with second persons; and interrogatives are categorically (100 percent) associated with second persons. Overall, the first-person and second-person opposition we saw in the subject form is further substantiated in the distribution of utterance types. Clearly, this skewed distribution of utterance types (especially the

TABLE 5.   Distribution of Negatives, Interrogatives, and Imperatives across Persons for *Remember*

	Negative		Interrogative		Imperative	
	N	Percentage	N	Percentage	N	Percentage
First person	65	89%	0	—	14	13%
Second person (Including null)	5	7%	27	100%	90	87%
Other	3	4%	0	—	0	—
Total	73	100%	27	100%	104	100%

association of negatives with the first person and of interrogatives with the second person), is an intriguing fact that needs to be explained. Later in this chapter, I will demonstrate how it can be accounted for from the point of view of interaction.

The Verbal Complex

When verbal predicates involving *remember* are examined in discourse, we find that the verb is seldom in simple form (i.e., consisting of a verb only); typically a variety of adverbs, modals, auxiliaries, and conjunctions cluster around the verb, making up a complex verbal expression (Hopper 1995). Such elements typically indicate the speaker's stance or attitude (Biber and Finegan 1988). Typical examples of such satellite elements in the database are listed in figure 1.

In general, these items are more frequently associated with first persons than with second persons, except for the following, which are more frequently used with second persons than with the first person: "but remember," "just remember," "so remember," "you may/might remember." In the following example, a variety of satellite forms are used in conjunction with the first-person subject.

8. *PT:*   and all of this with it. And I — there were some others. And *I can't even remember* what they all were . . . [But I] —
   DN: [I know, but it] was Evelyn who did it, and we ought to make her get her notes out again. [Because sh-] —
   PT: [Yes].
   X: [@@@]
   PT: [2 If you can find <X this X> 2].

Adverbs: *even, ever, exactly, quite clearly, actually, just, scarcely, probably.*

Modal auxiliaries: *do, have to, need to, trying to, can, could, may, might, will.*

Conjunctions: *but, if, as, so, and.*

Fig. 1. Satellite forms in the verbal complex

LS: [2 She probably re2]mem [3 bers 3].
MN: [2 @@@@ 2]
JN: [3 Uh Ev3][4elyn,
EV: [4 *I don't remember* 4].
JN: will you do that a4]gain <@ some[5 time- @>.
EV: [5 Oh,
JN: @@@@@@@@@@@@5]
EV: *I will remember.* <X *I just* 5] *I just* X> *can't remember* what it was.
        (CSAE)

Again, from a discourse perspective, the pervasive use of these satellite elements is hardly surprising. As a number of researchers have argued, language is used not only for information transfer but also for expressing speakers' subjectivity and perspectives (Finegan 1995; Hopper 1991, 1995; Iwasaki 1993; Ochs and Schieffelin 1989; Scheibman forthcoming; Stein and Wright 1995). These elements contribute to the expressive function of language (Jakobson 1960) in important ways. (See my following discussion of the discourse-pragmatic functions of *remember* for further elaboration on this point.)

Postverbal Elements

The postverbal elements of *remember*, which have been the center of attention for traditional grammarians and theoretical linguists, turned out some of the most surprising results in my analysis. In the spoken discourse data, we find that postverbal elements tend to be simple forms, not complex complements as previous studies have implied. Postverbal elements consisting of a zero form, simple NPs, and a simple clause headed by a relative pronoun (*that, who, what*, etc.) constitute a large majority of occurrences (74 percent), as opposed to the

TABLE 6.   Types and Distribution of Postverbal Elements of *Remember*

Postverbal Element	N	Percentage
Noncomplements	295	74%
Zero object	159	
Simple NP (including relative clause)	93	
Relative clause	43	
Complements	104	26%
Complement clause with *that*	77	
Complement clause with *-ing*	23	
Complement clause with *to* infinitive	4	
Total	399	100%

three much-discussed kinds of complement, which are clearly in the minority (26 percent).

The results suggest that complement-taking is, at least in spoken discourse, a marginal use of *remember* and that postverbal elements of *remember* can be characterized as having a simplex form. Even more striking is the fact that gerundial complement clauses with *-ing* and complement clauses with *to* + an infinitive, which are arguably the most studied types of postverbal elements of *remember,* account for only a small fraction (5 percent and 1 percent, respectively) of the postverbal elements. Once again the corpus data suggests that previous studies seem to have paid too much attention to some of the most rare, rather than common, properties of the verb *remember.*

Flexible Syntactic Positions

In terms of syntactic placement as broadly understood, *remember* is found to be very flexible. *Remember* can by itself be an utterance (see examples 4 and 7). *Remember* can be preceded by and can stand alone with a conjunction: for example, "so remember," "and remember," "but remember," "because remember."

9. Yes, *because remember,* Jay said — you said . . . (CSPAE)

Remember can be a parenthetical insertion by itself or a part of one.

10. For example, *remember,* Sharon gave the example. (CSPAE)
11. It's an important statement to make because *if you remember,* that was a relatively new concept. (CSPAE)

Remember can appear at the beginning of an utterance.

12. *Remember* a few months ago I used to go out dancing. (CSAE)

Remember can appear as part of an adverbial clause: for example, "as I remember," "if I remember correctly," "if I remember right."

13. *TZ:* I'd have to go back and look at the news release for you. I think she is getting paid and it's going to a charity, *if I remember correctly.* (CSPAE)

Remember can be attached to the end of a completed utterance, functioning as a "tag."

14. you see how Luther came to his reformation *remember,* (CSAE)
15. I don't think we heard a lot at the public hearing, *remember.* (CSAE)

These categories may not be always clear-cut, and borderline cases undoubtedly exist. But the data shows quite clearly that *remember* is used in a very flexible manner. Far from conforming to the configuration "S + V + Complement Clause" that previous research has implied, *remember* can be used in much smaller and simpler structures and can appear in a wide range of syntactic positions.

Prosodic Properties

The last feature I want to discuss concerns prosody. As far as the transcriptions show, *remember* often coincides with an intonation unit boundary. Out of the 339 instances of *remember*, 134 exhibit this pattern, which accounts for 40 percent of the data in a data set that is not always narrowly transcribed (especially the million-word CSPAE corpus). The notion of the intonation unit refers to a discourse prosodic segment. It is typically understood as any stretch of discourse falling under a single coherent intonation contour (Chafe 1987; Du Bois et al. 1993). In the transcripts I examined, it is indicated with a punctuation mark, which does not necessarily correspond to a grammatical unit.[3] The intonation unit boundaries with which *remember* coincides include both final (completion and appeal/question) and continuing types.

Table 7 gives a breakdown of *remember* correlating with different types of intonation unit boundaries. That 40 percent of the instances of *remember* coincide with a prosodic boundary—even in a data set that is not always narrowly transcribed—shows that, prosodically, *remember* frequently marks the end of a unit, rather than being embedded in a larger unit. This reinforces the impression that the structure in which *remember* is used is smaller and less complex than previous studies have implied, since the end of a prosodic unit is more likely to coincide with the completion of a grammatical unit than with the middle of a larger grammatical unit, as, for example, in the case of a main clause taking a complement clause.

The Discourse-Pragmatic Functions of *Remember*

The discussion above demonstrates that, in spoken discourse, *remember* and its associated structures tend to function as an independent, highly mobile unit of some sort. It is now our task to explore the exact nature of this unit and of the grammatical patterns I have reported. From a methodological point of view, I suggest here that while corpus linguistic tools can be useful in helping the researcher glean patterns out of massive amounts of data, a deeper understanding of such questions as why grammars behave the way they do needs a research methodology informed by discourse-pragmatic theoretical insights. In other words, I suggest that a combined approach to language where corpus linguistic evidence is viewed from a discourse-pragmatic perspective may be most fruitful. In this case, then, I explore the following question: Are there discourse-pragmatic functions that can be said to unify the unquestionably patterned and yet seemingly disparate surface manifestations of the grammar of *remember*? My contention is that there are some discourse explanations for why the grammar of *remember* behaves the way it does. My hypothesis follows.

TABLE 7.   *Remember* at Intonation Unit Boundaries

Remember at Unit Boundaries	N	Percentage
Remember + continuing intonation (,)	84	63%
Remember + completion intonation (.)	43	32%
Remember + appeal intonation (?)	7	5%
Total	134	100%

> *Remember* in spoken English is used mainly as (1) an epistemic marker, that (i) indexes epistemic stance and (ii) is constitutive of a variety of interactional acts; and (2) a metalinguistic device, that functions to regulate participant interaction in a direct way.

I will eventually explain that the grammatical form of *remember* accords well with these functions (see my discussion section later in this chapter). Before I move on to illustrate these functions, however, a brief introduction to some theoretical concepts is in order.

Crucial to our understanding of the epistemic function of *remember* in spoken discourse is the notion of indexicality in sociocultural linguistics. Ochs (1996) articulates this in terms of the Principle of Indexicality. According to Ochs' theory, linguistic signs can be understood as indexing conceptualizations of social situations. As used here, "social situations" subsumes a wide variety of features, including the temporal-spatial locus of communicative situations, the social identities of participants, the social acts and activities taking place, and participants' affective and epistemic stance. Of particular relevance to the discussion here is the notion of epistemic stance. Generally speaking, epistemic stance refers to speakers' knowledge, belief, and commitment regarding states of affairs or propositions made in the discourse (see, among others, Chafe and Nichols 1986; Biber and Finegan 1988). As suggested earlier, my contention is that *remember* functions as a linguistic marker indexing epistemic stance. Equally important is the view that stances are also performative, that is, that expression of stance is linked to or constitutive of social acts (see, among others, Austin 1962; Searle 1969, 1975; Halliday 1992; Ochs 1996). As I will show next, this line of thinking is highly relevant for one of the functions *remember* appears to perform in spoken English.

Function 1: Indexing Epistemic Stance

A prominent function of *remember* in my data is to index the speaker's epistemic stance toward certain states of affairs or propositions made in the discourse. Specifically, *remember* can be used to show both the speaker's certainty and his or her uncertainty about certain propositions. This may at first sound contradictory; however, a closer examination of the data shows that division of labor among different forms associated with *remember* eliminates the possibility of being contradictory. There is some close form-function pairing (even though the match is far from perfect) in the data (see fig. 2). Also, it is interesting to note that both certainty and uncertainty are linked to first-person constructions.

Before talking about this function of the use of *remember* in detail, it is useful to point out that, structurally speaking, *remember* is recurrently used in conjunction with other cognitive verbs to form a larger construction.

16. *I don't remember* the percentages, *but I know* that the — there are different kinds of — there are both agreements between . . . (CSPAE)
17. This is a comprehension test and not an informational search test. And *I don't know* the data on this, *but I do remember* that one of the first things that happened when we went to longer passages in Illinois was that . . . (CSPAE)

The preceding examples demonstrate that *remember* is not just used by itself to index epistemicity; it can also be part of a larger whole that indicates epistemicity.

When *remember* is used to show the speaker's certainty toward a state of affairs, this function is commonly expressed with a simple form: first-person subject + *remember*.

18. the woman mentioned the calculators and stuff like that, . . . But in my day, *I remember,* you know, writing a dissertation. My advisor, just to do a calculation, it took several pages like this. (CSPAE)

For expressing a speaker's uncertainty about a state of affairs, a wide variety of forms can be used. The most common form involves a negative construction, usually including *can't* or *don't.*

Function	Form
Indexing certainty	Affirmative, typically without adverb/modal auxiliary/conjunction
Indexing uncertainty	Negative, with adverb/modal auxiliary/conjunction

Fig. 2. Form-function pairing in indexing epistemic stance

19. *KF:* And thinking more of the usefulness of the test . . . But again,
    I don't remember well that context. (CSPAE)

A second strategy is to use certain modal auxiliaries.

20. *BK:* Barb, can you talk about the time burden it took to do
    this . . . ?
    BP: I wish *I could remember* exactly. It took about an hour.
    (CSPAE)

A third common strategy is to use *remember* as a parenthetical and/or
in *if*-clauses and other adverbial clauses. These parentheticals commonly end with an adverb, such as *right* or *correctly*.

21. *MT:* The question of speededness, number seven, traditionally,
    NAEP is not a speeded test. Some place, *if I remember the sta-
    tistics right,* between 90 and 92 percent of students have an
    opportunity. (CSPAE)

   Now that I have sketched the function of *remember* to mark epistemic stance in discourse—that is, to express the speaker's certainty
and uncertainty about the proposition made in the discourse—it is
necessary to explore why speakers mark epistemic stance in oral
interaction. Recall that from the point of view of the indexicality principle, stance-marking is seen as linked and constitutive of social acts;
that is, stance-marking is often best understood not simply as indicating the speaker's knowledge state or mental capacity but as a way of
acting or doing things with a communicative goal. As the following
discussion will demonstrate, this general understanding of the function of language applies extremely well to the case of *remember*. I here
characterize some of the social acts performed by using *remember*.
   One circumstance where speakers use a *remember* phrase is to
show agreement with other interlocutors. In this context, *remember* is
often accompanied by other agreement markers, such as assessments
(Pomerantz 1984; Goodwin and Goodwin 1992).

22. *PS:* They tended to be of the ilk of our short to medium informa-
    tional piece. They tended to be like 4- to 6-year-old current
    event type pieces . . .

ST: *Yes, I remember those. They were very manageable. They were interesting.* (CSPAE)

In the preceding example, the second speaker shows that she is in agreement with what the first speaker said. The second speaker not only confirms this by appealing to her memory of the state of affairs referred to in the first speaker's turn but also gives some further assessments in the following utterances ("very manageable," "very interesting"). Supplying and alternating assessments is a common way of showing affiliation or agreement (Pomerantz 1984; Goodwin and Goodwin 1992; Tao and McCarthy forthcoming).

A second context where a *remember* phrase is used is to build rapport with other interlocutors by adding more details about a topic initiated by others. This kind of act is similar to the agreement use but differs in that the speaker often uses "I remember" as an introducing device to bring about further events or states of affairs to support the previous speaker. In the following example, speaker 2 uses "I remember" to start her turn and provides new details of a situation that other speakers have been talking about, namely, the awkward situation of some holidays in different places and different times. (Notice also that earlier in line 3, with the agreement tokens ["yeah"], speaker 2 already showed her high involvement with the other speakers.)

23. (Talking about the history of the Thanksgiving holiday in the United States.)
    <3> Yeah but Lincoln declared it as a holi= a national holiday. It had been celebrated prior to that.
    <1> I think harvest festivals are pretty institutional around any country.
    <2> Yeah. Yeah.
    <5> Yeah I think so.
    <4> Ours happen to be quite late. Don't you think? I mean . . .
    <5> The — Yes definitely.
    <1> You know early harvesting right now.
    <4> In Canada they have it earlier. In Canada —.
    <1> damn cold.
    <2> *I remember* like when all of the American holidays merge. You know we've already got all the Presidents together.
    <5> ((laughs))

<2> Because then we would get months like months off. (CUP-CU)

In contrast with the previous situations, *remember* phrases can also be used by the current speaker to challenge other interlocutors or distance him- or herself from them—that is, stance-marking can also be used in a negative way. In the next example, which is a family conversation, parents (F and M) are talking with their children about the children's report cards. Amused by the children's attentiveness to their average scores, the father (F) uses a teasing tone of voice (indicated here by <@ @>), questioning why they talk so much about the details of their school reports.

24. <M> Annie what did you get?
    <A> A ninety.
    <B> Excuse me.
    <C> What?
    <A> Get away with your disgusting.
    <X> So what was your overall average?
    <A> Ninety-three point seven.
    <B> That was my overall average last year the second quarter.
    <F> <@ Do you *remember* all your little overall averages? @>
    <B> No I just *remember* that one because we had to know it for some. (CUP-CU)

Even though the syntactic form associated with the father's *remember* utterance is a question, it is clear from the context that the father is not interested in questioning the mental state or the mental capacity of the children, just as "Can you pass the salt?" kinds of question are not about the addressee's physical capacity (Austin 1962; Searle 1969, 1975). That B, the daughter, uses a *remember* utterance in her reply ("I just remember that one") constitutes a counterattack, so to speak, on her father.

Finally, another kind of social act associated with stance-marking with *remember* phrases is politeness. This use of *remember* typically occurs in face-threatening situations, especially when forgetting is considered embarrassing.

25. I think we've covered all the tangential issues that ... If you'll look at the middle column for grade 8, and *if you'll remember*, I had the

one transparency up there yesterday about — and I, on that transparency, had just put the 25, . . . (CSPAE)

In the preceding example, the speaker is giving a presentation. Since what he talked about yesterday is important for what he is about to say now, he needs to make sure that the audience remembers what he did yesterday. However, the speaker cannot be sure either that everyone remembers what he did or that everyone has forgotten what he did. The use of the *remember* phrase and the subsequent utterances (recapitulating what he said earlier) can be seen as a polite reminder designed to accommodate both situations.

Function 2: A Metalinguistic Device

The notion of metalinguistic device here refers to the function of using a form to focus explicitly on the interaction between participants. This notion is close to what Bateson (1972) and Ruesch and Bateson (1951) have called the metacommunicative function of language. In this regard, three subcategories are identified in the data.

The first use is drawing the interlocutor's attention to certain states of affairs or propositions. This is typically done with a lone *remember.*

26. WL: I think this is connected to the reporting issues that we're going to discuss.
    PL: You mean, within the district or the state? Because, *remember,* there's no data that comes back to the Federal Government for this test . . . (CSPAE)

In such a case, the current speaker calls the addressee's attention to the upcoming talk that is produced after the lone *remember,* and the current speaker typically continues the talk after uttering the *remember* phrase.

The second category has to do with what can be called a "tying" function (Sacks 1992), and involves participant interaction through topic negotiation. Specifically, the current speaker uses a *remember* phrase to tie an intended topic or proposition to the other participant, by referring either to an activity that they both participated in or to some speech that can be attributed to the other participant (or sometimes both), so that a new topic of conversation can be established.

27. *GR:*   I don't know *if you remember* when we were first thinking about trying to do the intertextual stuff on the IGA. Were you still working on it?

   Voice: Yes. (CSPAE)

In the preceding case, the current speaker ties his proposed topic to an activity (thinking) in which the other participant is alleged to have engaged with him or her. In such cases, recurrently the *remember* phrase is in the middle of a larger stretch of talk rather than at the beginning of an incoming flux of talk (as in the case of attention-getting discussed earlier).

Finally, another type of metalinguistic use is to elicit listener responses and to relinquish the conversation floor. In this usage, we typically find that the *remember* phrase appears at the very end of a turn, typically in an interrogative form and with or without a second-person pronoun.

28. *SL:*   In fact, there will be a new section on—a new little section within this chapter on that. The chapter is becoming two chapters. *Remember?*

   BR: Uh-huh. But we're worried now about what's existing here. (CSPAE)

In the preceding example, the addressee takes up the conversation floor from the current speaker, which is very typical in the data. With such an explicit solicitation of participation, it would be very difficult to imagine that the addressee does not respond.

Overall, the data seems to suggest patterns of form-function pairing, in the context of metalinguistic usage, which I summarize in figure 3. As the examples indicate, second-person subject forms, including zero subjects, are typically associated with this function.

Discussion: Form and Function

In the preceding sections of this chapter, I have shown that the recurrent patterns of *remember* in spoken discourse are strikingly different from the patterns posited by intuition-based studies, which assert that *remember* is a cognition verb with a complex grammar of complement-taking. In the remainder of the chapter, I will discuss the connection between the discourse grammar and discourse functions of *remember*

Function	Form
Attention getting	Lone *remember*, begin ning of chunk of talk
Tying	Utterance medial
Soliciting addressee response/ relinquishing conversation floor	Turn-final, question intonation

Fig. 3. Form-function pairing for metalinguistic usage

based on the data presented here. As you will recall, earlier in this chapter, I presented a grammatical profile of *remember* in conversational discourse showing that *remember* can be characterized by two features: (1) skewed grammatical structure and (2) smallness, simplicity, and flexibility. The skewed grammatical structure of *remember* refers to the following:

1. the pervasive use of first- and second-person subject forms
2. the predominant use of the present tense
3. first-person constructions that have more negative statements and are used with more adverbs, modal auxiliaries, and conjunctions than second person constructions
4. second-person constructions that have more interrogatives and imperatives than first person constructions

Discourse researchers have repeatedly found a strong correlation between the use of the first and second persons and the use of the present tense for indexing epistemicity. In their analysis of the epistemic phrase "I think" in English conversation, which shares many remarkably similar morphosyntactic properties with the grammar of *remember*, Thompson and Mulac (1991) state:

> As seemingly disparate as these factors are, their behavior finds a unified explanation in the acknowledgement that certain combinations of main clause subjects and verbs in English are being reanalyzed as unitary epistemic phrases. . . . As we have seen, the frequency of the subjects *I* and *you* and the verbs *think* and *guess* provides a strong push towards the reanalysis because these are just the subjects and verbs most likely to express epistemic meanings: speakers assert speaker commitment with *I* or question it with *you*. (249)

The similarity shared by first and second grammatical persons in expressing epistemicity has also been well documented crosslinguistically (e.g., Benveniste 1971; Woodbury 1986; Traugott 1989). In the data, moreover, in addition to the stance-marking function, *remember* utterances have the metalinguistic function of regulating participant interaction.

As for the heavy concentration on the simple present tense, it can be said that the simple present tense in English is the most neutral tense form in terms of expressing temporal meaning and is thus most suitable for direct interaction. Biber (1988) points out:

> Private verbs and present tense forms . . . can also be considered interactive or involved. Present tense refers to actions occurring in the immediate context of interaction. . . . Private verbs (e.g., *think, feel*) are used for the overt expression of private attitudes, thoughts, and emotion. First and second person pronouns, which also have large weights on this factor, refer directly to the addressor and addressee and are thus used frequently in highly interactive discourse. (105)

In terms of the convergence of directness with these various grammatical elements (subject form and tense), the data on *remember* provides further evidence in support of the findings of the aforementioned discourse researchers. This evidence is supportive on two accounts: expressing epistemic attitude and regulating participant interaction in face-to-face conversational situations, both functions that require direct interaction. At the same time, the data also shows clearly that *remember* utterances are not about a third person reporting a past event, or rather an observer's speculation about it, as the intuition data implies. From this perspective, it is no wonder that the kinds of grammatical phenomena syntacticians have a tendency to describe are rarely found in spoken discourse.

How can the feature of smallness, simplicity, and flexibility be understood to be motivated by discourse functions? Given the fact that *remember* in spoken discourse is heavily loaded pragmatically, this set of grammatical features can be straightforwardly linked to properties of other discourse elements in language systems. Universally, pragmatically loaded elements are small items or small structures that sometimes result from phonological and/or morphosyntactic reduction. Thus, in many Asian languages, pragmatic particles are realized by simple vocal forms (e.g., *a, ne,* and *me* in Mandarin Chinese and *la* in Singapore English [Gupta 1992]). In all languages where discourse markers have been studied (Schiffrin 1987), these pragmatic elements strongly prefer small items or simple structures, either in short vocalic forms (e.g., *oh* in English [Schiffrin 1987] and *joo* in Finnish [Sorjonen 1996]) or in reduced phrasal structures (e.g., "y'know," "I mean" [Schiffrin 1987], "I think" [Thompson and Mulac 1991], and "I don't know" [Bybee and Scheibman 1999] in English and "ni zhidao" [you know] in Mandarin Chinese [Tao and Thompson 1991]). Many of these items also have a strong grammatical mobility, which is not surprising given the highly grammaticized nature of these structures.

So far, my discussion about form-function pairing—that is, the understanding of the common grammatical features of *remember* in spoken discourse—has focused on features at the macro level. I now turn to some specific areas where similar effects of form-function pairing can be observed. In the preceding section of this chapter, I identified the specific grammatical patterns of *remember* under each of the two broadly defined discourse communicative functions. My discussion shows that there is a close correspondence between form and function. Figure 4 pieces together the forms under the two discourse-pragmatic functions. As the figure shows, the overall distinction is between first and second persons (with a lack of the third person). The data shows that the expression of epistemicity strongly tends to be realized with first-person constructions. This implies that, at least with *remember*, speakers use this form mostly to indicate their own epistemic commitment (i.e., certainty and uncertainty) toward the message expressed, rather than questioning the commitment of the addressee, as is the case with *think* (Thompson and Mulac 1991). In contrast, the second-person constructions heavily align with the metalinguistic function; that is, they are frequently used by the current speaker to attract the addressee's attention, to remind the addressee of a relevant state of affairs, or to solicit his or her responses. Hence, the imperative (lone *remember* forms) and interrogative forms are frequent.

To sum up, I have shown that at both the macro and micro levels, the common patterns of the use of *remember* are tightly linked to the discourse communicative functions that *remember* utterances recurrently perform in discourse, namely, marking epistemic stance and regulating interaction. The way *remember* behaves in the data is clearly motivated by discourse function. By way of contrast, the grammar of *remember* that syntacticians have imagined has more to do with

Function	Form
Epistemicity	First person
Indexing certainty	affirmative, typically without adverb/modal auxiliary/conjunction
Indexing uncertainty	negative, with adverb/modal auxiliary/conjunction
Metalinguistics	Second person
Attention-getting	Lone *remember*, beginning of chunk of talk
Tying	Utterance medial
Soliciting addressee response/relinquishing conversation floor	Turn-final, question intonation

Fig. 4. A summary of form and function correspondence

reporting or speculating about third-person, past events, which, as it turns out, speakers rarely, if ever, do with *remember* in face-to-face interaction.

Concluding Remarks

In this chapter, I have taken a corpus-based approach to identifying some common patterns of the use of *remember* in spoken interactive discourse and have found that they depart substantially from the kinds of patterns nonempirical studies have presented. Overall, *remember*-associated utterances are characteristically skewed in their grammatical structure; they are much smaller, much simpler, and more flexible than previously thought. I propose that *remember,* a cognition verb representing a mental state, is best analyzed as an epistemic marker and metalinguistic device in conversational English. Remembrance, or speaking of this mental process, just as forgetfulness, constitutes an interactional resource (Goodwin 1987).

By way of conclusion, I would like to discuss briefly how this study may bear on language research in general. As discussed in the beginning of this chapter, many syntactic approaches, such as Role and Reference Grammar, appeal to semantics to derive syntax. Since the decomposition of semantic properties of verbs is usually done out of context, there is always the question of whether semantic analysis based on isolated sentences is interactionally real for participants in social interaction. Thus, in the case of *remember,* many researchers have routinely treated it as a mental-state verb having to do with recalling states of affairs that presumably have happened in the past (see, e.g., Van Valin and Wilkins 1993). I call this the label-centric approach, since most of what the researcher does is look at the label (e.g., "mental-state verb") in isolation and try to construe the potential meanings the label might entail. The problem with this methodology is that analyses of labels often turn out to be at variance with how speakers actually use labels. In actual discourse, speakers may not use a label for the kind of activities the label designates, or when speakers do use it in that way, the connotation of the use may have some derivative or even opposite effects. I by no means suggest that there are no instances where the designation of a label and the use of the label converge. Rather, only when we pay attention to the actual use of a label in real communicative contexts can we tell whether or not there is indeed a convergence between the designation of the label and the use of the label. I believe that the distinction between deduction of label meanings and observing the use of labels has important implications for research on cognition verbs in particular and for research on lexico-grammar in general.

Notes

I am grateful to Sandra A. Thompson for her inspiration through various discussions in the process of my study of this topic and to Traci Suiter for her helpful comments and editorial assistance with this chapter. Standard disclaimers apply.
1. I thank the director of the project, John W. Du Bois, for making the data available to me.
2. In the CSAE transcription system, each utterance represents an intonation unit. Other special conventions are @: laughter; =: lengthening, []: overlaps; --: truncation.
3. Among the three spoken corpora, CSAE is strictly transcribed according to the intonation unit, while the CSPAE and CUP-CU corpora are done on the basis of the transcriber's individual judgment.

References

Austin, J. L. 1962. *How to Do Things with Words.* Cambridge: Harvard University Press.

Barlow, Michael. 1998. *The Corpus of Spoken Professional American-English* (CSPA). Houston: Athelstan.

Bateson, G. 1972. *Steps to an Ecology of Mind.* New York: Ballantine.

Benveniste, Emile. 1971. *Problems in General Linguistics.* Trans. Mary Elizabeth Meek. Coral Gables, FL: University of Miami Press.

Biber, Douglas. 1988. *Variation across Speech and Writing.* Cambridge: Cambridge University Press.

Biber, Douglas, and Edward Finegan. 1988. Adverbial Stance Types in English. *Discourse Processes* 11, no. 1:1–34.

Bolinger, Dwight. 1977. *Meaning and Form.* London and New York: Longman.

Bybee, Joan, and Joanne Scheibman. 1999. The Effect of Usage on Degree of Constituency: The Reduction of *Don't* in American English. *Linguistics* 37:575–96.

Chafe, Wallace. 1987. Cognitive Constraints on Information Flow. In *Coherence and Grounding in Discourse,* ed. R. Tomlin, 21–51. Amsterdam and Philadelphia: John Benjamins.

Chafe, Wallace, and Jane Danielewicz. 1987. Properties of Spoken and Written Language. In *Comprehending Oral and Written Language,* ed. R. Horowitz and S. Samuels, 83–113. San Diego, CA: Academic Press.

Chafe, Wallace, J. DuBois, and S. Thompson. 1991. Towards a Corpus of Spoken American English. In *English Corpus Linguistics: Studies in Honour of Jan Svartvik,* ed. K. Aijmer and B. Altenberg, 64–82. London: Longman.

Chafe, Wallace, and J. Nichols, eds. 1986. *Evidentiality: The Linguistic Coding of Epistemology.* Advances in Discourse Processes. Norwood, NJ: Ablex.

COBUILD. 1996. *Collins COBUILD Grammar Patterns 1: Verbs.* London: Collins.

Du Bois, John, W. S. Schuetze-Coburn, S. Cumming, and D. Paolino. 1993. Outline of Discourse Transcription. In *Talking Data: Transcription and Coding in Discourse Research,* ed. J. Edwards and M. Lampert, 45–90. Hillsdale, NJ: Lawrence Erlbaum.

Fanego, Teresa. 1996. On the Historical Development of English Retrospective Verbs. *Neuphilologische Mitteilungen* 97, no. 1:71–79.

Finegan, Edward. 1995. Subjectivity and Subjectivisation: An Introduction. In *Subjectivity and Subjectivisation: Linguistic Perspectives,* ed. D. Stein and S. Wright, 1–15. Cambridge: Cambridge University Press.

Francis, W. N., and H. Kucera. 1964. *A Standard Corpus of Present-Day Edited American English, for Use with Digital Computers.* Providence: Department of Linguistics, Brown University.

Goodwin, Charles. 1987. Forgetfulness as an Interactive Resource. *Social Psychology Quarterly* 50, no. 2:115–31.

Goodwin, C., and M. H. Goodwin. 1992. Assessments and the Construction of Context. In *Rethinking Context: Language as an Interactive Phenomenon,* ed. C. Goodwin and A. Duranti, 147–90. Cambridge: Cambridge University Press.

Gupta, Anthea F. 1992. The Pragmatic Particles of Singapore Colloquial English. *Journal of Pragmatics* 18, no. 1:31–57.

Halliday, M. A .K. 1992. The Act of Meaning. *Georgetown University Round Table on Languages and Linguistics,* 7–21.

Hopper, Paul J. 1991. Dispersed Verbal Predicates in Vernacular Writing. *BLS* 17:402–13.

———. 1995. The Category "Event" in Natural Discourse and Logic. In *Discourse Grammar and Typology: Papers in Honor of John W. M. Verhaar,* ed. W. Abraham, T. Givon, and S. Thompson, 139–50. Amsterdam and Philadelphia: John Benjamins.

Iwasaki, Shoichi. 1993. *Subjectivity in Grammar and Discourse.* Amsterdam and Philadelphia: John Benjamins.

Jakobson, Roman. 1960. Closing Statement: Linguistics and Poetics. In *Style in Language,* ed. T. Sebeok, 350–77. Cambridge: MIT Press.

Jorgensen, Erik. 1990. *Remember* and *Forget* with Gerund and Infinitive as Objects. *English Studies* 71, no. 2:147–51.

Lakoff, George. 1991. Cognitive versus Generative Linguistics: How Commitments Influence Results. *Language and Communication* 11:53–62.

Ochs, Elinor. 1996. Linguistic Resources for Socializing Humanity. In *Rethinking Linguistic Relativity,* ed. J. Gumperz and S. Levinson, 407–37. Cambridge: Cambridge University Press.

Ochs, Elinor, and Bambi Schieffelin. 1989. Language Has a Heart. *Text* 9, no. 1:7–25.

Ogura, Michiko. 1986. OE Verbs of Thinking. *Neuphilologische Mitteilungen* 87, no. 3:325–41.

Pomerantz, Anita. 1984. Agreeing and Disagreeing with Assessments: Some Features of Preferred/Dispreferred Turn Shapes. In *Structures of Social Interaction: Studies in Conversation Analysis,* ed. M. Atkinson and J. Heritage, 57–101. Cambridge: Cambridge University Press.

Quirk, Randolph, S. Greenbaum, G. Leech, and J. Svartvik. 1985. *A Comprehensive Grammar of the English Language.* London and New York: Longman.

Ruesch, J., and G. Bateson, eds. 1951. *Communication.* New York: Norton.

Sacks, Harvey. 1992. *Lectures on Conversation.* Ed. Gail Jefferson. Cambridge, MA: Blackwell.

Scheibman, Joanne. Forthcoming. Structural Patterns of Subjectivity in American English Conversation. Ph.D. diss., University of New Mexico.

Schiffrin, Deborah. 1987. *Discourse Markers.* Cambridge: Cambridge University Press.

Searle, John. 1969. *Speech Acts.* Cambridge: Harvard University Press.

———. 1975. Indirect Speech Acts. In *Speech Acts: Syntax and Semantics,* ed. P. Cole and J. Morgan, 3:59–82. New York: Academic Press.

Sorjonen, Marja-Leena. 1996. On Repeats and Responses in Finnish Conversations. In *Interaction and Grammar,* ed. E. Ochs, E. Schegloff, and S. A. Thompson, 277–327. Cambridge: Cambridge University Press.

Stein, Dieter, and Susan Wright, eds. 1995. Subjectivity and Subjectivization. Cambridge: Cambridge University Press.

Tannen, Deborah. 1982. Oral and Literate Strategies in Oral and Written Discourse. In *Literacy, Language, and Learning: The Nature and Consequences of Reading and Writing,* ed. D. R. Olson, N. Torrance, and A. Hildyard, 124–47. Cambridge: Cambridge University Press.

Tao, Hongyin, and Michael McCarthy. Forthcoming. Understanding Nonrestrictive *Which*-Clauses in Spoken English, Which Is Not an Easy Thing. *Language Sciences.*

Tao, Hongyin, and Sandra A. Thompson. 1991. English Backchannels in Mandarin Conversations: A Case Study of Superstratum Pragmatic "Interference." *Journal of Pragmatics* 16:209–23.

Tao, Hongyin, and Linda R. Waugh. 1998. The Cornell-Cambridge University Press Corpus of Spoken American English. Paper presented at the Teaching and Language Corpora Conference 1998, Keble College, Oxford, July 24–27.

Thompson, S. A., and A. Mulac. 1991. A Quantitative Perspective on the Grammar of Epistemic Parentheticals in English. In *Approaches to Grammaticalization 2,* ed. E. C. Traugott and B. Heine, 313–29. Amsterdam: Benjamins.

Traugott, Elizabeth. 1989 On the Rise of Epistemic Meanings in English: An Example of Subjectification in Semantic Change. *Language* 65:31–55.

Van Valin, Robert, and David Wilkins. 1993. Predicting Syntactic Structure from Semantic Representations: *Remember* in English and its Equivalents in Mparntwe Arrernte. In *Advances in Role and Reference Grammar,* ed. R. Van Valin, 499–534. Amsterdam and Philadelphia: John Benjamins.

Woodbury, Anthony. 1986. Interactions of Tense and Evidentiality: A Study of Sherpa and English. In *Evidentiality: The Linguistic Coding of Epistemology,* ed. Wallace Chafe and J. Nichols, 188–202. Advances in Discourse Processes. Norwood, NJ: Ablex.

Wu, Yidi. 1997. Higher Verbs and Their Nonfinite Complements. *Journal of English Linguistics* 25, no. 3:241–49.

Discourse Management and New-Episode Flags in MICASE

John M. Swales and Bonnie Malczewski
University of Michigan

The character of academic literacy in English has been heavily investigated over the last 20 years. Among the several consequences, there has emerged an increasing body of work, initiated and inspired by Bazerman 1998, on its rhetorical and stylistic evolution (Atkinson 1999; Valle 1999). Its major genres, such as the research article (Swales 1990), the doctoral dissertation (Bunton 1998), and the book review (Motta-Ruth 1998), have been analyzed in terms of both rhetorical organization and lexico-grammatical features. Studies of written discourses from particular disciplines abound, such as Myers 1990 on biology, Salager-Meyer 1992 on medicine, Dressen and Swales 2000 on geology, and McCloskey 1994 on economics. Analyses of particular features of written academic prose have also flourished; extensive book-length studies of this type include Mauranen 1993 on metadiscourse, Peck McDonald 1987 on sentence subjects, and Hyland 1998 on hedging. Although much remains to be done, our maps of this area of discourse are steadily improving.

Additionally, there is a growing body of work designed to illuminate how academic literacy is acquired, both at the undergraduate level and at the graduate level. For the former, one major early contribution has come from the work of Flower and Hayes (e.g., 1981) and their demonstration that immature academic writers produce "writer-based prose" while mature ones produce "reader-based prose." More recently, Geisler 1994 has shown how students cross "a great divide" and learn to occupy as writers a "rhetorical space." The overall conclusion from these and other studies would seem to be that this great leap forward typically occurs at around the junior year in selective institutions and somewhat later in less selective universities. At the graduate level, the major breakthroughs concern such matters as "graduate student positioning" (Swales and Feak 1994), the perceiving of an audience bigger than an individual instructor (Gosden 1995), and the acquisition of revision negotiating skills (Prior 1998). Throughout, we see at work processes of disciplinary socialization and the gradual, if at times uncertain, ascension of a ladder of genres starting from the term paper and concluding with the dissertation and published articles.

In contrast, our knowledge of spoken academic discourse per se, of its historical evolution, and of its individual acquisition is much more patchy and anecdotal, despite the fact that, in terms of academic socialization, writing represents "the tip of the iceberg" (Mauranen in this volume). Indeed, it is likely that a preponderance of situated learning, of "legitimate peripheral participation" (Lave and Wenger 1991), and of "learning the academic ropes" takes place via involvement in oral discussion, revelation, confession, and consultation. That said, there are some cartographic expeditions into this little-known territory. Dubois, in a major series of papers (e.g., Dubois 1987) has revealed much of what goes on when biologists give their short conference presentations. Tracy (1997) has provided an important study of academic colloquia in her own field of communication studies. There are strong traditions of work on the basic undergraduate lecture, especially outside the United States (e.g., Flowerdew 1994), and, in the United States, on research designed to attack the so-called international teaching assistant problem. For the latter, the annotated bibliography by Briggs et al. (1997) lists some 45 dissertations on aspects of this complex issue.

In this chapter, in an attempt to throw a little more light on academic spoken discourse, we focus on a cluster of features that constellate around discourse management across a wide range of university speech events. With a few exceptions, such as certain lab sessions, academic speech events are "activity types" (Levinson 1979) in which language is the prime vehicle for getting things done (as opposed to such activity types as gardening or fishing). This language can also be highly reflexive, for there is much discourse about discourse, from both retrospective and prospective points of view (Mauranen in this volume). Further, academic language is complexly dilemmatic (Tracy 1997), being both complicitous and contestatory: "This is good/interesting/okay, but . . . " is a major trope, which in some fields, such as general linguistics, can morph into "the tyranny of the counter-example" (Sinclair, personal communication). Just as importantly, if perhaps more mundanely, academic discourse has to deal with many different kinds of "business." There is the business to be got through in organizing teaching, studying, and learning—questions to be posed, deflected, or answered; displays to be evaluated; advice to be given, taken, or rejected; progress to be assessed; tasks to be assigned and managed; visuals to be integrated; assurances to be offered; and warnings to be issued. However, it is by no means the case that all this business is somehow orchestrated with seriousness and solemnity; quite the contrary, humor provides much of the lubrication for this complex rhetorical and educational machine.

Academic speech is, in consequence, variously monologic and dialogic, and in the transitions between these two basic modes, there is much negotiative work to be done in obtaining, retaining, and relinquishing the discoursal floor. How and with what linguistic resources is this work achieved? In this chapter, we focus on how academic speakers recover attention in these transitions and concomitantly or consequentially signal some change of "footing," glossed by Goffman (1981) as "participant's alignment, or set, or stance, or posture, or projected self" (128). Goffman goes on to argue, "one can get at the structural basis of footing by breaking up the primitive notions of hearer and speaker into more differentiated parts, namely, participation framework and production format" (153). Since we believe that most participants in university speech events have acquired a strong, intuitive sense of these frameworks and formats, such speech events provide a rich context for studying how various aspects of discourse management are typically—and atypically—realized in actual speech. One class of footing changes that we are particularly interested in are what we call here new-episode flags (NEFs). In brief, these linguistic signals (doubtless sometimes supported by paralinguistic elements) indicate that the speaker wants the discourse to move on or the participants to do something else (e.g., break into discussion groups). Before we look at these NEFs in some detail, we need first to offer some comments on two types of contextual frame: the first concerns the location of the data source, and the second provides some preliminary comments on the general nature of academic spoken discourse, more particularly, whether it is more like casual conversation or more like academic prose.

The University of Michigan and MICASE

The rationale for the MICASE (Michigan Corpus of Academic Speech in English) project has been discussed elsewhere in this volume (Powell and Simpson). Here we focus on the nature of the institution wherein the corpus is being assembled. The University of Michigan is one of the best-known public research universities in the United States and offers degrees in practically all fields except for agriculture and veterinary medicine. It has about 36,000 students, about 10,000 of whom are graduate students. The university is highly successful in obtaining research grants and produces about 700 doctoral graduates a year. About 70 percent of its undergraduates are from Michigan, the remainder being from other states or international. The percentage of graduate students who are nonnative speakers of English varies greatly from one department to another, being highest in science and engineering and lowest in departments like English. Considerable efforts have been made in recent years to increase the representation of minorities (especially African Americans and Hispanics) within the student body, although these efforts are being challenged in court at present. The university is a member of the Big Ten, a consortium of other flagship public universities in the Midwest plus the private Northwestern University. The university's main campus is in Ann Arbor, a fairly large university town of 120,000 situated in the southeast corner of the state. In effect, then, although MICASE has been restricted to a single institution, that institution seems to have a profile that differs in degree rather than in kind from that of many other major public research universities. Extrapolations to other broadly comparable U.S. academic contexts cannot, of course, definitively be made but can certainly be suggested.

Preliminary Observations on Spoken Academic Discourse

As we have mentioned, one obvious area for early investigation is whether—to put it a little crudely—spoken academic discourse is more like informal conversation or more like academic prose. For example, Biber has been showing (e.g., Biber 1999) that verbs taking *that*-clauses, such as *think, say,* and *know* are much more common in conversation than in expository writing. The MICASE data so far shows that spoken academic English occupies a firmly intermediate position in this regard, such clauses being there less common than in conversation but more frequent than in academic prose. In contrast, the MICASE data for verbs governing *to*-clauses (such as *want, try,* and *like*) offer a different perspective. Biber showed that these again were more common in conversation. However, rather than again falling in an intermediate position, they are actually considerably more common in MICASE than in Biber's conversational data. Presumably, this has something to do with the didactic nature of the specialized corpus and the managerial exigencies of those didactic settings. These exigencies often involve prospective and retrospective discourse, as in the following extract from an undergraduate lecture: "okay. alrighty what *I want to do* is continue with this discussion that *we've been trying to show,* between the interaction of history, and language change . . ."

There are two further small pieces of the puzzle. First, we can show that certain productive adjectival suffixes well-attested in informal English are very rare in MICASE. These suffixes are *-ish,* as in *middayish* and *urgentish,* and *-y,* as in *cutesy, dressy,* and *bluesy.* For the first suffix, there were only two innovative uses in the first 39 speech events in MICASE (some 350,000 words): "it looks meadowlarkish" (from the Bird Walk at the Biological Station) and "a reddish brownish object twentyish feetish from me" (from a philosophy seminar). For the second suffix, we can take the case of *alrighty,* since it occurs in the previously cited quotation from the corpus. Although *alrighty* can be frequently attested in service encounters in the city of Ann Arbor, it has occurred only four times so far in MICASE (some 600,000 words) in contrast to the 610 examples of *alright.* It would seem there are constraints on the use of certain kinds of colloquial forms. Second, we take the case of epistemic parentheticals, the uses of *I think, I guess,* and so on without *that.* Thompson and Mulac (1991) showed that at least in colloquial conversation, these uses were predominant and becoming grammaticalized or "pragmatized" (see also Mauranen in this volume). The MICASE data confirms this trend and extends it to academic speech. To date, there are 323 examples of the verb-lemma *guess,* of which as many as 256 were *I guess/I'm guessing,* not one of these was followed by *that,* and nearly half of them did not occur in the canonical initial position in the utterance. (*That* is slightly more likely to occur after *I guessed* or *I would have guessed*—12 instances.) So, with regard to what academic speech is "more like," an interesting mixed picture is emerging from our first expeditions into this discoursal territory.

New-Episode Flags

Our focus in the remainder of this chapter is on the linguistic resources used by participants in a wide variety of university speech events to, say, move from lecture format to group discussion (or the reverse) or change the direction of the lecture or discussion. We have called these moves new-episode flags. They are comparable to the framing and focusing moves posited by Sinclair and Coulthard (1992) as realizing the "boundary exchanges" in classroom discourse. However, we have opted here for a new label for several reasons. First, the term *frame* is interpreted very differently in discourse analysis. Second, Sinclair and Coulthard's use of *exchange* is highly technical, being a middle-level unit in a five-level ranking scale. Finally, the term *exchange* might be (wrongly) taken to imply a necessary change of speaker. To handle this last confusion, we have adopted the more neutral term *episode*, while *flag* is here seen as indicating that there is some metaphorically verbal "waving" going on. All the same, we concur with Sinclair and Coulthard that there are potentially two consecutive elements in an NEF. The first is the attention-getting element (e.g., "okay now"), while the second is the NEF itself (as in "let's move on"). Although the two often occur together, either element can occur on its own.

We now need to offer some caveats about our data and its analysis. First, the nature of any functional analysis based on corpora that cannot easily be tagged for pragmatic or discoursal features leads to some inevitable incompleteness. In our case, in our search for attention-getting language, we may simply have missed something; in effect, necessary reliance on our intuitions about possible surface forms may have led us to overlook a relevant verbal item or two. We have not looked, for instance, at a word like *yet*, which with suitably high volume and emphasis might in theory function as an attention-getting device. Second, many common exponents of NEFs, such as the word *okay*, can also have several other functions (e.g., as a back-channel), and subcategorization may at times be uncertain. Third, gestural signals can certainly play important roles in discourse management but will likely be missed by transcribers relying principally on audiotapes. Fourth, a specialized corpus of under a half-million words may have absences that would be attested in a database several times larger, and it may overprivilege the idiolectal preferences of certain clusters of main speakers. Our final caveat is rather different, since it concerns application. As several researchers have recently pointed out (McCarthy 1998; Partington 1998), the uptake of frequency data, especially for educational purposes, is not simply a matter of simple application but requires complex mediation via an array of features, including semantic salience, teachability, learnability, and sociolinguistic appropriacy.

Less Common New-Episode Flags

We start with the rare and uncommon devices for indicating a new episode and then move to the common. Although there has been some concern about negative evidence in corpus linguistics, we believe that this concern has been largely misplaced, given the close attention paid in areas of the language sciences—such as the rhetoric of science (Gross and Keith 1997) and genre analysis (Swales 1990)— to the interpretation of silence, to the noting of the unsaid, and to selectivity in paradigmatic choice.

One of the most famous attention getters is the opening to Mark Anthony's speech in *Julius Caesar*.

1. Friends, Romans, countrymen, lend me your ears.

This does not occur in MICASE (yet), but, somewhat more surprisingly, neither does anything like

2. Ladies and gentlemen, your attention please.

Indeed, with one exception to be discussed shortly, group nominations (group vocatives) are almost never used. There are no occurrences of *team, class, gang,* or *friends* used in this way, only one of *group*, and a handful of *folks*.

3. so let's let some other *folks*, jump in . . .

As might be expected, the exception is *guys*, especially in the formula *you guys*, which occurs 272 times in the current 614,000 word corpus, of which approximately half form part of NEFs.

4. alright *guys.* deep breaths, we can do this . . .
5. how about *you guys,* anything?
6. nice, *you guys* have any of you guys done five?
7. that's it . . . so uh . . . *you guys* all did a very good job today. I'm proud of you.
8. [In Kant's case you're trying to get to the existence of the categories] . . . so do *you guys* see the structure here? this making sense? okay. so somebody explain to me how it is . . .

Another obvious category for NEF membership would be the small group of directive or vocative verbs, *say, listen (up),* and *look.* As might be expected, the phrase *listen up,* associated with younger schoolchildren or students, does not occur at all, while there are only three instances of *say* as an unembedded directive, four of *listen,* and five of *look.*

9. *say* what's the answer to number two?
10. okay *listen* I'm gonna reward you for your patience, if I start the next topic I'll never get it finished.
11. well *look* it's basically all in the test-tube anyway.

However, where *look* as a directive occurs in MICASE, it is more often found (12 instances) as part of the onset of a quotative.

12. the epidemiologists were going in there saying well *look* we have to see how much risk there really is here.

These directive verbs would thus appear to be too admonitory for university-level academic speech. Further, *look* would seem to be more characteristic of British English than of American English (see Fairclough and Mauranen's 1997 discussion of *look* in Prime Minister Margaret Thatcher's hortatory television interview style).

Another possible outside candidate would be the attention-getting *hey.* Of its 85 instances in the first corpus, a sizable minority are again quotative.

13. you could contact the state D-N-R and say *hey* I'd like to be involved in . . .

However, as many as 19 of the remaining 30 instances come from a single interactive speech event, a session of a chemistry lab recorded toward the end of semester and focusing on the interactions of two groups of senior undergraduates who seem to know each other pretty well.

14. *hey* Brian did you wanna get the reference point . . .
15. *hey* wait this contradicts that because it says . . .

Again, apart from this kind of context, *hey* would seem too abrupt and "streetlike" for at least our particular grove of academe; we note that there were only three instances in close to 13 hours of lectures.

A Middle-Frequency New Episode Flag: The Case of *Let*

One further option that is picked up quite frequently in our data is the exhortative or jussive imperative *let*. In the corpus, there are about 850 tokens of *let,* comprised principally of 542 instances of *let's* (but including only 10 tokens of the unreduced form *let us*) and 201 instances of *let me.* A few instances have a quotative feel to them, one of the most engaging being

16. but some of the faculty are not exactly, um, warm fuzzy hand outstretched *let me* help you, kinds of individuals . . .

Although there a fair number of ambiguous or uncertain cases, attention-getting and new-episode-flagging uses comprise about 50 percent of the total. ("Let me digress" is clearly an NEF, but "Let me rephrase" is much less certainly so.) If we make a rather crude distinction between realigning to the ongoing discourse ("let me start by introducing myself") as opposed to realigning to nonverbal actions or real-world conditions ("let's meet tonight"), then *let me* is considerably more metadiscoursal than *let's;* about half of the former realize this function, while just under a third of the latter do.

17. so *let me* once again plunge us into darkness.
18. *let me* just refresh your memory about . . .
19. *let me* digress a little here.
20. boy things are all bollixed up *let's* quit out of *let's* quit this, it's not working.
21. um, okay *let me* get into sort of the more serious stuff.
22. right okay *let's let's* think about this for a sec.
23. yeah um okay well alright, *let me* explain this to you.

The last three examples, with their increasingly complex arrangements of markers of discourse management, point to the most striking feature of our NEF data, which is discussed in the next section.

Frequent New-Episode Flags

Okay

An even more frequent item in our NEF data is *okay*. Like *alright*, it can serve a number of functions, including adjectival and adverbial forms ("This is okay stuff"), responses to questions, indicators of assent or agreement, question tags, back-channels, and, in certain cases otherwise hard to interpret, fillers. Moreover, a single instance of usage may serve more than one function, and the definition of that function may vary depending on whether the utterance is perceived from the speaker's or the audience's perspective. Nonetheless, despite these uncertainties and ambiguities, we can still sketch a rough portrait of its usage. In fact, there were some 1,875 instances of *okay*; as best we can determine, the functions distribute approximately as illustrated in table 1.

There are a number of observations that can be made here. First, most of the native speakers we informally queried about the functions of *okay* in academic speech cited question tags and adjectival/adverbial descriptors as the common uses of *okay*. However, at least according to our data, these intuitions seem somewhat astray. As can be seen from table 1, only about 10 percent of the MICASE uses were question tags.

24. but I'll be with you in a minute *okay*?

TABLE 1. Functional Distributions of *Okay*

Function Type	Percentage of Total
New episode flag	35
Back channel	30
Response	15
Question tag	10
Filler	6
Descriptor	3

Furthermore, very few of these tags seemed to elicit a direct verbal response. The least common use of *okay* (3 percent) was as a descriptor.

25. so it functions *okay* as a primer?

A further 30 percent were back-channel cues, where the listener was merely prompting or agreeing with the main speaker while not attempting to take the floor, and some 6 percent were fillers (or filled pauses), in much the same way as *kind of* and *sort of*—and their reductions—can function as floor-maintaining fillers (Poos 1999).

26. cuz here we've got *okay* the first sentence which is to me a really
     . . .

Some 15 percent were in response to a previous utterance, in agreement with, assent to, or at least acknowledgment of the preceding speaker's ideas.

27. *S1:*   . . . and then it can lead to a whole new set of things.
     S2:   *okay* but what about this I mean, how do folks, deal with this
             question . . .

Interestingly, about 10 percent of these responsive examples of *okay* were doubled ("okay okay"), and this combination, without pause or phrasal separation, seems to be used almost exclusively in this function. Finally, it would seem that the most common use of *okay,* the remaining 35 percent, or approximately 650 tokens, is as an NEF, either embedded within an utterance to show embarkation on a new topic or utterance-initial to signal an attempt to take the floor.

28. the negative impacts are too minor. *Okay,* another group of managed species . . .
29. *Okay,* so how do you think you did?
30. keep your eyes on your own paper . . . *okay* are we ready or are we not . . .
31. as I develop the pieces. *Okay* first of all, there are two major . . .
32. collecting information over time. *Okay* the next thing that I want
     . . .
33. it has to be doesn't it? *Okay,* what I need to know is . . .

In this context, it is also worth nothing that about 30 of these instances signaled the onset of a summation.

34. *Okay* I think that I've covered everything . . .
35. you heard about it here first. *Okay* I think, that may be my last . . .
36. specifically interested in. *Okay* I'm gonna start off my next lecture then . . .
37. or someone else's research. *Okay*. It's time to go to lunch . . .

The most remarkable feature of our NEF data for *okay* involves the term's co-occurrence with other items. Of the 1,875 examples found, *okay* was followed by at least 20 instances of each of the following words: *and, but, okay, this, that('s), so, uh/um, well, yeah* (see table 2). By far the most common second element was *so*. Further, the great majority of the instances of *so* used in conjunction (more than 90 percent) were employed as NEFs, a much higher proportion than is found among uses of *okay* in total (where approximately one-third of the overall instances were flags). Other significant findings include the fact that *okay okay* and *okay yeah* were much more often used as a response than as anything else and that *okay but* was used either as a response—meaning something to the effect of "I see your point; however, I do not agree"—or occasionally with an adjective.

38. If it did I'm *okay* but if it didn't . . .

Curiously, *okay this* was used almost entirely in flags, while *okay that('s)* was used almost entirely in response.

39. *Okay this* afternoon uh, my plans are to talk to you about avian . . .

40. *S1:* which could have any number of evidence, yeah.
    S2: Okay that's what I didn't understand . . .

As best as we can see, this difference likely arises because of the tendency to use *this* to refer to a concept that is close to the speaker, such as a new idea to be presented, and *that* to refer to one that is more distanced, such as one just presented by an interlocutor.

In addition to these "doublets," there were a number of longer

TABLE 2.   Items Directly Following *Okay* in MICASE

	Total Tokens	Distribution of Functions			
		NEF	Descriptor	Filler	Response
So	200	187	2	8	3
Uh/um	72	59	4	4	5
Well	43	35	1	1	6
And	39	19	1	16	4
Okay	33	3	—	—	30
That('s)	27	3	1	3	20
Yeah	25	1	2	—	22
But	22	—	5	2	14
This	22	21	—	1	—

clusters of words including *okay,* usually prefacing a new idea and/or initiating an utterance. Here are three examples:

41. and I imagine a straight edge. *Okay um uh but now so* all I'm saying is . . .
42. Presumably this part is also, *okay so now* we have now . . .
43. money was appropriated. *Okay so now* we're, at a time . . .

While it can be argued that some of these clusters are essentially fillers (marking time while the speaker gets his or her thoughts sorted out), they seem, because of their initial positioning, to be serving as complex NEFs. Furthermore, aside from hesitations of the *um* and *uh* type, there would seem to be some lexical patterning in these clusters, such as runs of *okay so now.* Because of these kinds of phenomena, we will now look at the occurrences of *so* and *now* a little more closely.

So

The little word *so* was considerably more frequent in our data, with some 5,100 entries, than was *okay.* Flowerdew (1993), in his corpus of biology lectures, found 1,183 instances of *so* but only four instances of *as a result.* The same plurality of function—and difficulties in categorization—that we encountered in looking at *okay* is again present in the case of *so.* The term might serve as a flag.

44. here at the bottom. *So* I've already talked about . . .

It might serve as an indicator of causation.

45. disturbed these colonies, *so* that birds were deserting . . .

Or it might serve as a descriptor.

46. fascinating and at the same time *so* frustrating, for a lot of people
. . .

We found that, like *okay*, about one-third of *so*'s uses can be classified as NEFs. As in the case of *okay*, *so* can regularly be found in collocation with certain words (see table 3). In addition, *so*, just like *okay*, is one of the items frequently employed in flag-type clusters.

47. that is awesome. *Okay so anyway*, actually that concludes the tour.
48. *alright. Okay. Um uh alright so* um what I'm trying . . .
49. *so alright anyway. So okay* there's a lot of different . . .

The *(okay) so anyway* combination, as in example 47, often seems to function as what Thomas (1983) calls an "upshot," or as some kind of summative evaluation.

50. it was the untenured women because of the tenure clock that was to be the big issue. Um but we never thought that they would exclude tenured women from these policies. Don't ask me the logic of all this. Engineers can be real logical about some things but not other things. *Um so anyway* my work on this policy is an example of where I felt I was helping someone in need rather than helping the Women's Movement.
51. and I really think that with kids if you want, to have them understand that you can't talk to them in these really broad terms and give them these things that mean nothing to them really and these

TABLE 3.   Common Items Preceding *So*

Okay	392*
And	240
Um/uh	234
Right	145

*This number is higher here than in table 2 because the corpus from which these data were taken was larger than when *okay* was surveyed.

stories you have to, somehow find a way to get them . . . to feel it through someone they care about. *So anyway.* That's what my selection was about.

Interestingly, *so* often acts in a way in which *okay* does not: it will repeat several times in succession, occasionally serving as the only word in a cluster.

52. yeah, *so so* that was really neat . . .
53. talk about explaining it. *So so so* just you can have . . .
54. in Kuwait or whatever *so so so so, so so so* this part of . . .

Overall, it seems that, in flagging a change of footing, *so* acts very much like *okay,* not only in terms of its frequency of use in this function, but also in regard to the words that tend to appear with it. It may be that these features are broadly characteristic of academic NEFs as a class. However, we finally and briefly turn to some complicating findings raised by the case of *now.*

Now

A third main candidate for NEF status is the little word *now.* Of course, in our data, it often serves its traditional function as a temporal marker.

55. all these babies are *now* emerging . . .

But it can also serve as a flag.

56. independent. *Now* my father was almost twenty . . .
57. unless you want to. *Now* tomorrow morning . . .

These last two examples demonstrate somewhat different functions; the first is a flag in an expository participation framework, the second in a management one.

We calculate that nearly half of the occurrences of *now* can be categorized as flags. While this is a larger proportion than those found in the *okay* and *so* data sets, we do not find the same patterns of collocation. Indeed, *now* does not collocate frequently with either of these items; rather, *now* seems to be typically followed by a definite noun phrase of some sort.

Final Considerations

An unaddressed question is where NEFs tend to occur and not to occur. As table 4 suggests, they tend to occur more frequently in interactive contexts. However, the evidence for this is impressive for *okay* (with all five top events being interactive), fairly convincing for *so* (four out of five), and rather unconvincing for *now* (with three out of the top five being in fact monologic). A similar picture emerges for the speech events with the least occurrences of these three NEFs. By and large, occurrences here are smaller by an order of magnitude. In the case of *okay*, the lowest numbers (0.53 to 0.08 per 100 words) occurred in three lectures and two colloquia. However, the situation for both *so* and *now* was much more mixed, with two labs, two discussions, a lecture, a set of student presentations, a colloquium, an interview, a meeting, and an office hour. At present, we have no coherent explanation for these findings.

A number of further questions arise from our preliminary study. One is whether these attention-getting and change-of-footing particle usages are transparent to nonnative speakers. Problematic usages might include the use of *okay* as a preface to criticism.

58. *Okay*, but I'm looking through my notes . . .

Another possible test case would be the atemporal and slightly admonitory use of *now*.

59. *Now* tomorrow morning . . .

TABLE 4. The Five Speech Events with the Most NEF Occurrences (per thousand words)

So		Okay		Now	
1. Office hour	19.27	1. Tutorial	8.73	1. Lab	3.15
2. Tutorial	17.44	2. Tutorial	6.23	2. Lecture	2.82
3. Lecture	16.4	3. Tutorial	5.59	3. Colloquium	2.56
4. Meeting	12.41	4. Office hour	4.93	4. Tutorial	2.55
5. Discussion	12.41	5. Meeting	4.51	5. Lecture	2.48

More broadly, and as we have been at pains to point out, categorization has proved to be particularly tricky in a preliminary pragmatic investigation of the kind we have presented, and there have been a larger number of ambiguous or doubtful cases than we would have liked. Further, we do not in fact really know whether such uncertainties or multivalencies lie in the discourse itself, are an artifact of insufficient analysis, or both. Moreover, this is an area of considerable idiolectal variation; in effect, many (academic) speakers have marked individual preferences for NEFs. The first author of this chapter, for example, is often teased about his frequent use of *right* to move the discourse or nonverbal action along; we can easily recognize other speakers as "alrighters" and yet others as "okayers." The data we have presented has smoothed out any possible peaks and valleys of individual usage, and yet again we remain unsure of how to weigh the possible advantages and disadvantages of this blending process. We can claim, with some confidence, that showing what does not occur—negative evidence if you will—is one of the great benefits of a corpus approach, especially when we consider the pedagogical implications of those dispreferences. We can see this most clearly in the relative absence of attention-getting realizations that involve imperatives (e.g., *listen*), group vocatives (as in "okay class"), or more formulaic utterances (e.g., "May I have your attention please").

Finally, we are aware that investigating discourse markers has become something of a minor industry over the last 15 years or so. We do not yet know whether academic discourse differs in degree or in kind or hardly at all in its use of such markers from other varieties of English, and certainly a comparative study of academic and business discourse, for example, might be instructive in this regard. As far as we are aware, most studies of discourse particles have treated particles one by one (as in Schiffrin's 1987 monograph). However, the MICASE data seems to suggest that focus on single discourse markers, while fully understandable in the context of the pioneering nature of the earlier studies, may have its limitations. As we have tried to show, perhaps the combinations of discourse markers should now be catching our interest. Indeed, Fraser (1999) concludes that one of the things we still do not understand about discourse markers, despite much progress, is which markers can or cannot co-occur with which. As we have tried to show, analysis of the MICASE data is beginning to open a window on this phenomenon.

References

Atkinson, D. 1999. *Scientific Discourse in Sociohistorical Context: The Philosophical Transactions of the Royal Society of London, 1675–1975.* Mahwah, NJ: Lawrence Erlbaum.

Bazerman, C. 1998. *Shaping Written Knowledge: The Genre and Activity of the Experimental Article in Science.* Madison: University of Wisconsin Press.

Biber, D. 1999. A Register Perspective on Grammar and Discourse: Variability in the Form and Use of English Complement Clauses. *Discourse Studies* 1:131–50.

Briggs, S. L., P. Aldridge, R. Beal, V. Clark, S. Hyon, C. G. Madden, and J. M. Swales. 1997. *The International Teaching Assistant: An Annotated Bibliography.* 2d ed. Ann Arbor: University of Michigan Press.

Bunton, D. 1998. Linguistic and Textual Problems in Ph.D. and M. Phil. Theses: An Analysis of Genre Movement and Metatext. Ph.D. diss., University of Hong Kong.

Dressen, D. F., and J. M. Swales. 2000. "Geological Setting/cadre geologique" in English and French Petrology Articles: Muted Indications of Explored Places. In *Analysing Professional Genres,* ed. A. Trosberg, 57–76. Amsterdam: John Benjamins.

Dubois, B.-L. 1987. "Something on the Order of Around Forty to Forty-Four": Imprecise Numerical Expressions in Biomedical Slide Talks. *Language in Society* 16:527–41.

Fairclough, N., and A. Mauranen. 1997. The Conversationalization of Political Discourse. *Belgian Journal of Linguistics* 11:89–119.

Flower, L., and J. R. Hayes. 1981. A Cognitive Theory of Writing. *College Composition and Communication* 32:365–87.

Flowerdew, J. 1993. Concordancing as a Tool in Course Design. *System* 21:231–44.

———, ed. 1994. *Academic Listening: Research Perspectives.* Cambridge: Cambridge University Press.

Fraser, B. 1999. What Are Discourse Markers? *Journal of Pragmatics* 31:931–52.

Geisler, C. 1994. Literacy and Expertise in the Academy. *Language and Learning across the Disciplines* 1:37–57.

Goffman, E. 1981. *Forms of Talk.* Philadelphia: University of Pennsylvania Press.

Gosden, H. 1995. Success in Research Article Writing and Revision: A Social Constructionist Perspective. *English for Specific Purposes* 14:37–57.

Gross, A. G., and W. M. Keith. 1997. *Rhetorical Hermeneutics: Invention and Interpretation in the Age of Science.* Albany: State University of New York Press.

Hyland, K. 1998. *Hedging in Scientific Research Articles.* Amsterdam: John Benjamins.

Lave, J., and E. Wenger. 1991. *Situated Learning: Legitimate Peripheral Participation.* Cambridge: Cambridge University Press.

Levinson, S. C. 1979. Activity Types and Language. *Linguistics* 17:356–99.

Mauranen, A. 1993. *Cultural Differences in Academic Rhetoric.* Frankfurt: Peter Lang.

McCarthy, M. 1998. *Spoken Language and Applied Linguistics.* Cambridge: Cambridge University Press.

McCloskey, D. N. 1994. *Knowledge and Persuasion in Economics.* New York: Cambridge University Press.

Motta-Roth, D. 1998. Discourse Analysis and Academic Book Reviews: A Study of Text and Disciplinary Cultures. In *Genre Studies in English for Academic Purposes,* ed. I. Fortanet, S. Posteguillo, J. C. Palmer, and J. F. Coll, 29–58. Castello, Spain: Jaume I University Press.

Myers, G. 1990. *Writing Biology: Texts in the Social Construction of Science.* Madison: University of Wisconsin Press.

Partington, A. 1998. *Patterns and Meanings: Using Corpora for English Language Research and Teaching.* Amsterdam: John Benjamins.

Peck McDonald, S. 1987. Problem Definition in Academic Writing. *College English* 49:315–31.

Poos, D. 1999. A Question of Gender? Hedging in Academic Discourse. Paper presented at the annual meeting of the Michigan Linguistics Society, Michigan State University, East Lansing, October.

Prior, P. A. 1998. *Writing/Disciplinarity: A Sociohistoric Account of Literate Activity in the Academy.* Mahwah, NJ: Lawrence Erlbaum.

Salager-Meyer, F. 1992. A Text-Type and Move Analysis Study of Verb Tense and Modality Distribution in Medical English Abstracts. *English for Specific Purposes* 11:93–114.

Schriffrin, D. 1987. *Discourse markers.* Cambridge: Cambridge University Press.

Sinclair, J., and M. Coulthard. 1992. Towards an Analysis of Discourse. In *Advances in Spoken Discourse Analysis,* ed. M. Coulthard, 1–34. London: Routledge.

Swales, J. M. 1998. *Other Floors, Other Voices: A Textography of a Small University Building.* Mahwah, NJ: Lawrence Erlbaum.

———. 1990. *Genre Analysis: English in Academic and Research Settings.* Cambridge: Cambridge University Press.

Swales, J. M., and C. Feak. 1994. *Academic Writing for Graduate Students: Essential Tasks and Skills.* Ann Arbor: University of Michigan Press.

Thomas, J. A. 1983. Cross-Cultural Pragmatic Failure. *Applied Linguistics* 5:226–35.

Thompson, S. A., and A. Mulac. 1991. A Quantitative Perspective on the Grammaticization of Epistemic Parentheticals in English. In *Approaches to Grammaticalization,* ed. E. C. Traugott and B. Heine, 2:313–29. Amsterdam: John Benjamins.

Tracy, K. 1997. *Colloquium: Dilemmas of Academic Discourse.* Norwood, NJ: Ablex.

Valle, E. 1999. *A Collective Intelligence: The Life Sciences in the Royal Society as a Scientific Discourse Community, 1665–1965.* Turku, Finland: University of Turku.

Reflexive Academic Talk: Observations from MICASE

Anna Mauranen
University of Tampere

Although academic writing has been thoroughly studied in the last 10 to 15 years, academic talk has been the subject of serious investigation much more sporadically. Yet it is clear that socialization into the shifting, evolving identities that (hopefully) coalesce in some kind of graduate student identity or persona takes place primarily through speech and that the much-researched writing is but the tip of the iceberg.

Although written texts are the most visible aspects of academic subcultures, representing basically what Gilbert and Mulkay (1984) called the "empiricist repertoire," academic oracy combines this repertoire with the "contingent" one, thus representing much more heterogeneous and more varied sets of discourses. To modify Wittgenstein's famous utterance: "Wovon man nicht schreiben kann, daruber muss man sprechen" [What we cannot write about, we must speak about]. We could therefore tentatively conclude that speech and writing engage in and sanction different kinds of discoursal silences—both in the basically positive sense that Becker (1995) and Swales (1999) among others have used the term *silence* and in the more negative sense of Huckin (1996, 1999) and other members of the Critical Discourse Analysis movement. Written academic discourses leave things unsaid not only because they are shared or known but also because speakers or writers may not want to get into issues too complicated (theory disputes), too contentious (personal animosities), or too dangerous (weaknesses in their research design) for them to handle. But spoken discourse in mainly pedagogic contexts may well turn out to be different; there is more asymmetry in participant positions but less peer competition and rivalry. Power asymmetries between participants are not made explicit in everyday university discourses—

yet they seep into the language, as we can see, for instance, in the connections between reflexivity and hedging discussed in this chapter.

In this chapter, I first offer some brief comments on some aspects of the Michigan Corpus of Academic Speech in English (MICASE), particularly with regard to what I believe to be certain strengths that have not been elaborated on by others in the present context. I then look into its research potential by way of an example, some findings on discourse reflexivity, often also called metadiscourse (or talk about talk/text about text). I suggest that this phenomenon is a striking and important aspect of academic speech in ways that are not paralleled in academic writing. It also seems that even when we look at the same kinds of language use in writing and speech, new distinctions and relevant categories for analysis are called for.

The Michigan Corpus of Academic Speech in English

Because MICASE (<http://www.lsa.umich.edu/eli/micase/micase. htm>) aims at depicting how English is used on a campus, instead of providing a model of correct or ideal usage, it includes, among other things, a good deal of English spoken by people who would not fit into the category of speakers known as "native speakers." In other words, the data has not been subjected to any linguo-ethnic cleansing, but rather it actually seeks to reflect the reality of English spoken in the characteristic activities of a major American research university. That this corpus has different speaker categories included in their natural mix is one of its major strengths, especially because it has been common for corpora to be compiled separately for "nonnatives," as is the case, for example, with the ICLE corpora (see Granger 1998).

As has often justifiably been argued (e.g., Sinclair 1991), large corpora should preferably be composed of complete texts, that is, texts that are not truncated, or "extracts" of some predetermined length, such as 2,000 words. Of course, determining what constitutes a "complete" text is never easy, but with some speech events, such as lectures, it is reasonably easy to see—on one level—at least the limits of a particular session in terms of beginning and end. Yet academic speech events are commonly organized in chainlike formations either within one genre (e.g., a lecture course or a linked series of seminars) or across different genres (e.g., lectures, followed by an examination; supervision and consultations, followed by a thesis defense and its important prior text, the thesis itself). Thus, each of the recorded events has a history and a future—they are part of a network of related discourses in a very concrete sense (see Bazerman 1994 for one of the first attempts to conceptualize systems of genres).

Although this issue may be relatively irrelevant for many research questions, this is not at all true of discourse reflexivity, which needs a borderline to be drawn between what counts as "current text" and what does not. A good deal of discourse-organizing talk refers to previous or later events that can be, in an important way, thought part of the ongoing discourse—as, for instance, in the case of a lecture series. For example, the words *next* and *last* in the corpus overwhelmingly refer to earlier or later events in a sequence, typically next week's or last week's session of a lecture course, rather than to immediately following or preceding discourse segments as they do in writing (e.g., "In the next chapter . . .").

Some Kinds of Questions to which MICASE Lends Itself

In general, descriptive or applied linguists could have two main kinds of research interest in academic spoken discourse: (1) to look at the linguistic elements emerging from the data, that is, investigate language as a resource; and (2) to investigate the kinds of discourse practices that are characteristic or less characteristic of university settings. The tension between these two broad approaches is also very much in the forefront when we confront the MICASE transcript files and use concordances for their analyses (Mauranen 1998).

Questions of Linguistic Description

Some questions that remain open about the general characteristics of academic speech are hard to answer without the help of large quantities of data. These are broad questions about register or the linguistic characteristics of speaking in this field. In which ways does its lexico-grammatical patterning resemble everyday talk? In which ways is it close to academic writing? It is possible (and interesting) to address such questions as the relations of grammar and lexis in speech and the phraseological patterning that is found in the data but is not described in grammars or teaching materials. For example, a study of *just* shows that it occurs very frequently in the corpus but rarely (only 3 percent of its occurrences) in its traditional and typically taught usage—for "hot news" (e.g., "they have just signed the contracts")—which is not infrequent in written texts. Rather, it would seem that the primary function of *just* in the evolving corpus is to soften suggestions or proposals, as in "if we could just move on to the second issue" (Lindemann and Mauranen 1999).

Questions of Language Use in Social Activity (Discourse Practices)

A second set of questions that can be addressed to this data concerns the social uses of language—more precisely, the discourse practices—in the university community. Thus, we can ask generally what sorts of identities, social relations, epistemic positions, and beliefs are there coconstructed and negotiated—how participants coconstruct the situations that they find themselves in and act out their institutionally given positions, each of these situations being the intersection of a number of positional trajectories.

More specifically, the corpus has been compiled to enable a developmental angle on the academic speech used by participants at different stages of their socialization into the academic community. The idea is thus to explore how, when, and perhaps why academic speech evolves as experience of the academic world increases and the speaker's position changes. For this, a number of speaker classes have been established with respect to academic position, from junior undergraduates to senior faculty. It is to be expected that people speak differently from different positions; thus, the separation between faculty and students constitutes a major dividing line. However, there is clearly a more or less continuous cline in the categories established, and where major jumps occur (if any) will only be seen when a larger database can be analyzed. As of late 1999, the only preliminary study run on different speaker categories was Poos 1999, which shows, among other things, that the classic hedges *sort of* and *kind of* are associated less with female speech (as often claimed) and more with terminological difficulties—difficulties that tend to afflict the social sciences and humanities much more than the sciences and engineering. However, many other linguistic features, particularly in their clustering, lend themselves to investigations where the questions relate to differences in speaker positions. The question I am addressing in the latter part of this chapter, about discourse reflexivity, is a case in point.

Hypotheses concerning the social significance of reflexive discourse are seen in a new light when speech features can be systematically related to the speech events they occur in (e.g., is the speech feature most typical of monologues?), the participant positions that permit their use (e.g., is the feature used mainly by professors?), and the developmental continuum (e.g., is it a speech feature gradually acquired?). With this data, then, we can relate microlevel patterns of difference to the larger patterns of social action that are being constructed and maintained within the university.

Discourse Reflexivity in General

Discourse reflexivity, or metadiscourse, is discourse about the discourse itself. It can in principle be distinguished from the propositional content (or the "ideational" matter) of a text or discourse, together with other interpersonal aspects of language. The specific domain of reflexivity is therefore the organization of discourse. In this sense, it also clearly carries a "textual" function. The main tasks of metadiscourse can be summarized very briefly.

a. It organizes, describes, comments on the ongoing discourse.
b. It guides the hearer in the interpretation of the discourse.
c. Its expressions vary in size and rank of linguistic unit.

The four main types of discourse reflexivity derived from work on written language (e.g., Mauranen 1993b) can be illustrated with examples from MICASE.

I.   References to the ongoing discourse
  1. and *today* we're gonna talk a little bit about, epidemiology
  2. excuse me i'm not following *this,* is it
  3. scale of one through five basically for the *following* reasons,
  4. what i'm hoping to do with the remainder of of *this first hour,* is just give you some uh bit of perspective, show where biology fits into,

II. Speech function indicators
  5. that's a really good *question*
  6. okay. all right a few last sort of *nags and reminders*
  7. I really want to *get across* to you the . . .

III. Addressing the hearer/interlocutor explicitly
  8. and, *you guys might remember* from a couple of times ago when we talked about ( ), that we talked about, the design argument,
  9. *you* taking any teaching time this summer *Mary*
  10. okay so *remember* back to last week on the Play-doh machine? um . . .

IV. Internal connectors
  11. um our, MELAB um testing program is undergoing some changes, um, *first of all i* should tell you what is not changing
  12. one of the um more interesting differences between *let's say* France and Spain, and even between, *let's say* Spain France and Italy in this regard

What, then, is interesting about reflexivity in academic discourse? We can look at it from both major angles or approaches sketched out earlier. One source of interest lies in precisely the expressions themselves and how they may differ from expressions used with comparable functions in writing. The other is in seeing how the use of reflexive language functions in social reality: how it constructs, maintains, reflects identities, ideologies, worldviews. From this latter perspective, discourse reflexivity can be seen as a strategy for organizing the discourse and directing (manipulating) the interlocutor's attention toward the speaker's topics and points of focus and, at the same time, away from other potential topics and foci. In this context, we might assume, as a working hypothesis, that those in a dominant position in any speech event will use more reflexive expressions.

In organizing and focusing the discourse, the speaker not only—if at all—clarifies it in a neutral, reader- or hearer-friendly manner but rather imposes the speaker's point of view on the discourse. Reflexivity is a way of imposing authority on the discourse—giving hearers the limits of their interpretative freedom. There is, then, an ongoing struggle for space: as the speaker's space increases with the use of reflexivity, the hearer's space is reduced.

My earlier interpretations of the effects of reflexivity, with written language and relating specifically to cultural differences (Mauranen 1993a, 1993b), were that reflexive discourse imparts a flavor of, on the one hand, "didactic" and, on the other hand, "marketing" discourse. In the context of academic speaking, the didactic aspect is fairly obvious, and the speaker's authority can be relatively freely imposed by members of the teaching staff. This reflects essentially an epistemic set of positions—those who know and those who ought to know something—deriving from the basic function of a university; as a result, the activity can be framed as lecturers "imparting knowledge and skills."

The marketing aspect seems at the outset a less plausible role relationship to apply to the academic setting. However, an aspect of promotional discourse applies to much of current academic life, including teaching situations. Constructing students as *clients* implies that their evaluation of, say, the courses given is influential and that lecturers have to take this into account. So there is also a set of client-service positions, in addition to the epistemic ones, that may affect the ways in which language is used in academic speech.

Discourse Reflexivity in MICASE

After working on the corpus for a while, starting from the typical expressions of discourse reflexivity found to be characteristic of written academic discourse in the literature (e.g., Bäcklund 1998; Crismore 1989; Mauranen 1993a, 1993b; Vande Kopple 1985), it began to seem more appropriate to try out other bases for categorization than have been found relevant to the written mode. Indeed, it does not take long to recognize that one crucial difference between spoken and written discourse is the presence of listeners in speech situations. As far as reflexivity is concerned, this seems to imply that the ongoing discourse that gets organized and commented on can have different origins and different targets among the discourse participants.

Targeting

Reflexive expressions can be classified according to their target in the interactive situation; they can be targeted on the speaker's own discourse, on that of another participant, or on the discourse situation more generally. This targeting reflects on the speaker's choices by which he or she explicitly positions himself/herself in relation to the discourse and the participants. In this way, three main types of targeted expressions can be distinguished: the monologic, the dialogic, and the interactive. These labels are not ideal, since it can justifiably be argued that all discourse is dialogic and interactive; scientific lecturing has also been called "dialogical monologue," since it incorporates the interlocutors' perspective even without their verbal responses (Parpette 1999). Nevertheless, the labels used here are chosen for their ability to capture relevant distinctions vis-à-vis each other, not to characterize the discourse exhaustively.

Monologic targeted expressions (organizing the speaker's own ongoing speech) include prospections of what is to come and what is not going to come up and tactics for putting aside issues that might arise but are judged by the speaker to be distractions. The latter type, what might be called negative prospection, is of course highly loaded with hidden dialogicality, showing speaker awareness of the hearer's position.

13. his book, about that. *after, that i'll talk about* coherent states, and then . . .
14. *i've already mentioned,* um, that i i think, there's, one
15. here, that we'll have to deal with, but *i want to look at this phase first.*
16. deals with Spanish not with Basque *we're not trying to say,* that Basque, changed
17. *is an issue perhaps worth mentioning* within this broader framework *but not today.* maybe next class.
18. you remind me sometime when we're not being taped *i'll tell you* a Feynman story

Dialogic targeted expressions refer and respond to interlocutor's talk.

19. what *you're talking about,* well, *you're talking about* both fields acting at the
20. oh i'm sorry i see what- i see what *you mean*
21. yeah yeah, *as Glenda mentioned.* right. yeah. so, the
22. to understand why coherent- *you mentioned* that, coherent states have to
23. thanks *for mentioning* oh yeah one other thing, the

Interactive targeted expressions elicit response from an interlocutor (e.g. asking questions, choosing the next speaker) and generally organize the interlocutor's talk, not just one's own.

24. Jane. oh yes *Jane you can talk about* the co-ops, Jane *you can talk*
25. let's begin. uh, *any questions* on the last class or anything on the

readings [Here, of course, *Let's begin* is monologic, but *any questions* is interactive.]
26. and, it doesn't always fit, mhm *you following*?
27. we can . . . okay *anything else*?

These types of targeting can be seen to constitute a cline where space is increasingly allocated to participants other than the current speaker. At the same time, both the monologic and the interactive types particularly strongly act out the speaker's structuring of the ongoing discourse. Yet each interactively targeted reflexive act carries the potential for the next speaker turning the flow of the discourse, thereby risking the current speaker's monopoly over it.

Some linguistic characteristics in the data immediately strike the observer as being different in comparison to written discourse. These include the absence of typical internal connectors, such as *firstly, second(ly), finally.* Such connectors as *next* and *last* were virtually always used to refer to preceding or forthcoming speech events, usually in the course. It must be noted at this point that comparisons of this kind are necessarily based on earlier work on written academic texts, since there is no direct written counterpart of MICASE available, that is, one that would represent all major types of writing on campus.

Since the corpus is in the process of construction, there is little point in presenting numerical evidence from the findings so far. However, the monologic type is overwhelmingly the most common. Consider, for example, the uses of the lemma *tell.* In early 1999, there were 86 instances altogether. Twenty-four were used in a reflexive way, and of these, 15 were monologic, 4 dialogic, and 5 interactive.

The tendency to favor monologic targeting varies, however, with the reflexive element itself. Thus, one exception to the general tendency is the lemma *mention.* The dominant use in the corpus seems to be reflexive, since out of 25 instances found in the corpus, 19 were reflexive. Among these reflexive uses, monologic and dialogic types were quite evenly represented, as there were 10 monologic and 9 dialogic cases.

Reflexivity and Hedging

Apart from the typology of targeting, which is different from that attested for written discourse, a very interesting connection is emerging between reflexivity and hedging. It is typical of many of the reflexive expressions to attract hedges around them. A typical instance is "let me just rephrase." Moreover, reflexive nouns (e.g., *point*) also appear to attract hedging expressions around them. Such clusterings of interactive elements suggest different pragmatic functions in the spoken and written modes for expressions with the same reflexive core.

28. now, *i do- i wo- don't want to go through and bore you but*
29. so, let me spend *a little bit of* time and I mean a little bit of time, talking about um *a little bit* about the continuous methods
30. other thing that i, *just* wanted to *(quickly)* mention um, is that, we are trying,
31. okay. um, okay let me get into *sort of* the more serious stuff, and, um, what i'm hoping to do with the remainder of of this first hour, is *just* give you *some uh bit of* perspective, show where biology fits into, *sort of* the rest of your education, and *hopefully* i can, um begin that framework that we're gonna fill in in the rest of the term. so i i have entitled this lecture, philosophy of science . . . or *at least* that's the point i'm talking about now,

Example 31 is a particularly rich and elaborated instance of hedged discourse reflexivity that encapsulates in a rather wonderful fashion the argument that I have been making. Quite a few of the other instances were semifixed multiword units, such as *let* + first-person pronoun + *just* + verb of communication.

32. alright well **let me just tell** you this
33. **let me just mention** one
34. **let's just call** it a statistical approach
35. **let's just say** we have a two level system

In all, it was common for reflexive examples to co-occur with hedges. Why should this be so? One possible reason is that since discourse reflexivity and hedging are both largely interpersonal aspects of language use, they like to cluster together on account of a certain functional similarity: they provide indicators of speaker orientation toward the ongoing dialogue. This explanation keeps well within the domain of "the linguistic."

Another possible explanation can be derived from the authority function of discourse reflexivity. As was pointed out earlier, reflexivity implies a speaker's assuming of authority over the discourse, not just authority over his or her own discourse, but management of the interaction. This imposing of the speaker's order on other participants involves using power and therefore calls for mitigation, for redressing some of the power balance.

In view of the complex relations between professors and lecturers and students (i.e., the epistemic positions in combination with the client and service positions), the assuming of authority and the simultaneous need to mitigate it on the part of the instructors are particularly salient. The teaching staff are educators and authorities in their field and thereby gatekeepers in the degree system. At the same time, they are increasingly in a service position with respect to their students, who are positioned as clients; students evaluate the service they receive and thereby possess power in relation to their instructors. Lastly, the finding is also interesting in view of Crismore and Vande Kopple's 1997 conclusions concerning hedges; hedging may make controversial messages more palatable, and thereby more persuasive, than unhedged texts expressing full certainty. Thus, even the persuasive tactics employed by speakers could come in as a factor.

Some questions that remain open in the current state of the data concern the use of reflexivity by nondominant participants. Although reflexivity seems to be used by nondominant parties as well, this use appears from the present data to be less frequent. To what extent can reflexivity be defensive as well? Clearly, one defensive strategy is to explain all the things you are not going to talk about and what you are not trying to say. It can be speculated that certain speaker positions— such as student presenters, dissertation defendants, people offering their own thoughts while thinking on their feet—could be defensive, or self-protective, whereas explaining "safe" views, based on the speaker's own authority (as in the case of professors lecturing on their own field) or the authority of others (presenting thoughts by authorities in the field), is not risky and can be performed in a different manner.

Conclusion

In this chapter, I have tried to show that even with a limited amount of data, we can begin to generate new insights into academic discourse by looking into corpus data. It has been possible to at least tentatively identify recurrent units in discourse that are very hard to detect without the kind of data (repeated lined-up examples) that a corpus throws up. By going through repeated instances and simultaneously having access to the social context of their use, it is also possible to set up hypotheses concerning the workings of language in these social contexts.

I have been arguing that reflexivity is a way of imposing the speaker's authority on the ongoing discourse and that it is therefore natural to assume that it is used by dominant participants in abundance. It also appears natural that the power balance should be redressed in some way, and the combination of reflexivity with hedging could be explained as one device for doing so. Thus, reflexivity embodies power relations that exist but are not directly referred to— in short, about which tacit discoursal silences prevail. It therefore offers a means of incorporating into the discourse matters we do not talk about.

I would like to conclude with a couple of remarks about the MICASE project and its relationship with the study of spoken discourse in general. Earlier research into casual conversation has been criticized on two accounts by Eggins and Slade (1997, 7): first, analysis has been fragmentary, dealing only with selected features; second, it has not sought to explore the connections between the social work achieved through the microinteractions of everyday life and the macrosocial world. Much the same criticism is easily extendable to a good deal of other spoken discourse analysis. One realistic way of overcoming the first criticism, fragmentary analysis, is to set up larger projects or have teams of researchers working on related problems on the same data. This is an important aspect of the MICASE setup: one of my roles as external consultant to the project is to try to involve a number of people (not necessarily in the same place) working as a team on the same data. Addressing the second criticism is crucial if we are to achieve a greater understanding of the discourses we are describing. I believe the searches over speaker categories and event types enable the achievement of meaningful results if combined with our current knowledge of the university community as described in sociological, ethnographic, and discourse-analytical studies. Thus, as it continues to evolve, the corpus of academic talk will be a very useful database for testing a number of hypotheses concerning the use and nature of discourse. More specifically, it should provide new information about the kinds of linguistic units that emerge through patterned repetition in speech data, as well as furnishing us with new insights into the processes of academic socialization and of negotiating complex positions and identities.

References

Bäcklund, I. 1998. Metatext in Professional Writing: A Contrastive Study of English, German, and Swedish. Texts in European Writing Communities 3. *TeFa* 25.

Bazerman, C. 1994. *Constructing Experience*. Carbondale: Southern Illinois University Press.

Crismore, A. 1989. *Talking with Readers: Metadiscourse as Rhetorical Act*. New York: Peter Lang.

Crismore, A., and W. Vande Kopple. 1997. The Effects of Hedges and Gender on the Attitudes of Readers in the United States towards Material in a Science Textbook. In *Culture and Styles of Academic Discourses*, ed. A. Duszak, 223–47. Berlin: Mouton de Gruyter.

Becker, A. 1995. *Beyond Translation*. Ann Arbor: University of Michigan Press.

Eggins, S., and D. Slade. 1997. *Analysing Casual Conversation*. London: Cassell.

Gilbert, G. N., and M. Mulkay. 1984. *Opening Pandora's Box: A Sociological Analysis of Scientific Discourse*. Cambridge: Cambridge University Press.

Granger, S., ed. 1998. *Learner English on Computer*. London: Longman.

Huckin, T. 1997. Cultural Aspects of Genre Knowledge. *AILA Review* 12:68–78.

———. 1999. Using Text Corpora to Identify Textual Silences. Paper presented at the North American Symposium on Corpora in Linguistics and Language Teaching, University of Michigan, Ann Arbor, May.

Lindemann, S., and A. Mauranen. 1999. It's Just Real Messy: The Occurrence and Function of *Just* in a Corpus. Paper presented at the AILA Congress '99, Tokyo, August.

Mauranen, A. 1998. Another Look at Genre: Corpus Linguistics vs. Genre Analysis. *Studia Anglica Posnaniensia* 2:303–15.

Mauranen, A. 1993a. *Cultural Differences in Academic Rhetoric: A Textlinguistic Study*. Frankfurt: Peter Lang.

Mauranen, A. 1993b. Contrastive ESP Rhetoric: Metatext in Finnish-English Economics Texts. *English for Specific Purposes* 12, no. 1:3–22.

Parpette, C. 1999. Le discours pédagogique scientifique: Caractéristiques et implications didactiques. Paper presented at the international colloquium "La Didactique des langues en Europe au seuil du 3 millénaire: Des réponses, des questions," University of Nancy, France, May 27–29.

Poos, D. 1999. A Question of Gender? Hedging in Academic Spoken Discourse. Paper presented at the annual meeting of the Michigan Linguistics Society, Michigan State University, East Lansing, October.

Sinclair, J. M. 1991. *Corpus Concordance Collocation.* Oxford: Oxford University Press.

Swales, J. 1999. Textual Silence: An Approach to Disciplinary Culture. Paper presented at the seminar "Disciplinary Cultures," Cornell University, June.

Vande Kopple, W. J. 1985 Some Exploratory Discourse on Metadiscourse. *College Composition and Communication* 36:63–94.

Rethinking French Grammar for Pedagogy: The Contribution of Spoken Corpora

Aaron Lawson
Textwise Labs, Syracuse, New York

Recent innovations in French-language textbooks used in the United States have concentrated almost exclusively on the form of presentation of language to the learner. Approaches to teaching and the teaching philosophies either presented or implied in textbooks have progressed from a more overt teaching of grammar and vocabulary to a more contextualized and covert manner of presenting aspects of language. A large part of this movement has been a willingness to take into consideration the authenticity of materials to which learners are exposed in the classroom. Another key element in this pedagogical sea change has been the emphasis that French teachers and textbooks have placed on oral proficiency, the notion that language learners should have the opportunity to acquire the ability to express themselves orally in a native-like way.

Given that communicative approaches to language teaching have placed such great emphasis on both authentic materials and oral proficiency, one would expect that a major concern of French teachers and publishers of French textbooks would be ensuring that the grammar they present to students reflects authentically the language that native speakers use when they speak. In large part, however, this is demonstrably not the case. Indeed, as others have previously noted (Walz 1986; Di Vito 1998), most language textbooks and almost all university-level French textbooks used in the United States present a single version of French to serve as the model of both speech and writing. The authenticity and veracity of this version of the language is rarely contested, despite the fact that the form of the language presented in French textbooks has depended, at best, on intuition and hunches and, at worst, on simple tradition—that is, following what other textbooks have previously done. Many researchers have assumed that textbook grammar is a reflection of the standard written language, but the recent work of Nadine Di Vito (1998) has demonstrated empirically that this is not the case.

Textbook publishers and developers of teaching materials are not the only language professionals who have neglected to critically examine the linguistic data on which they base their work. The vast majority of academic research in the field of second language acquisition (SLA) has focused on the manners of presentation of the L2 to the learner. Be it debate over whether input alone is sufficient for acquisition (Krashen 1981, 1985; Krashen and Terrell 1983; Barasch and James 1994; Huebner and Ferguson 1991) or output is essential as well (Swain 1985; Swain and Lapkin 1995); over the structuring of input for processibility (e.g., VanPatten 1986) or over parameter resetting (Eubank 1991), the issue of the linguistic nature of input/output in terms of native-like authenticity has largely been ignored. The impact on second language learning is that while enormous amounts of research have been done to investigate how to maximize and make authentic the means of getting learners to appropriate the language to which they are exposed, SLA researchers and textbook writers have virtually ignored the nature of the language itself, rarely, if ever, questioning the authenticity or reality of the grammar and vocabulary they treat in textbooks and research studies.

Some researchers have attempted to address the issue of pedagogically oriented language authenticity, especially in analyzing the presentation of materials in language textbooks. Walz (1986) concluded that oral proficiency in phonology, morphology, and syntax in French would not be possible using the 22 textbooks he examined, since aspects of the spoken language were almost never presented: "they [students] study forms that are not used by native speakers and that have little communicative value" (14). Walz found that the sound system of French was presented as abstract articulatory information, a form that appeals to many linguists but would not be usable for most students. In terms of morphology, adjectives were grouped together as irregular according to spelling, even though they were perfectly regular in speech, and the texts concentrated on listing as many morphologically odd forms as possible, rather than on useful vocabulary, all the while claiming that the main goal of the textbook was conversational proficiency. Walz noted that in cases where the oral language is more complicated than the written (e.g., numbers), "books often teach written forms twice and oral forms not at all" (15). The syntax of French was also heavily, if not exclusively, oriented toward the written language, even for syntactic elements, such as question formation by inversion, which has been shown to impede acquisition and is also almost never used in the spoken language. Walz demonstrates that the same neglect for presenting useful facts about real discourse is true for explanations about the differences between the immediate future and the simple future and that, especially egregious, textbooks make no mention at all of dislocation, "the most striking feature of spoken French" (17). This kind of misleading information came out of textbooks that claimed, according to Walz, to present "elements most frequently used by native speakers in daily life" and "a practical, functional knowledge of French as it is spoken by native speakers in real life situations" (16).

Likewise, Glisan and Drescher (1993) examined 24,500 words of spontaneous Spanish conversation that they collected from native speakers from eight different countries. They focused on the frequency and occurrence of (1) double-object pronouns, (2) nominalization with *lo*, (3) demonstrative adjectives/pronouns, and (4) possessive adjectives/pronouns in the spoken language. Their findings show that textbooks spent enormous amounts of space teaching oral proficiency for elements that almost never occur in the spoken language (e.g., double-object pronouns, possessive pronouns, and the demonstrative *aquel*), while spending no time at all on extremely common and useful items (e.g., the neuter demonstrative pronouns and nominalizations with *lo*). Glisan and Drescher noted that the presentation of object and demonstrative pronominal forms in textbooks did not in any way resemble actual use as determined by consulting the corpus of native spoken Spanish. They concluded that the principle of construction for language textbooks should be based on native speaker usage in different genres as opposed to categorical teacher intuitions.

This work of Walz and of Glisan and Drescher has demonstrated that the content of textbooks does not reflect the realities of actual language use. Similarly, the recent work of Di Vito (1998) questions whether the one language–one grammar approach to language teaching used by textbooks could ever successfully provide realistic input for either speaking or writing. The way textbooks are currently constructed makes it difficult or impossible for language teachers to effectively prioritize the grammar and vocabulary items presented in the textbooks they use. The textbooks do not provide information about whether a given structure is part of the written language, part of the spoken language, or common to both, nor do they provide any information about the relative frequency of structures. Knowing the frequency of the subjunctive, for example, in the spoken language compared to the written can provide information allowing a teacher to decide how much time should be spent on oral versus written practice of this feature. This sort of information cannot be found in today's French textbooks, nor can it ever be a part of them if they continue to be constructed based on intuitions about language or through appeals to tradition. The only way we can provide authentic information to students about the language they are learning is by empirically studying that language as it is used. The tool that can best accomplish such a task is corpus linguistics.

Large corpora of language use now form a major part of the production of textbooks and teaching materials for English as a second language (ESL), especially in Britain. Corpus linguistics has much to offer foreign language teaching of all languages, primarily because it can inform us about essential aspects of the target language, which intuition alone cannot do. There are four areas in particular where corpora can provide invaluable insight into the grammatical features and functions of a language and allow teachers to better target and prioritize what they teach.

First, and perhaps most important, corpora can provide information about frequency, which is almost always lacking in textbook descriptions of the target language. Teachers and students are presented with a certain set of features of a language (tenses, moods, prepositions, pronouns, etc.), usually in a particular order, but with no information about whether this feature occurs frequently or whether it occurs frequently in some genres or registers and not at all in others. As this study will demonstrate, there are enormous frequency differences between those items textbooks spend a lot of time on and what speakers spend a lot of time using. In some instances, textbooks stress oral usage of features that are practically never used orally by native speakers.

Second, ethnographic information about language genre and register is readily obtained through the analysis of corpora. This information can tell materials developers, teachers, and students about the social contexts in which constructions tend to occur, as well as whether the feature in question is typical of spoken or written language and whether it is only used in specific genres. Some elements of a language have different meanings and different grammatical functions depending on the genre in which they are found. Some features of a language, such as the French pronoun *ça* (to be discussed later), are virtually absent from most written genres yet are among the five most common words in spoken French conversation.

Third, corpus linguistics can provide language professionals information about the salience of a particular feature. While textbooks present many aspects of the target language, with each aspect having, for example, its own section of a chapter, there is no way of knowing whether the feature at hand is productive in the language or whether it is productively used only under certain circumstances or in certain contexts. An example of this would be the French pronoun *y*. It is quite common, yet it is very unproductive in that it tends to occur overwhelmingly in the fixed expressions *il y a*, "there is/are," and, to a lesser extent, *y aller*, "to go there." Without this information, a student would reasonably expect that *y* is likely in any locative expression. An important distinction to make here is that while this feature of French (and many others, of course) are logically possible in an infinite number of combinations, in reality they only occur with any frequency in a select few. This points up the grave limitations of native speaker intuitions; they may be able to tell one what is possible in a language but not what actually does occur.

Finally, corpus analysis is especially well suited to provide essential knowledge about the discourse properties of structures and functions in a language. Knowledge of discourse properties, such as collocation (i.e., with what other words a given word tends to occur), is important to understanding vocabulary as it is used. Moreover, many very common elements of language, such as tense, aspect, and pronominal reference, depend almost entirely on discourse structures larger than the sentence or immediate utterance. Thus, in French one cannot tell in most cases whether to use the compound past *(passé-composé)* or the imperfect *(imparfait)* without having the larger context in which a given utterance is placed. As Hopper (1997) notes, native speaker intuitions are especially problematic when one is seeking to understand discourse-based elements, such as verbal categories.

The major objective of this study is to demonstrate the usefulness of corpus linguistics in allowing teachers to reevaluate the actual language they teach, not just the methods by which they teach it. To this end, I examine two grammatical items—the subjunctive and demonstratives—and compare real-life contextualized spoken usage with information in textbooks for teaching the French language.

I have chosen to investigate these two grammatical aspects of the French language because they demonstrate very clearly just how important empirical research can be to improving our understanding of language as we teach it. Both the subjunctive and demonstratives show the wide gap between textbook descriptions of the target language and actual usage. In the case of the subjunctive, corpus evidence reveals how relatively small the functional space of this mood is, compared to the enormous amount of time textbooks spend having students practice this mood orally. Demonstratives in French exemplify the opposite situation: while the main demonstrative form, *ça*, is incredibly frequent in spoken French, it is virtually absent from the textbooks I examined.

The Data

The data on which this study is based was provided by the Barnes Corpus of Spoken French Language, collected in 1984 by Betsy Barnes of the University of Minnesota for use in her study *The Pragmatics of Left Detachment in Spoken Standard French* (1985). As the name of the book implies, the data she collected is from well-educated speakers speaking in a standard conversational mode. Aside from a few words by Barnes herself, all of the speakers in the corpus are native speakers of continental French (most from Paris) who were currently teaching French at the University of Minnesota. The section of the corpus that I used for this study comprised 75,000 words (about eight hours) of natural dinner conversation collected from various gatherings organized by Barnes. The computerized texts were analyzed with the help of the Concorder demo program and WordSmith.

The textbook characterizations of the forms I examined in the Barnes corpus were drawn from nine different recently published university-level textbooks distributed by five different publishers and in common use around the United States. Since they were basically homogenous in their treatment of the subjunctive and demonstratives, I will not point out the specific textbooks I looked at, as this would be, in a sense, misleading. All introductory French textbooks in the United States that I have seen have had a similar approach to the

French language as was presented in the nine textbooks I looked at. The textbooks all claimed to be communicative in their approach to teaching and placed a strong emphasis on oral proficiency and speaking in class.

Research Issues

In the body of this study, I empirically investigate five research questions concerning the usage of the subjunctive and demonstratives in the French language. The first three deal with the subjunctive.

1. How frequent is the subjunctive compared with other verb modalities and relative to the time textbooks devote to it?
2. Which verb lexemes are most frequently employed in the subjunctive?
3. After which expressions is the subjunctive most used?

The last two questions pertain to demonstrative usage.

4. How often and in what way are demonstratives used as pronominal referents?
5. What is the difference in usage between distal and proximal forms of demonstratives in French?

I treat each of these issues separately in a different section. In each section, I characterize the textbook presentation or (lack thereof) of the linguistic feature in question, followed by what is revealed about the feature in looking at actual usage in the spoken French language.

The Subjunctive

In French, the subjunctive mood occurs, for the most part, obligatorily after certain fixed expressions; those most frequently discussed are expressions that indicate doubt, emotion, will, or necessity. In addition, many possible expressions that do not fit into these categories are said to be followed obligatorily by the subjunctive. These expressions include, for example, *pour que,* "in order that," and *bien que,* "although." For many English-speaking learners, learning the French subjunctive is a major task: there are well over 50 expressions that trigger the subjunctive, there is a new set of verb forms to learn, and the raison d'être of the subjunctive (which in French is presented as largely redundant and not actually contributing any meaning when it is used) is often difficult for students to grasp.

Frequency of the Subjunctive

My first research question in this study deals with the frequency of the subjunctive relative to other verb modalities. In textbooks, the subjunctive is dealt with extensively in 3 to 4 (out of 12 to 16) chapters, in conjunction with over 50 expressions. All sections dealing with the subjunctive emphasize largely oral practice, and all textbooks devote sections to the oral practice of the past subjunctive. In most textbooks, the subjunctive is given as much or more space than the imperfect and the compound past verb modalities combined.

In the Barnes corpus, the subjunctive makes up only 1 percent of all verb forms (see fig. 1; Di Vito [1998] similarly found that only 2 percent of verb forms in the written language are subjunctive). The past subjunctive never occurs in the corpus. In contrast, the compound past and imperfect make up 33 percent of all verb forms. Surprisingly, the past perfect (pluperfect) is almost 50 percent more common than the subjunctive in the spoken French corpus, yet some introductory textbooks do not even mention it. Even when it is dealt with, the pluperfect is often presented as a written form that the student needs only passive command of; for example, one textbook states: "You should be able to recognize and understand the *plus-que-parfait* when you encounter it, especially in written French." Students and teachers would profit from knowing that this tense is more common in educated native oral production than is the subjunctive.

Subjunctive Verb Forms

This section addresses which forms of the subjunctive are most frequently used. This is potentially important information because textbooks rarely, if ever, indicate which forms of the subjunctive are most used; in general, the implied message to the students is "memorize them all as soon as possible." For many verbs, the subjunctive is not distinct from the indicative except in the first-person and second-person plurals. For this reason, I refer to the unique forms of the subjunctive as "distinctive" and to the forms identical to the present as "isomorphic."

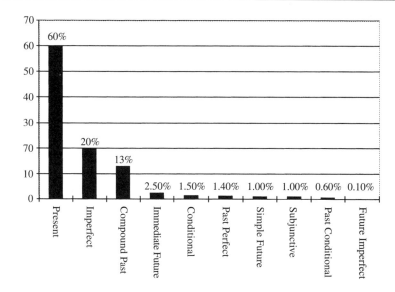

Fig. 1. Frequency of the subjunctive compared with other verb modalities in the Barnes corpus

As is shown in figure 2, just four forms (phonetically [swa], [fas], [e], and [aj]) make up 66 percent of the distinctive forms in subjunctive usage in the corpus. These four forms make up 51 percent of all usage, including the isomorphic forms. All the expressions that triggered the subjunctive in the data where based on a singular verb in either the first or the third person. Surprisingly, none of the verbs in the subjunctive were first- or second-person plurals.

Frequency of Expressions Triggering the Subjunctive

While there are more than 50 expressions presented as triggering the subjunctive, textbooks do not give any indication as to whether one expression is more common than any other. While textbooks do present certain sets of expressions (those indicating necessity) before others (those indicating doubt, emotion, etc.), they do not provide any information about which expressions are extremely rare (most of them never occurred in the data examined) and which are quite prevalent. Moreover, there is nothing to indicate whether some expressions are only literary, journalistic, written, and so on. In other words, the student and teacher is left with the understanding that all

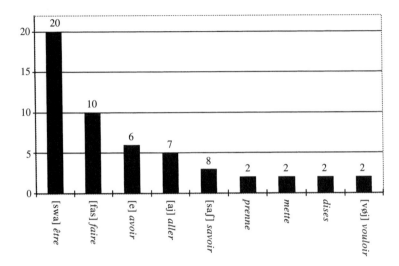

Fig. 2. Frequency of subjunctive verb forms used in the Barnes corpus

of these expressions are more or less equally frequent and probable in all genres of French.

In the corpus, more than 50 percent of all uses of the subjunctive were triggered by one expression, *falloir que,* "one must," and 73 percent of all instances of the subjunctive followed three expressions: *falloir que; que,* "that"; and *quoi que,* "whatever" (see fig. 3). The use of *que* + subjunctive is not dealt with in the textbooks examined, despite its productivity in the spoken corpus. The expression *quoi que* is not dealt with until the very end of most textbooks, and it is of note that *quoi que* occurred only with the verb *être* in the Barnes corpus, almost always in the fixed expression *quoi que ce soit,* "whatever it might be."

Demonstratives

Implicit in all grammar and textbooks is the notion that French has a two-way system of demonstratives, with forms indicating that a referent is near to the speaker (proximal) or distant from the speaker (distal). The various forms of the demonstrative system of French are outlined in figure 4.

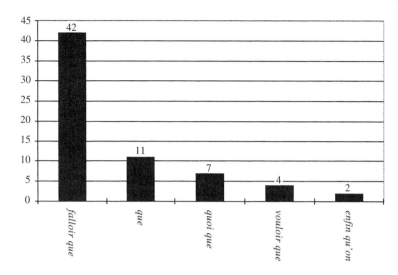

Fig. 3. Most common expression triggering the subjunctive in the Barnes corpus

	Proximal	**Distal**
Adverb	*ici,* "here"	*ici,* "here"
Pronoun	*ceci,* "this"	*cela (ça),* "that"
Long-form pronoun	*celui (-ci),* "this one"	*celui (-lá),* "that one"
Adjective	*ce* [noun] *-ci,* "this *[noun]*"	*ce* [noun] *-lá,* "this *[noun]*"

Fig. 4. Demonstratives in French

Frequency of Types of Demonstrative Pronominal Reference

Figure 4 indicates that there are many possibilities for using demonstratives as pronouns in French. Textbooks deal mainly with *celui* and its various forms (*celle, ceux, celles,* etc.). The other demonstrative forms are at best mentioned in passing, and none are treated in a separate section with any kind of explanation. In short, these demonstratives are assumed to be the lexical equivalents of the English demonstratives, ostensibly because they do not change for gender as do the long-form demonstratives.

The form *ça* is only mentioned once or twice in the textbooks I examined, always only in passing as part of a collocation, such as *ça va*, "it goes." Its usage as a productive form is never discussed, and textbooks with a presumably strong emphasis on oral proficiency seem to be oblivious to its incredible prevalence and versatility of function in the spoken language.

In the data I examined, *ça* (N = 1,546) is the second most used pronoun in conversational French, after the first-person singular *je*, and is the fourth most commonly used word overall, after *c'est* (3,022), *je* (2,478), and *oui* (1,729). For example, *ça* is six times more frequent in conversation than the similarly functioning clitic object pronouns *(le, la, les)* and enjoys a much wider scope of usage, being able to refer to chunks of speech as well as to words and objects. The enormous frequency of *ça* compared to the other demonstratives is clear in figure 5. *Ça* is by far the most common productive third-person pronoun in spoken French, yet it is virtually ignored in French textbooks.

Distal Conspiracy

In textbooks, nothing is said about usage differences between distal and proximal forms of demonstratives in French; they are treated as being functionally equivalent to the English forms. Further, no infor-

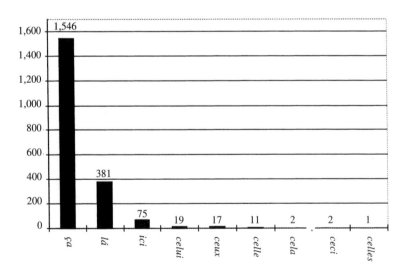

Fig. 5. Frequency of demonstratives in the Barnes corpus

mation is given about the relative frequency of the different demon-stratives. One is left to assume that distal forms refer to "far" things and proximal forms refer to "close" things.

In the corpus, however, distal forms actually make up 96 percent of all demonstrative use. Proximal forms are either not used at all (as is the case of the pronoun *ceci*) or only used contrastively with distal forms (e.g., *ici et là*, "here and there"). Moreover, it is obviously rarely the case that spatial distinctions determine the choice between proxi-mal and distal forms in spoken French. In fact, a normal initial exchange over the telephone in French would be "Jean est là? Oui, il est là" [Is John **there**? Yes, he is **there**]. Figure 6 demonstrates that spo-ken French is well on its way to having a demonstrative system where spatial distinctions are irrelevant and where only distal forms are pro-ductively employed.

Conclusions

I believe the data presented in this study speak largely for themselves and that it is not necessarily the place of the corpus linguist to pre-scribe a pedagogical approach based on their findings. Rather, I hope to have here demonstrated in general how important it is to base the

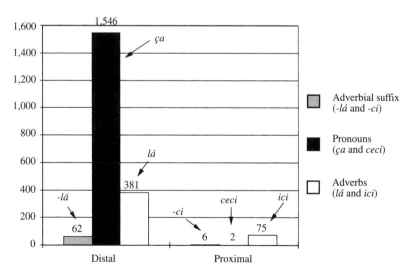

Fig. 6. Frequency of proximal versus distal demonstrative forms in the Barnes corpus

language we teach on the language native speakers speak, rather than relying on hunches or tradition. It goes without saying that many other textbook aspects of French and other languages (as Glisan and Drescher [1993] have demonstrated) do not reflect actual usage and require much more research. The important contribution of corpus linguistics can allow students, teachers, and materials developers to have accurate information about the target language they work with. In this way, they will be able, in their approach to the language in question, to make personal decisions that are grounded in an understanding of the empirical realities of language use. For these reasons, I leave it up to the readers of this study to draw their own conclusions about what they feel they should do in light of my findings.

However, we should definitely not fall into the trap of assuming that because the status quo is adequate, there is no need for improvement. The quick and dismissive answer to all of the research presented in this study, my own as well as that of other researchers, would be that some students do eventually learn French from contemporary textbooks. But just as students certainly learned French from the grammar-translation method, the audio-lingual method, and many others, language teachers came to see that students had the potential to learn better from other approaches to language. We have at our disposal for perhaps the first time in the history of French-language teaching the technological means to reevaluate our currently adequate teaching practices so that they fit more closely with the way native speakers actually use their language.

Prioritizing What We Teach with the Help of Corpora

In more general terms, how can information about frequency and distribution from corpora help us with language teaching? First and most obviously, authenticity can be enhanced, such that we teach what native speakers actually use, in the way(s) that they actually use it, and present it in its natural context. Further, with corpora, we can better reevaluate the order of presentation of linguistic features in such a way as to teach rare, trivial, or functionally marginal elements of the language later, after students have a grasp on the productive and frequent core items in a language. Finally, teachers may have the information necessary to focus in and localize, targeting the forms we teach to their proper context. For example, if a form occurs only in literary writing, one knows to focus on reading comprehension and writing with this aspect of the language. In this way, we can avoid wasting time teaching students to orally produce complex grammatical elements that native speakers themselves rarely ever orally produce. Above all, teachers will be able to prioritize what they teach, and students what they learn, with priorities derived from actual native speaker usage.

The Future of Authentic Materials Development

At one time, due to technological obstacles that have since been overcome and to misconceived theoretical notions that have been largely discarded, it was adequate to speculate about how speakers spoke. I believe that this study, together with others mentioned in it, shows that language professionals can now do much better, but improvement must start with a demand for, or at least an open-mindedness toward, change on the part of language teachers. While textbook editors also play a role in maintaining the traditional outlook,[1] it is ultimately up to the teachers and students to demonstrate a desire for access to information that will provide a more authentic language experience in the classroom.

Note

1. Bull and Lamadrid (1971; cited in Glisan and Drescher 1993, 25) point out, "publishers hesitate to change the traditional grammar rules because they can't sell books with rules which upset the teachers."

References

Barasch, R., and C. James. 1994. *Beyond the Monitor Model.* Boston: Heinle and Heinle.

Barnes, B. 1985. *The Pragmatics of Left Detachment in Spoken Standard French.* Amsterdam: John Benjamins.

Di Vito, N. 1998. *Patterns across Spoken and Written French: Empirical Research on the Interaction among Forms, Functions, and Genres.* Boston: Houghton Mifflin.

Eubank, L. 1991. *Point Counterpoint.* Amsterdam: John Benjamins.

Glisan, E., and V. Drescher. 1993. Textbook Grammar: Does It Reflect Native Speaker Speech? *Modern Language Journal* 77:23–33I.

Hopper, P. 1997. When "Grammar" and Discourse Clash. In *Essays on Lan-*

guage Function and Language Type, ed. J. Bybee, J. Haiman, and S. Thompson. Amsterdam: John Benjamins.

Huebner, T., and C. Ferguson. 1991. *Crosscurrents in Second Language Acquisition and Linguistic Theories.* Amsterdam: John Benjamins.

Krashen, S. 1981. *Second Language Acquisition and Second Language Learning.* Oxford: Pergamon.

———. 1985. *The Input Hypothesis: Issues and Implications.* London: Longman.

Krashen, S., and T. Terrell. 1983. *The Natural Approach.* Hayward, CA: Alemany.

Swain, M. 1985. Communicative Competence: Some Roles of Comprehensible Input and Comprehensible Output in Its Development. In *Input and Second Language Acquisition,* ed. S. Gass and C. Madden. Rowley, MA: Newbury House.

Swain, M., and S. Lapkin. 1995. Problems in Output and the Cognitive Processes They Generate: A Step Towards Second Language Learning. *Applied Linguistics* 16, no. 3:371–91.

VanPatten, W. 1986. Second Language Acquisition Research and the Learning/Teaching of Spanish: Some Findings and Their Implications. *Hispania* 69:202–16.

Walz, J. 1986. Is Oral Proficiency Possible with Today's French Textbooks? *Modern Language Journal* 70:13–20.

The Lexical Phrase as Pedagogical Tool: Teaching Disagreement Strategies in ESL

Stephanie Burdine
Rice University

Pawley and Syder's 1983 seminal paper was the first to claim that successful L2 learning requires nativelike selection (the ability to choose idiomatic expressions in the correct pragmatic context in lieu of grammatical but nonnativelike or marked paraphrases) and nativelike fluency (the ability to produce spontaneous strings of connected speech, despite a limited speaking ability). The core of this argument is that idiomatic control and fluency rests considerably on knowledge of lexical phrases. A lexical phrase is defined here as a frequently recurring chunk of language (varying in length), whose meaning is not (totally) predictable from its form, and designates a culturally accepted term for "a socially recognized conceptual category" (Pawley and Syder 1983, 209). Pawley and Syder explain that what distinguishes a nonce form (e.g., *footache, thighache,* and *toeache*) from a lexicalized form (e.g., *backache* and *headache*) is a question of conventionality. While *footache, thighache,* and *toeache* might label common enough ailments, they have not been institutionalized like *backache* and *headache* have been and are therefore considered marked forms. For this reason, we are more likely to hear the expressions "my thigh hurts," "I have an aching toe," and so on, whereas "I have an ache in the head" is a peculiar paraphrase for "I have a headache." Of course, part of successful L2 learning is the capacity of the student to recognize the markedness of the sentence "I have an ache in the head" and avoid using it.

Nattinger and DeCarrico (1992) made further contributions to research on lexical phrases with their extensive typology that classified phrases according to structural and functional criteria. Distinctions were made between less variable and fixed forms (e.g., "in a nut-shell"; "this is a piece of cake"; "get a life") and more variable, non-canonical forms (e.g., "as far as [I know/I can tell]"; "that reminds me of X [a movie I once saw]"), as well as among pragmatic roles (e.g., "so far so good" [marker of approval]; "all in all" [summarizer]; "by the way" [topic shifter]; "in part" [qualifier]) (Nattinger and DeCarrico 1992, 34). In addition, a substantial portion of Nattinger and DeCarrico's 1992 study outlined the practical applications for lexical phrases in teaching spoken and written discourse with the aim to help students understand the value of lexical phrases as part of spontaneous social interaction.

The two influential studies I have just described support the claim that fluent, connected speech depends on substantial knowledge of lexical phrases and that therefore the lexical phrase is an ideal unit to exploit in L2 instruction. Pawley and Syder (1983, 215) emphasize that "by far the largest part of the English speaker's lexicon consists of complex lexical items including several hundred thousand lexicalized sentence stems." Lexical phrases are often easy for students to store and retrieve and have the added benefit of

> being familiar to the hearer as well as to the speaker. . . . [providing] con-venient ways of referring to [salient concepts] which are not provided for by the stock of unitary lexical items. (Pawley and Syder 1983, 218)

In addition, a further advantage is that students do not need to com-pletely understand each of the component units to achieve functional usage of the phrase in a communicative situation (cf. Hakuta 1976, 333). Thus, even in the early stages of L2 instruction, students' fre-quent exposure to lexical phrases will help prevent them from becom-ing bogged down by the lexical patterns that native speakers regu-larly exploit in the course of speaking. Based on the research of Pawley and Syder and Nattinger and DeCarrico, we can also assume that students will be able to produce these same patterns by them-selves, including such phrases as "Did you hear about X?" as a device to introduce a topic, "Do you follow me?" to verify or acknowledge listener comprehension, and "Well, that's about it" to end a conversa-tion.[1]

Given this preamble on the value of the lexical phrase in L2 instruction, it may strike some readers as surprising to discover that the lexical phrase has been largely neglected in mainstream ESL mate-rials. As a consequence, students often lack knowledge of the prefabricated forms they encounter in conversations with native speakers and either ignore or misunderstand their meaning. For instance, while Azar's 1989 *Understanding and Using English Grammar*, widely used in American intermediate-level ESL classes, aims to "promote vocabulary development" (xiii), new vocabulary is restricted to the amount necessary to exemplify formal patterns. The textbook has no focus on lexis and no lexically based activities. Function words are treated in the traditional grammar way; for example, prepositions are separated into prepositions of place, prepositions of time, and miscellaneous prepositions. Lewis (1993, 110) believes that this is a mistake and that these "typically high-frequency, de-lexicalised" words "deserve lexical rather than grammatical treatment," because they "enter into the widest range of patterns, and are thus usefully if not maximally generative." Azar's activities on miscellaneous prepositions appear at the end of chapters, often seeming out of place, and students are asked to choose a preposition from a list in the appendix to complete various sentences.

Are you ready _____ the test?
I'm angry _____ Greg.
I'm mad _____ Greg. (Azar 1989, 17)

This type of exercise leads students to believe that these small words are some of the most difficult to master in English and, at the same time, fails to illustrate the powerful extent to which the words generate patterns (cf. Lewis 1993, 143). A more pedagogically effective activity would be to collect some of the more important patterns and arrange them in a nonlinear format so that words occurring together are recorded together and are thereby illustrated as part of lexical phrases with functional purposes. Sentences illustrating the important patterns of *with* might include: "I'm with Compaq now," "she was on a trip with the Junior League" (when talking about an institution); "he's at home with the flu," "she's in the hospital with pneumonia" (when talking about an illness); and "they shivered with fright," "he shook with anger," "she agreed with reluctance," "she squealed with delight" (when talking about showing a mood) (adapted from Lewis 1993, 144).

Determining exactly which lexical phrases should be presented to students becomes an altogether separate matter. Williams's 1988 research has shown that when textbooks teach lexical phrases for functional purposes, the structures chosen for inclusion may be infrequent in actual language or never used at all. Focusing on disagreement, Williams compared the language used in business meetings with the structures included in English for business textbooks and concluded that the variation found in actual usage is not adequately and accurately represented by examples included in the textbooks. The structures found in the transcripts of business meetings consisted mostly of lexical phrases (e.g., "well/yes, [I can see that] but X" or "wouldn't it be better to X"), rather than complete sentences. The structures presented in the textbooks, however, were strictly isolated sentences, such as "I disagree with that." While offering students complete sentences to work with seems rather unproblematic—after all, many routinized forms can be analyzed sententially (e.g., "I'm grateful for your help," "I'm sorry"; cf. Aijmer 1996)—textbooks' lack of variants represented in actual usage is somewhat discouraging. Williams has suggested that teaching students to express opinion in isolation underestimates their abilities as learners to select strategies and use them in the appropriate pragmatic context and is an inaccurate representation of how native speakers actually use language.

Perhaps even less helpful to students, however, is being taught only one strategy for expressing opinion. It seems quite predictable that students who only learn the construction "I disagree with that," as opposed to a range of frequent constructions applicable in diverse situations, will overuse the single phrase, applying it to incorrect contexts and consequently creating the wrong impression with the native speaker. Equally problematic is the possibility of students who misunderstand the recurring variants they encounter in everyday conversation (e.g., "that makes me uncomfortable") and risk interpreting a phrase in only its literal sense. Teachers can do more to minimize the occurrence of such difficulties for students by providing them with extensive opportunities in the classroom to explore the meaning and application of useful variants.

With these factors in mind, the goal of the present study is to compare the expression of disagreement in various communicative situations (other than in business) with the information contained in ESL textbooks. After analyzing spoken corpus data and comparing the findings to five intermediate-level textbooks, I propose a lexically based framework (one that relies on concordancing) for teaching students disagreement strategies.

In my analysis, I used a combination of three genre-specific corpora, taken from Switchboard Transcripts (Linguistic Data Consortium 1994) (hereinafter SWB), a two-million-word corpus of spontaneous telephone conversations of over 500 speakers representing all regional American dialects, and from the Corpus of Spoken Professional American English (CSPAE) (Barlow 1998), a two-million-word corpus divided into transcripts of White House press conferences (hereinafter WH) and transcripts of faculty/academic committee meetings (hereinafter FM). The combination of these corpora offers the researcher a diverse collection of genre-specific texts from which to gather empirical data on the range of variation in disagreement strategies that would be useful for ESL students.

In keeping with Williams's 1988 findings on disagreement, I surmised that a wide variety of lexical phrases used to mark disagreement would occur in the corpora and that the majority of the ESL textbooks examined would have little or no mention of the recurring phrases found in the corpora. In the appendix, I list all of the disagreement markers I arbitrarily chose and searched for in the corpora, accompanied by a concordance example illustrating their usage (sentences were randomly chosen from one corpus). Table 1 displays the raw frequencies and percentages of those markers with an overall total of ten or more occurrences.[2] As the reader will see, the data confirms the first point in my hypothesis; there is strong variation in disagreement forms, and more noteworthy for my purposes, the data show different usage frequencies for different expressions and variation across text types.[3]

While my list is by no means exhaustive, it is a starting point from which we can work to classify disagreement strategies. The data reveal four basic strategy types: explicit/strong, implicit/strong, explicit/weak, and implicit/weak. These strategies are affected by the degree of directness, emotion, and personal style of the speaker, which are all tied to specific genre. Students will benefit from knowing about these strategies, based on pragmatic principles, and can use them to classify the variation in disagreement forms they encounter. Like any conversational act in English (e.g., inviting, greeting, introducing), the strategy by which a speaker chooses to mark disagreement is influenced by the (in)formality of the speaker-listener relationship. The general (in)formality of the genre, as well as the topic of conversation, are other sociolinguistic features contributing to the overall register of the conversational act. Thus, an explicit/strong disagreement might be considered rude and inappropriate in one con-

TABLE 1. Disagreement Markers in the Corpora (in descending order of total frequency)

	WH		FM		SWB		All
	N	%	N	%	N	%	Total
No	756	.008	507	.006	1288	.054	2551
Don't think X	127	.013	249	.003	138	.006	514
Concern	29	.003	317	.004	62	.003	408
That's not X	55	.006	20	.002	32	.001	107
Don't see X	10	.001	40	.005	30	.001	80
Problem	0	—	35	.004	31	.001	66
Don't believe X	18	.002	14	.002	21	>.001	53
Thing	0	—	23	.003	25	.001	48
Yes but	22	.002	22	.003	3	>.001	47
Don't understand	1	>.001	6	>.001	30	.001	37
Well, no	13	.001	16	.002	6	>.001	35
Look	32	.003	1	>.001	0	—	33
Disagree	9	.001	12	.001	10	>.001	31
Uncomfortable	6	.001	22	.003	3	.001	31
Against X	4	>.001	6	.001	18	.001	28
Trouble	0	—	18	.002	8	>.001	26
Wrong	2	>.001	1	>.001	20	.001	23
But see	0	—	8	.001	13	.001	21
Idea	5	.001	10	.001	6	>.001	21
Don't agree	2	>.001	5	.001	10	>.001	17
Ridiculous	4	>.001	8	>.001	0	—	13

Note: The items listed represent what are considered to be the major or basic components of the disagreement phrases and encompass the variant forms of the basic words found in different disagreement phrases, including all lemmas. Thus, *concern* also encompasses *concerns, concerning,* and *concerned; thing* encompasses *the thing is, the thing that; idea* encompasses any adjectives that may qualify it, as in *bad idea.* The reader may consult the appendix for concordance examples.

text, while being perfectly acceptable in another. It is the task of the language teacher to provide students with enough examples of actual usage so that the various contexts are exemplified as much as adequately possible, enabling students to see how the strategies are generally employed and to spot patterns among them. For instance, teachers can display several scripts in which the choice of lexical phrase alters the dynamics of the disagreement situation with regard to register, style, or pragmatics. In so doing, the teacher demonstrates to students the extensive variation possible within the same basic script (e.g., husband and wife disagreeing about X versus boss and employee disagreeing about X or two colleagues disagreeing about X). Ideally, the instructor requires a range of genre-specific texts or corpora to present students with a variety of contexts and speaker-listener relationships. Depending on the language goals of the students (i.e., conversational English or ESP), the teacher can present the range of disagreement variation and then concentrate more on the production of the variants that will be of most use to the group of students. Some of the disagreement patterns I identify in the corpus analysis that follows are viable candidates to use in such an exercise.

The WH data generally indicate more explicit/strong disagreement than do the other corpora, as evidenced by the higher usage of *look, oppose,* and "that's not *X*." This is to be expected, since the press secretary's aim is to provide details to satisfy reporters in a manner that precludes ambiguity and speculation, which will affect how dissenting opinion is presented. Turn-taking is a struggle in this forum, so reporters necessarily prepare a condensed line of questioning and wait to be called on. Generally, the briefings tolerate much less time for lengthy expressions of disagreement and personal positions than does a faculty meeting or telephone conversation. This might explain why we do not find any occurrence of "the problem with *X*" or "the problem is *X*," both of which might signal a drawn-out explanation. One the other hand, we have a very frequent usage of *no* plus a short explanation or "I don't think *X*." The occasional usage of more emphatic phrases, such as "that's ridiculous," "that's bogus," and "that's crazy," reveals the candor of the press secretary. After perusing longer excerpts of the transcripts, one's first impression is that most of the White House reporters are regulars and that the press secretary feels at ease with the familiar faces, which may explain the occurrence of these phrases. However, the use of these phrases is much more likely attributed to the press secretary's feeling the pressure of being in the "hot seat." In other words, the press secretary is not at ease and wants to make certain that some stories or lines of inquiry are effectively "killed."

Directing our attention now to the FM corpus, we find that this corpus allows for the extensive two-way exchange of opinion that is more or less absent from the WH. Although the corpora do not mark overlaps, several speakers appear to be talking at once in both the WH and the FM, but in the FM, speakers are more gracious in letting others finish their turn. While we might assume that personal feelings, as well as perhaps conflicts between colleagues, have a greater chance of surfacing in this corpus given the closeness of the group, the disagreements here actually seem less personal than those in the WH, and a certain etiquette appears to compel individuals to maintain their composure and provide others with an equal opportunity for expression. As a consequence, we find a predominant usage of direct/weak disagreement strategies, with a preference for such phrases as "I'm uncomfortable with," "I'm concerned that," and "I am troubled by," which are quite polite, comparatively speaking. The use of "The thing is . . ." is another more humbling approach to disagreement that allows the speaker to mitigate his or her apparent forwardness toward the listener. If faculty members care to exercise a stronger, more formal expression of disagreement, the rather academic "I disagree" is used.

The SWB corpus is comprised of the most informal dialogues of the three corpora. The speakers broach a variety of topics and converse freely about them. My findings here are in some respects similar to those from the WH corpus in that these speakers also seem less inclined to frame disagreement in terms of how much X concerns or troubles them; they are more apt to employ direct strategies that provide an immediate position (e.g., "I'm against X" or "I don't agree with X"). If an SWB speaker wishes to demonstrate sensitivity, there is a tendency toward "the problem with X" or "I don't believe X." Alternatively, the use of a somewhat weaker expression using *thing* (i.e., "The thing is . . .") may also be applied, similar to the FM corpus. That the SWB corpus does not have any occurrences of "that's ridiculous" (nor are there any instances of "that's stupid" or "that's crazy") suggests that a telephone conversation with a perfect stranger is not necessarily reason to speak frankly or, one might say, naturally. So, while the SWB strategies are direct and opinions are explicitly provided, they preclude any boorish remarks, since the speaker-listener relationship is guided by a different etiquette than the WH or FM corpora.

All of my findings appear to fit accordingly with the fundamental dynamics of the genres captured by the corpora: disagreement in the WH data is direct and explicit, while in the SWB it is informal, yet still direct and explicit; the FM data indicate primarily formal expressions of disagreement that are, at times, inflated for politeness. It is interesting to note that the phrases "I don't think X" and "I don't believe X" are the two disagreement markers "neutral" enough in kind to cut across all three corpora rather equally. To briefly summarize the findings from the entire set of corpora, *no* is the default marker by a significant margin (2,551 occurrences) and is quite often applied in sequence with other disagreement markers, as in "No, I don't think so" (SWB) and "No, that's not what I meant" (FM). Markers based on the phrase "don't think X" (514 occurrences), the word *concern* (408), the phrases "that's not X" (107) and "don't see" (80), and the word *problem* (66) round out the top five markers based on frequency.

Having looked at the corpus data to see how disagreement is signaled in actual usage, I now focus on my survey of five ESL textbooks. The reader will recall that the second element of my hypothesis states that the majority of the textbooks would have little or no mention of the recurrent lexical phrases found in the corpora. In fact, my examination of the textbooks does not completely confirm this statement. Barnard and Cady 1992 provides students with several variants to work with, a total of five: "I disagree" and "I'm afraid I disagree" (both used in imaginary dialogues), "Actually, I don't think that's quite correct" (characterized as "polite"), and "That's wrong!" and "You're wrong!" (both characterized as "impolite"). While some of the phrasing in the textbook variants is a little wordy, the structures are basically congruent with the corpus results. "I disagree" occurs verbatim in the corpora 31 times, while there are 514 cases of "I don't think X" and 23 cases of "That's wrong." Further corpus work may reveal usage of the other variants mentioned in the textbook, but it is still encouraging to find the majority of the variants in the textbook represented in the corpus data.

McKay 1993, in a lesson on stating opinions, also includes five disagreement variants for students to work with: "I don't agree," "I don't think so," "I don't believe that," "you can't say that," and "No way!" While "I don't agree" was a more marked choice in our corpora (six occurrences), "I don't believe X" occurred quite frequently, and "I don't think X" was the second most widely used variant. Although "you can't say that" and "No way!" did not occur in our data, this is not to say that they would not be found in other corpora; presumably they would. On the basis of the corpora examined here, however, it is worthwhile to reiterate that only two of the five variants included in the textbook were frequent in actual usage. This suggests that there needs to be a better selection of variants in the textbook, which would be accomplished by making corpus analysis an integral part of materials preparation. As a secondary observation, I add that, unlike Barnard and Cady 1992, the presentation of the variants in this textbook is inadequate because the phrases are simply listed. No explanations are given as to which contexts would be appropriate for use of the phrases (i.e., which are considered more polite, etc.), and therefore the students are not shown the value of the phrases in natural conversation.

It is almost difficult to criticize the third textbook in my survey, Carter and McCarthy 1997, because each chapter is based on a conversation transcript from the CANCODE project and is used to demonstrate real language usage. The transcripts are followed by the authors' descriptions and comments about the data, and this format allows students to first have exposure to the data contained in authentic texts and then be presented with information specific to some of the common constructions included therein. The constructions discussed are ultimately chosen by the authors, and, unfortunately, the textbook is not especially helpful for our purposes, because out of twenty transcripts, none deals with a situation that clearly invites disagreement. In a radio call-in show transcript, there is one marker of disagreement, "But I don't understand how . . . ," uttered by the radio host. However, no explanation in the commentary section of this unit accounts for its presence, and no mention of disagreement strategies is found elsewhere in the textbook.

The final two textbooks examined are the least impressive in the area of teaching disagreement. In Richards et al. 1990, no disagreement marking strategies are mentioned, even in unit 4, where students are supposed to discuss their reasons for agreeing or disagreeing with the question of whether television is good or bad. Similarly, in Kozyrev 1998, no disagreement strategies are provided, despite an activity in chapter 6 that intends for students to engage in a debate on "consumer boycotts."

The selection of lexical input is a necessary part of any teaching or any textbook. Whether exclusion of disagreement strategies was a mere oversight of authors or a deliberate decision, less than half of the textbooks we surveyed provided students with these strategies. There is also a concern about which variants were presented in the textbooks. Given the small amount of time spent on teaching this function, there is little evidence that textbooks are including the best or most worthwhile examples, since few frequent phrases are being included. Not only should students be given large quantities of frequent lexical phrases to work with, but they should also be exposed to a great deal of the lexical phrase variation that arises out of genre-specific contexts.

I propose the use of concordancing, first, to organize disagreement strategies to introduce students to variants used in actual discourse and, second, to illustrate how disagreement markers are strung together in routinized forms and applied in genre-specific contexts. A typological framework of disagreement strategies is outlined in table 2 with examples taken from the CSPAE.

Within this framework, type A variants can be characterized as somewhat polite because they increase the buffer zone between the speaker and listener by acknowledging the opinion of the listener first and then proceeding with disagreement. The variants in type B are more assertive, provide less of a buffer zone, and can be characterized as mainly opinion-driven. The varying degrees of types C and D are contingent on the use of mood, qualifiers, and/or an appeal to the notion of reality. Type E strategies essentially involve hesitations prior to disagreement and are made up of the expression of slight, indirect disagreement plus a follow-up point. The speaker might employ this strategy in the anticipation of a negative reaction from the listener. Type F is very direct in that it introduces the speaker's opinion as correct. One might rely on this strategy in the attempt to close an ongoing debate with one final remark. The last strategy, type G, comprises questions, in the conditional and negative, that serve to invite the agreement of the listener. The questions appear biased, however, inasmuch as their formulation may reveal the interrogator's expected or desired response.

This typology is useful from a teaching standpoint because it exemplifies that although the concept of disagreement is no different between genres, there is variation among strategies, as well as among the various constructions used to express disagreement. Students can therefore utilize the framework as a means to classify strategies according to type (assertive disagreement, weak, etc.), using the concordance lines as samples of each type. With some modifications, the instructor could also make use of this framework in a discussion on the frequency of various disagreement strategies and tailor the information and concordance examples to the needs of the individual ESL class.

Perhaps in the near future instructors will be able to access relevant corpus data on demand to provide students with examples of actual usage (when textbooks fail to do so) or simply to give students additional data to explore. In these still early stages of corpus-assisted language teaching, however, where teachers often need to call up data in advance of teaching the lesson, a lexically based classification via concordancing, such as the one I have described here, is a valuable

TABLE 2. Typology of Disagreement Strategies, with Corpus Examples

Type A: Short acknowledgment + disagreement
1. *That's true. But the major issue is the Puerto on the . . .*
2. *Right. But we won't have all the other things that . . .*
3. *Yes, but LEP is sort of considered a negative . . .*
4. *Correct. But we want the list of people who will be there tonight.*

Type B: Doubt + opinion
1. <voice>: *Ed, we're voting on whether you want the examples intact, sitting in the middle of the thing, or do you want them all in one place. —*
   <turn>: *No, that's not exactly it. We're voting do you want them to interrupt . . .*
2. *We're creating a Lake Woebegon effect of educational quality. I don't see the point.*
3. *I don't think that's likely to happen. I think some . . .*

Type C: Stronger disagreement
1. *Barbara, I disagree with you on that one.*
2. *It's a very bad idea . . .*
3. *Well, we would disagree. We believe the FEC can.*
4. *I strongly disagree and strongly disagree with those groups.*
5. *That's ridiculous.*

Type D: Absolute disagreement
1. *And I totally disagree with the premise of your question . . .*
2. *No, no. But Marilyn is assuming that it's a more literal activity. And that's not true.*
3. *That's where you're wrong.*

Type E: Slight disagreement + addition of point
1. *There's a couple of things I'm uncomfortable with. One of them . . .*
2. *because I guess I'm troubled by us taking the position that we will . . .*
3. *Well, my concern is, quite frankly, we need to work on . . .*

Type F: Introduction of opinion as correct
   <voice>: *Is there going to be closer scrutiny of briefs and legal papers filed in this case, in the future, to avoid the kind of opportunities that this—*
   <turn>: *Look, lawyers have to file legal arguments in front of courts and that happens a lot in our government.*

Type G: Questions
1. *Well, do you dispute that he was looking for access and looking for favors in return?*
2. *Is it true that she is looking for a permanent family vacation home here on this off-shore island?*
3. *Is there any concern about how the federal government will . . . ?*

tool. Its content becomes the input that helps students to manage the various connections they uncover as they work through data illustrating the ties between function and register, function and genre. With the exception of Carter and McCarthy's 1988 transcript-based textbook, the overall format of the input I am suggesting is quite distinct from that found in the textbooks I surveyed. First, and most obviously, the raw number of variants the students are being given to work with is higher, and because we are working from data of actual usage, it is guaranteed that the selection of the variants will be among the most widely used. Moreover, the variants are shown to be functional in a range of genres, and the number of concordance lines can be increased to reveal more of the surrounding text so that genre-specific information is made more explicit, if necessary. Also, since the information is being extracted from actual data, any categorizations the students make will be more accurate than what would come from intuition-based information, better preparing students to deal with native speakers.

As the results of my corpus analysis on disagreement reveal, corpora not only illustrate the ubiquity of the lexical phrase in natural discourse but challenge our intuitions about the nature of language. My search list of disagreement phrases is by no means complete but serves as a starting point into this area of study. From it, I have been able to begin to answer the question of how disagreement is marked in actual usage in genre-specific contexts. A survey of additional corpora will be useful in order to add to the list and recognize new strategy types. Research extending into various paralanguage phenomena, including the use of hesitation forms, pauses, and coughing as expressions of disagreement, might also be useful, albeit a challenge to collect, since such phenomena are not always marked in corpora.

The lexical approach emphasizes the importance of classroom input and activities that reflect "the pervasive role that ritualization plays in language behaviour" (Nattinger and DeCarrico 1992, 1) and resemble the natural patterns of language as much as possible. If language description is destined to become more concerned with empirical data and actual pattern usage than with intuitions (cf. Biber 1996), it should be expected that so must the method by which language patterns are taught to ESL students. While the present study focused exclusively on patterns of disagreement, multitudes of conversational routines can be presented to students in a lexically based framework. Introducing the L2 instructor to the value of corpora for identifying and exploring lexical phrase patterning is one way to help teachers promote accuracy in their lessons and provide students with input that most closely resembles actual usage in a variety of genres.

Appendix: Alphabetical List of Disagreement Markers Arbitrarily Selected for Corpus Study, with Corpus Examples

absurd	I mean, to me, that's *absurd,* never works. (FM)
against X	I was very *against* our involvement . . . (SWB)
bogus	That claim is *bogus.* (WH)
but see	*But see,* the one difference with the . . . (FM)
concern	And my *concerns* center around some things . . . (FM) Note: Out of 304 hits in the WH, only 29 were statements using *concern,* but the majority were questions, for example, "Do you share a *concern* that the Fed might step in again . . . ?"
crazy	We were not too *crazy* about number 27. (FM)
disagree	I *disagree* with your premise. (WH)
disturb	I'm *disturbed* by a country that attempts to . . . (SWB) Note: In the WH there were three cases of *disturbed* used in questions, for example, "But is the White House *disturbed* by its findings?"
don't agree	I, I *don't agree* with that at all. (SWB)
don't believe X	I *don't believe* that's correct. (FM)
don't buy X	I *don't buy* the argument that I can't understand. (FM) Note: In the WH, there were 3 cases of *buy* used in questions, for example, "Do you *buy* into any of those characterizations?"
don't see X	I *don't see* what the big deal is . . . (SWB)
don't think X	I *don't think* that Ed has made a compelling case to begin with. (FM)
don't understand	I *don't understand* why they charge you . . . (SWB)
give me a break	Oh, good grief. *Give me a break.* (SWB)
idea	I think that's a terrible *idea.* (SWB)
look	*Look,* this really borders on being outrageous . . . (WH)
not convinced	And I'm *not convinced* that any of them work a hundred percent. (SWB)
oppose X	We strongly *oppose* any effort to . . . (WH)
problem	Well, the *problem* is it's hard to define exactly . . . (FM)
ridiculous	You know, don't be *ridiculous.* (WH)
right but	*Right. But* this sentence isn't about that. (FM)

that's not X	*That's not* a fair characterization at all. (WH)
thing	The *thing* is if you're going to introduce those . . . (FM)
trouble	I really have *trouble* with that adjective there. (FM)
uncomfortable	There's a couple of things I'm *uncomfortable* with. (FM)
wait a minute	Well, *wait a minute.* Dee Dee, nobody is even talking about the . . . (WH)
well, no	*Well, no.* I'm trying to say where I think we . . . (FM)
wrong	That's where you're *wrong.* (FM)
yes but	*Yes, but* if a process that had credibility could . . . (WH)

Notes

My sincere appreciation goes to Michael Barlow for his insightful comments on earlier drafts of this chapter.

1. For more discussion on conversational patterns in English, see Aijmer 1996; McCarthy 1988.
2. The only way to initiate a study like this is to begin with personal intuitions about disagreement. Presumably, even if I was able to use a corpus that provided markups indicating disagreement markers, the original author would have had to proceed in the same manner as I have.
3. Sentence-initial *actually*, *but*, and *well* (except *well, no*) were omitted from the analysis. This decision was made based on the idea that since these items often function as discourse markers (cf. Helt 1997), it is generally difficult to determine if they remain discursive or whether they indicate disagreement in cases where they occur sequentially with (other) markers of disagreement, as in "Well, the problem with that . . ." (SWB). This issue is reserved for future study.

   Each occurrence of a disagreement marker was recorded separately, regardless of whether the speaker used more than one marker sequentially. This sequential patterning, while outside the scope of this chapter, merits attention in future research. In particular, it would be interesting to study which marker, if any, signals a stronger sense of disagreement.

References

Aijmer, K. 1996. *Conversational Routines in English: Convention and Creativity.* New York: Addison Wesley Longman.

Azar, B. 1989. *Understanding and Using English Grammar.* 2d ed. Englewood Cliffs, NJ: Prentice-Hall.

Barlow, M. 1998. *CSPAE* (Corpus of Spoken Professional American English). Houston: Athelstan.

Barnard, R., and J. Cady. 1992. *Business Venture 1*. Oxford: Oxford University Press.

Biber, D. 1996. Investigating Language Use through Corpus-Based Analyses. *International Journal of Corpus Linguistics* 1, no. 2:171–97.

Carter, R., and M. McCarthy, eds. 1988. *Vocabulary and Language Teaching*. London: Longman Group.

———. 1997. *Exploring Spoken English*. Cambridge: Cambridge University Press.

Hakuta, K. 1976. Becoming Bilingual: A Case Study of a Japanese Child Learning English. *Language Learning* 26:321–51.

Helt, M. 1997. A Corpus-Based Analysis of *Well, Actually,* and *Like*. Ph.D. diss., Northern Arizona University.

Kozyrev, J. 1998. *Talk It Up! Oral Communication for the Real World*. New York: Houghton Mifflin.

Lewis, M. 1993. *The Lexical Approach*. Hove, UK: Language Teaching Publications.

Linguistic Data Consortium. 1994. Switchboard Transcripts. University of Pennsylvania. <http://morph.ldc.upenn.edu> (May 1, 2000).

McCarthy, M. 1988. Some Vocabulary Patterns in Conversation. In *Vocabulary and Language Teaching,* ed. R. Carter and M. McCarthy, 181–200. London: Longman Group.

McKay, I. 1993. *Beginning Interactive Grammar: Activities and Exercises*. Boston: Heinle and Heinle.

Nattinger, J., and J. DeCarrico. 1992. *Lexical Phrases and Language Teaching*. Oxford: Oxford University Press.

Pawley, A., and F. Syder. 1983. Two Puzzles for Linguistic Theory: Nativelike Selection and Nativelike Fluency. In *Language and Communication,* ed. J. Richards and R. Schmidt, 191–226. London: Longman.

Richards, J., J. Hull, and S. Proctor. 1990. *Interchange: English for International Communication*. Cambridge: Cambridge University Press.

Williams, M. 1988. Language Taught for Meetings and Language Used in Meetings: Is There Anything in Common? *Applied Linguistics* 9, no. 1:45–58.

Writing Development among Elementary Students: Corpus-Based Perspectives

Randi Reppen
Northern Arizona University

Over the last thirty years, many researchers have studied writing development from a number of perspectives. Much of the research on writing development has focused on young children as they move into the school world. Most of these studies have used a case-study approach to discover the changes that happen as a child moves from pictures to written language (e.g., Bissex 1980; Dyson 1989; Edelsky 1986). Studies that have examined the writing of school-age children have taken several approaches. Some of these studies have compared the effect of different writing tasks, such as narrative or exposition (e.g., Crowhurst 1983, 1987, 1990; Martin 1985; McCutchen 1987). Some studies have explored the impact of writing in a second language (e.g., Carlisle 1983; McClure and Pratt 1988). There have also been a few longitudinal studies that collected student writing samples at different grade levels (Hunt 1965; Loban 1976). However, to date, there have been few empirically based studies of writing development that have included both a large number of texts and a large number of linguistic features.

This chapter will begin to close some of that gap by reporting on the results of a corpus-based study investigating the writing development of third- and sixth-grade students—both first and second language learners (L1 English and L1 Navajo). This investigation involves the use of multi-dimensional analysis (Biber 1988, 1995) to provide a picture of writing development across the grades and language groups. The study relies on the use of a corpora and corpus-based techniques (Biber, Conrad, and Reppen 1998), allowing us to look empirically at the linguistic changes that take place between third and sixth grade for these groups of students from two different first languages. However, before any claims about writing development can be made, it is necessary to establish an anchor against which development can be measured. This is accomplished through the construction and multi-dimensional analysis of a corpus of fifth-grade language. This analysis is used to construct a model of student language that will serve as an anchor for comparing the changes that take place in the writing of third and sixth grade for the L1 English and L1 Navajo students.

Description of the Corpus

Unlike adult language, very few corpora of children's written or spoken language exist. As a result, the first step for this analysis was to construct the CESSW (Corpus of Elementary Student Speech and Writing). This corpus was designed to be a representative collection of fifth-grade student language.

The corpus consists of two parts (spoken and written). The written material comes from three sources: textbooks and fiction produced for students (MacWhinney 1991; Reppen 1994) and in-class essays written by students (Reppen 1994). The oral material is a subset of spoken texts from the CHILDES project (MacWhinney 1991). See table 1 for a detailed description of the corpus.

The selection of fifth-grade textbooks encompasses a variety of subjects. These texts were scanned and edited before being tagged for linguistic features. The fiction texts consist of books that fifth graders commonly read. This was determined through an informal survey of teachers throughout the state of Arizona and by looking at lists of recommended reading (Reppen 1994). The fiction texts are a subset of the Cornell corpus (Hayes 1988).

The in-class essays are a subset from the ACESW (Arizona Corpus of Elementary Student Writing) constructed by Reppen and Grabe over a six-year period. This principled text collection from grades 3 through 6 in classrooms throughout the state of Arizona (Reppen 1994) consists of writing from students in participating classes responding to a particular prompt each month (see appendix). Since all the classes wrote on the same prompts, comparisons across grades and student groups are controlled for the influence of task on student writing. All of the texts were entered as ASCII texts, edited to

TABLE 1. Corpus of Fifth-Grade Student Language

	Number of Texts	Approximate Number of Words
Texts published for children		
Basal readers	23	5,000
Science textbooks	25	5,000
Social studies textbooks	24	5,000
Children's fiction	53	16,000
Texts written by children		
Student writing	179	14,000
Texts spoken by children		
Interaction	21	9,000
Monologue	14	8,000
Total	339	62,000

Sources:
Basal readers: Holt; HBJ; Ginn; Scott Foresman; Houghton Mifflin.
Science textbooks: Holt; Heath; HBJ; Scott Foresman; Silver Burdett
Social studies textbooks: American Book Co.; Holt; Houghton Mifflin; Macmillan (1978 and 1982).
Children's fiction: Cornell Corpus (Hayes 1988) from CHILDES.
Student writing: Pinedale and Sundance fifth-grade students (only text > 60 words).
Spoken texts: Carterette and Jones 1974; Hicks 1990 (from CHILDES).

standardize spelling, then tagged with an interactive tagging program developed by Biber (1988). This tagging program was used to tag all the texts in this study (see Biber, Conrad, and Reppen 1998 for more details). In this portion of the study, all texts written by fifth-grade native English speakers and over 60 words in length were selected from the corpus for analysis.[1]

The spoken corpus is from two studies included in the CHILDES project (MacWhinney 1991). The first set of spoken texts are from Hicks 1990. Students performed various types of retellings after watching a silent movie *(The Red Balloon)*. These retellings were categorized as monologues, since the students were not interacting with another speaker but rather retelling a story. The second portion of the spoken corpus is made up of texts from the Carterette and Jones 1974 study. These are transcribed dialogues of students sitting around a table and chatting about various topics. Only texts produced by students in the fifth-grade age range (10 to 11 years old) were selected for the present analysis. Even though this corpus does not include certain types of student language (e.g., notes, group work), it does reflect typical student language, since the parts that are not represented account for only a very small portion of student language.

Description of the Multi-dimensional Study

The corpus described in the previous section (which consists entirely of texts produced by or for fifth graders) was analyzed using a multidimensional approach (Biber 1988). After the corpus was tagged for over 65 linguistic features and interactively edited (see Biber, Conrad, and Reppen 1998 for more details), a factor analysis was performed. Factor analysis is a statistical procedure that allows us to see what linguistic features co-occur (see table 2). In this study, five factors were identified. These factors (or groups of co-occurring features) were then interpreted based on both previous research and the distribution of texts along the factor. Once the factor is interpreted and assigned a label, it is called a dimension. Each of the five dimensions were studied to determine the best explanation of the features and of the distribution of texts along the dimension. The five dimensions that were identified were assigned the following labels:

> Dimension 1: Edited informational discourse versus on-line informational discourse
> Dimension 2: Lexically elaborated narrative versus nonnarrative
> Dimension 3: Involved personal discourse versus uninvolved nonpersonal discourse
> Dimension 4: Projected scenario
> Dimension 5: Other-directed idea justification/explanation

Table 2 shows the groups of co-occurring linguistic features for each of the five factors. These linguistic features also occur in complementary distribution. In other words, when you have a high number of a set of features from one end of a factor, you tend to have few features from the other end of that factor. For example, if a text had a high number of nouns, long words, and many nominalizations, all features associated with the upper end of factor 1, then that text would tend to have an absence of the features associated with the opposite end of factor 1—initial *and*s, sentence initial non-*and*s (e.g., *then*), and time adverbials. A detailed example of this with text excerpts is provided later in this section.

TABLE 2. Summary of the Linguistic Features for Each Factor in the Model of Student Language

Factor 1		Factor 3	
Nouns	.719	Causal subordination	.501
Word length	.701	*That* deletion	.467
Nominalizations	.558	Private verbs	.447
Passives	.427	(Present-tense	.443)
Attributive adjectives	.423	Contractions	.438
Prepositions	.415	*Do* as pro-verb	.402
(Type/Token ratio	.367)	(First-person pronouns	.331)
(Once-occurring words	.330)	(Necessity modals	.323)
		(General emphatics	.322)
Initial *ands*	−.503		
Other initial words	−.483	(Time adverbials	−.405)
Time adverbials	−.453		
Third person pronouns	−.413		
(Adverbials	−.327)	Factor 4	
(*It* pronouns	−.323)	Prediction modals	.971
(First-person pronouns	−.320)	*Be* as main verb	.814
(Participials	−.305)		
		No negative features	
Factor 2		Factor 5	
Once-occurring words	.704	Second-person pronouns	.883
Type/token ratio	.671	Conditional subordination	.623
Past tense	.670	Possibility modals	.353
Public verbs	.666	(First person pronouns	−.305)
(Perfect aspect	.335)		
(Verb complements	.320)		
Present-tense verbs	−.540		
Infinitives	−.376		

Note: Features in parentheses are not used to compute dimension scores.

Although five dimensions were identified, due to space constraints, this study will focus on dimension 1, edited informational discourse versus on-line informational discourse. This dimension represents a literate/oral continuum that will provide a useful platform for exploring writing development and for comparing student texts across grades and L1 backgrounds. Figure 1 shows the distribution of texts along dimension 1.

From the distribution of texts, it is clear to see that the upper end of dimension 1 represents highly informational and edited language.

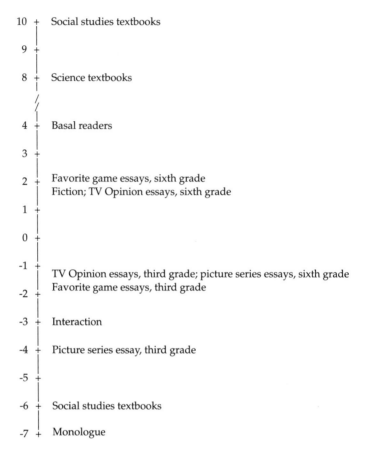

Edited Informational Discourse

```
10  +   Social studies textbooks
         |
 9  +
         |
 8  +   Science textbooks
         |
       /
      /|
 4  +   Basal readers
         |
 3  +
         |
 2  +   Favorite game essays, sixth grade
         |   Fiction; TV Opinion essays, sixth grade
 1  +
         |
 0  +
         |
-1  +
         |   TV Opinion essays, third grade; picture series essays, sixth grade
-2  +   Favorite game essays, third grade
         |
-3  +   Interaction
         |
-4  +   Picture series essay, third grade
         |
-5  +
         |
-6  +   Social studies textbooks
         |
-7  +   Monologue
```

On-line Informational Discourse

Fig. 1. Distribution of texts along dimension 1

The texts in the upper portion of the dimension are social studies and science textbooks. These textbooks might also serve as models of literacy. The spoken and written texts that were produced by the students fall onto the lower end of dimension 1.

Texts at the upper portion of dimension 1 are high in the features from the positive or upper end of dimension 1 (e.g., many nouns, long words, passives). Texts at the other end of dimension have few of these features and a high number of negative features—the features that occur below the dashed line in table 2 (e.g., initial *and*s, third-person pronouns). As I mentioned already, the distribution of features along the dimensions tend to be complimentary, so that when you have high frequencies of features associated with one end of a dimension, you have relatively low frequencies of features associated with the other end of the dimension. The following two text samples illustrate this.

Text sample 1: Social studies textbook (fifth grade)

Slavery in the Americas grew out of a need
for cheap labor. The large farms or plantations
that **had been founded** in the Americas needed
many workers. At first the Spanish tried to
force American Indians into slavery. When this
did not work *they* brought slaves from Africa.
By 1600, there were 40,000 Black slaves in Spanish
America. In 1619 the first Africans **were brought**
to English settlements in America.

Text sample 2: Student essay (fifth grade; L1 English)

One day some kids went to a circus. *And* a clown
was catching plates. *And he* did not drop one.
And then the kids put up the plates where *they*
belonged. *And* then the kid thought *he* could do it.
but he was not as good as the clown who did it.
These were *his* mom's plates. *And he* tried. *He* got
it going. *And* then *he* dropped *them*. *And they* all
broke. *His* mom came in. *She* was very mad.

Text sample 1, the excerpt from the social studies book, has many of the positive features associated with dimension 1, including nouns (e.g., "Americas," "slaves," "Africa," "settlements"), many long words, two passives (in bold), and one third-person pronoun (in italics). However, text sample 2, the student essay, has a low frequency of features associated with the positive end of dimension 1. There are relatively few nouns, few long words, and no passives. The student essay has a high frequency of features from the lower end of dimension 1, such as 12 third-person pronouns (in italics) and 7 sentence initial *and*s. These texts provide a nice example of the complimentary distribution of linguistic features at the ends of a dimension. Along dimension 1, these suites of linguistic features work together to create texts that are either more literate and edited or more oral in nature. When we read these two text samples aloud, the student essay has a more "oral" flavor, while the social studies text sample sounds like written text. From the placement of the texts along dimension 1, we see that student essays responding to a picture series are toward the lower end of dimension 1, while social studies textbooks actually define the upper end of dimension 1.

Student Writing Development and L1 Variation

Using dimension 1 as an anchor, we can compare the texts of third- and sixth-grade students to explore the linguistic changes that take place between third and sixth grade for both L1 English speakers and L1 Navajo speakers. A subset of the ACESW was used in this portion of the study. The essays come from four different classes: two third-grade and two sixth-grade classes, with one class in each grade being L1 English and the other being L1 Navajo. These essays were written and collected as part of the same corpus project described earlier in this chapter.

From the nine months of essays that the students wrote, three sets of student essays are plotted on the figure of dimension 1. All of the student writing in the ACESW is from in-class writing that was collected each month in response to specific writing prompts (for further details on the collection of the writing, see Reppen 1994; Biber, Conrad, and Reppen 1998). The three sets of essays selected for this analysis represent both essays collected throughout the academic year (i.e., October, December, and May) and the range of writing assignments that students are often asked to do in school. The topics and tasks of the selected essays follow. Full descriptions of the writing prompts are provided in the appendix.

Topics and Tasks

TV: Should kids watch a lot of TV? Why or why not?
Task: taking a stand/position

Game: Choose your favorite game or sport. Describe how to play your game or sport to someone who has not played it.
Task: explanation

Picture: Write about what is happening in the picture series. Write
so that someone who has not seen the pictures will know what
happened.
Task: description

To investigate the question of writing development from third
through sixth grade across the two language groups, the dimension 1
scores of the three essay tasks are plotted for the third-and sixth-grade
students according to their L1 (figs. 2 and 3). In figure 3, the picture
task for the third-grade students could not be plotted due to the small
amount of writing that the task elicited. As mentioned at the beginning of this chapter, only texts of 60 or more words could be analyzed
using the multi-dimensional approach.

Both figures 2 and 3 indicate that between third and sixth grade,
there are major changes in the way that students use language. The
upward lines between the third-grade scores and the sixth-grade
scores show that the students' writing is moving toward the upper
end of dimension 1—toward literate forms and away from spoken
forms. From third to sixth grade, the L1 Navajo speakers show
marked changes on the TV task. This task involves taking a position
and defending it. The difference between third- and sixth-grade
essays for the L1 Navajo speakers on this task demonstrates a remarkable change in the linguistic resources that are used. Although the L1
Navajo speakers make the greatest changes as measured by dimension 1, the essays of the sixth-grade students are still in the lower half
of dimension 1. This indicates that there are still many features associated with on-line, nonedited texts.

The three text samples below are from third- and sixth-grade student essays responding to the TV prompt. Text samples 3 and 4 are
from L1 Navajo students, while text sample 5 is from a sixth-grade L1
English speaker.

Text sample 3: Student #1823 (third grade; L1 Navajo)

Do you think kids watch too much TV? Yes because
they have a TV. They like to watch TV all the time. They
like to watch too much TV a lot. Kids just like to watch TV.

Text sample 4: Student #2296 (sixth grade; L1 Navajo)

If you watch TV too much you can get your brain crazy.
And you will be doing drugs and wearing short clothes.

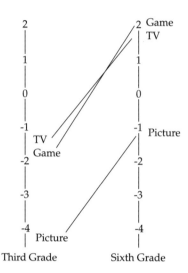

Fig. 2. Dimension 1 scores of L1 English for three writing tasks

When you go to school you won't have the brain to
think after watching all those scary movies. But at the same
time it can be good because you can learn a lot like news, 911,
and good movies that have no fighting, killing, and sex. Watching
the
good movies is good. But don't watch too much of violence.

Text sample 5: Student #4016 (sixth grade; L1 English)

Do you know that the average kid spends at least 5 hours in front
of the television each day. I don't think kids should watch a lot of
TV because it can cause bad eyesight. And it can get as bad as los-
ing the chance of having a baby because it can damage or effect
the ovaries in your body. If watching television many hours a day
is a habit, then you don't take the time to do outdoor activities and
other things besides TV.

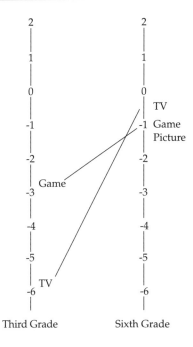

Fig. 3. Dimension 1 scores of L1 Navajo for three writing tasks

Although a simple reading of these three texts gives the reader a sense of the differences that exist among them, it is useful to quantify some of these differences in relation to dimension 1. The text written by the third-grade student is short compared to that of the texts by the sixth-grade students; the sentences (i.e., t-units) are also short and are not complex. In contrast, both sixth-grade students use several complex sentences. The L1 Navajo speaker uses both complex and simple sentences in her essay, while the L1 English speaker uses no simple sentences in her essay. Both sixth-grade essays make use of a greater variety of words than does the third-grade student and therefore have a higher type/token ratio. They also have a higher density of nouns and use longer words, attributive adjectives (e.g., "*average* kid," "*scary* movies"), and prepositions to a greater degree. These text samples highlight some of the differences that are found between third- and sixth-grade writers and also some of the differences that are found between the L1 English and L1 Navajo texts.

Conclusion

This study illustrates how using a corpus-based approach and analysis of a principled collection of texts provides more generalizable information about the writing development of both L1 and L2 English speakers. Through the creation of a multi-dimensional model of student language at a fifth-grade level, an anchor is provided against which developmental changes in other grades can be measured.

From this chapter, we see that several developmental changes take place from third to sixth grade, as students move closer to more literate uses of language in their writing. The lexical variety and the complexity of written constructions are areas that show major developmental changes between these grades. The degree of linguistic development between the L1 English and L1 Navajo students also provides interesting information about the differences between L1 and L2 speakers. Further study of different groups of students from different L1 backgrounds will provide a more complete picture of the linguistic development of L2 English students.

Many aspects of writing development can be productively explored through the use of a corpus of student writing. As the information from the studies of these aspects becomes available, the picture of writing development will be more accurate, helping teachers and materials writers become more effective in moving toward realistic goals as they guide students toward literacy.

Appendix: Student Writing Prompts and Teacher Brainstorming Activities

September
You can be any famous person: Describe who you would be.

Brainstorm: Talk about famous people (historical, scientific, popular, etc). List some on the board if you desire. Ask: "What would your life be like if you were_____?"

October
Should kids watch a lot of TV? Why or why not?

Brainstorm: Discuss how much TV students watch.
Talk about different types of shows (cartoons, talk shows, news, movies). What are some advantages and disadvantages of watching a lot of TV?

November
What will you do for Thanksgiving?

Brainstorm: Discuss different Thanksgiving plans and different traditions.

December
Choose your favorite game or sport. Describe how to play your game or sport to someone who has not played it.

Brainstorm: List games or sports on the board. Discuss how to describe a game/sport that someone has not played.

January
Explain what the ideal school would be like. How would this ideal school be similar or different to the school you are in?

Brainstorm: List what you like about your school. What would you include in your ideal school? What else would you put in your ideal school?

February
You have traveled back 200 years in a time machine. What did you see? Tell a story about what happened?

Brainstorm: Discuss what a time machine is. Where can you go in a time machine? List some places that students would like to go if they had a time machine. Relate to social studies and what it was like 200 years ago. Emphasize this is 200 years back, not "back to the future."

March
Describe your best friend.

Brainstorm: What is a good friend? How do you decide who is your friend? Discuss ways to describe friends (e.g., physical characteristics, inner qualities).

April
What is your favorite subject and why? What is your least favorite subject and why? Be sure to say why you like or do not like the subjects.

Brainstorm: No preactivity. Remind students that there are no right or wrong answers.

May
Write about what is happening in the picture series. Write so that someone who has not seen the pictures will know what happened.

Brainstorm: Discuss how to write so that people who do not see something can understand what happened. Relate it to a news report. If possible, read a news article to the class. Discuss what the students understood? What did they "see"?

Note

1. Texts need to be at least 60 words in length to provide stability for the statistical procedures that are used in the factor analysis.

References

Biber, D. 1988. *Variation across Speech and Writing.* New York: Cambridge University Press.

Biber, D. 1995. *Dimensions of Register Variation.* New York: Cambridge University Press.

Biber, D., S. Conrad, and R. Reppen. 1998. *Corpus Linguistics: Exploring Language Structure and Use.* Cambridge: Cambridge University Press.

Bissex, G. 1980. *Gyns at Work.* Cambridge: Harvard University Press.

Carlisle, R. 1983. The Writing of Anglo and Hispanic Elementary School Students in Bilingual, Submersion, and Regular Programs. *Studies in Second Language Acquisition* 11:257–80.

Carterette, E., and M. Jones. 1974. *Informal Speech: Alphabetic and Phonemic Texts with Analyses and Tables.* Berkeley: University of California Press.

Crowhurst, M. 1983. Persuasive Writing at Grades 5, 7, and 11: A Cognitive-Developmental Perspective. Report CS-207719. Paper presented at the annual meeting of the American Educational Research Association, Montreal, Canada. ERIC Document Reproduction Service no. ED 230 977.

———. 1987. Cohesion in Argument and Narration at Three Grade Levels. *Research in the Teaching of English* 21:185–201.

———. 1990. The Development of Persuasive/Argumentative Writing. In *Developing Discourse Practices in Adolescence and Adulthood,* ed. R. Beach and S. Hynds, 200–223. Norwood, NJ: Ablex.

Dyson, A. 1989. *Multiple Worlds of Child Writers.* New York: Teachers College.

Edelsky, C. 1986. *Writing in a Bilingual Program: Habia una vez.* Norwood, NJ: Ablex.

Hayes, D. 1988. Speaking and Writing: Distinct Patterns of Word Choice. Journal of Memory and Language 27:572–85.

Hicks, D. 1990. Kinds of Texts: Narrative Genre Skills among Two Communities. In *Developing Narrative Structure,* ed. A. McCabe and C. Peterson, 55–87. Hillsdale, NJ: Lawrence Erlbaum.

Hunt, K. 1965. *Grammatical Structures Written at Three Grade Levels.* Research Report 3. Urbana, IL: NCTE (National Council of Teachers of English).

Loban, W. 1976. *Language Development: Kindergarten through Grade Twelve.* Research Report 18. Urbana, IL: NCTE (National Council of Teachers of English).

MacWhinney, B. 1991. *The CHILDES Project.* Hillsdale, NJ: Lawrence Erlbaum.

Martin, J. R. 1985. *Factual Writing: Exploring and Challenging Social Reality.* Oxford: Oxford University Press.

McClure, E., and E. Pratt. 1988. The Development of Expression of Temporality in Written English Narratives of Monolingual American and Bilingual Mexican Pupils. *World Englishes* 7, no. 2:197–210.

McCutchen, D. 1987. Children's Discourse Skill: Form and Modality Requirements of Schooled Writing. *Discourse Processes* 10:267–86.

Reppen, R. 1994. Variation in Elementary Student Language: A Multi-Dimensional Perspective. Ph.D. diss., Northern Arizona University.

Glossary for Part I

annotation. A type of **markup** that usually refers to the linguistic (as opposed to structural) information added to a **corpus** to enhance its usefulness for linguistic analysis. A corpus may be annotated manually or automatically; in the latter case, the output usually needs to be corrected or checked for accuracy. The most common type of corpus annotation is the addition of *part-of-speech* **tags,** followed by *syntactic* annotation, or **parsing.** *Semantic, anaphoric,* and *prosodic* annotation are less common, and *discoursal,* or *pragmatic,* annotation is rare.

ASCII (American Standard Code for Information Exchange). An international standard for the storage and transfer of characters. An ASCII file is a plain text file consisting of characters conforming to this standard.

base tag set. In the **TEI** conventions, this refers to the minimum set of required **tags** used for a particular kind of text (e.g., prose, poetry, drama, speech).

batch concordance program. A **concordance program** that carries out its searches on the **raw text** of an entire set of files at one time, without continuous interaction with the user.

batch file. A computer file that contains instructions for the computer to execute without further interaction with the user.

collocation. Combinations of two or more words that commonly occur together, either adjacent to or in proximity to each other.

command language. A formal language consisting of sets of commands or instructions that can be issued to an operating system or application program.

concordance program. A program designed for a range of text analysis tasks, including executing a word or pattern search and presenting a list of all instances (tokens) of a specified word within a certain amount of surrounding context. Also called *concordancers.*

corpus. Loosely, any body of texts; most commonly, a collection of machine-readable texts compiled according to some set of principled criteria and provided with some kind of **markup** or **annotation.**

data-driven learning. Term used in language teaching to refer to the use of tasks that encourage learners to explore a **corpus** or subcorpus for the purpose of discovering generalizations about word or phrase meanings or about usage patterns, such as common **collocations.**

DTD (document type definition). A file that is the heart of **SGML,** the DTD is a kind of template that describes the structure of a set of related documents and provides a hierarchical framework for the **elements** that constitute those documents. A DTD also specifies rules for the relationships between elements that help ensure that related documents have a consistent, logical structure.

element. A textual unit or structural component of a text in **SGML** (e.g., title, chapter, paragraph, utterance, pause, etc.), delimited by a **tag** or set of tags surrounding the content.

encoding. The process of inserting codes into a document, or the codes used; often used interchangeably with **markup.**

encoding scheme. The conventions and set of codes used for a particular text or **corpus,** specifying exactly what information is to be encoded, how the structural **elements** are defined, and what the **tags** look like.

header. The beginning section of a text document (preceding the body of the text) that contains relevant descriptive information about the document contents. See also **metadata.**

HTML (Hypertext Markup Language). The markup language most commonly used to encode Web pages; a subset of **SGML.**

index. A table providing fast access to a collection of data items by listing features used to look up data items in a way suitable for fast search. In the context of a **corpus,** an index is the entire set of texts converted into such a database form.

interactive text analysis program. A computer program that retrieves information from a text or **corpus,** requires interaction with a user to accomplish its tasks, and operates on an **index** that has been built from the corpus files.

KWIC (key word in context). A format for displaying the results of a search in which the search word is lined up in the middle of the screen or page with a certain amount of context shown to the left and right.

markup. Everything in a document that is not content. *Descriptive* markup is based on the structure of a document and identifies **elements** within that structure, using codes that describe what the elements are, not how they appear. The process of inserting markup into a document is often called **encoding.** Linguistic information, such as a *part-of-speech* **tag,** is sometimes referred to as markup but more commonly as **annotation.**

metadata. Data that give information about other data, such as the information provided in the **header** of a document characterizing relevant aspects of the document contents (e.g., author, subject, speakers, date of publication, etc.) and serving as an aid for users in accessing parts of the data of interest.

modular system. A set of related computer programs consisting of individual modules or applications that can be interlinked or used separately.

off-line browser. A browser designed for viewing **HTML** and Web image files without being continuously connected to the Internet, by recording Web sites and storing them locally for later viewing.

parsed. Refers to a **corpus** that has been annotated with syntactic information; often called a *treebank*.

parser. A tool or program used for syntactic **annotation**. A parser assigns a phrase marker, usually in the form of a labeled bracket, to the grammatical constituents of each sentence.

query. A request or interrogation of a database for information retrieval that allows users to count, sum, and list selected records or data items contained in it.

raw text. Text that has not undergone any additional conversions, translation, or processing by a computer.

regular expression. Programming constructs used to search for a string or pattern of characters in texts by specifying the rules for the set of possible strings that the program user wants to match. For example, the regular expression *wom*n* will find the words *woman* and *women,* while *g[eo]t** will find *get, gets, getting, got, gotten.*

search parameter. Any value, from the available options supported by the **markup** of the **corpus,** chosen by the user to customize a search for a particular purpose: for example, any speaker or author variable, text type variable, or text segment.

SGML (Standard Generalized Markup Language). An internationally recognized standard for the description of electronic texts; a generic **markup** language that defines a standard method and format for describing the structure of a document and inserting descriptive markup. SGML texts are comprised of plain **ASCII** text, combined with items delineated by angle brackets, called **tags,** that define or enclose structural **elements.**

SGML-conformant markup. Any **encoding** scheme that uses **tags** and other **markup** conventions in accordance with the methods and format standards defined for SGML.

tag. A code or label associated with a word or other unit of text and providing information about the word or unit of text. A tag can mark the beginning and end of each part of a structural unit of text or can in itself comprise an **element** of the document structure (e.g., the tag "<PAUSE>"). Other tags, called *part-of-speech* tags, provide grammatical information about the word. The latter are usually attached to the end of the word and preceded by an underscore, while the most common convention for separating other kinds of tags from the document contents is to enclose them in angle brackets.

tagged. Refers to a **corpus** that has been **annotated** with *part-of-speech* **tags.**

tagger. A computer program used for **annotating** text that automatically assigns *part-of-speech* **tags** or other grammatical category tags to each word of a text or batch of texts. Taggers use a lexicon of words with their possible parts of speech combined with a set of rules produced by a probabilistic model to assign each tag. Most current taggers are between 94 and 97 percent accurate on written texts and considerably less so on spoken texts, therefore usually requiring some manual or interactive correction after the tagger is run.

tag set. The entire set of **tags** used in a particular **corpus** for structural **markup** or *part-of-speech* **annotation.**

TEI (Text Encoding Initiative). An international project to develop guidelines for the preparation and interchange of electronic texts for scholarly research. The main objective of the TEI was to define standardized **encoding** practices so that electronic texts could be both more universal and more versatile.

text retrieval program. Any program, including **concordancers,** used for text analysis functions, such as searching, retrieving, sorting, and so on.

Sources Consulted

ArborText, Inc. 1995. *Getting Started with SGML: A Guide to the Standard Generalized Markup Language and Its Role in Information Management.* White Paper. <http://www.arbortext.com/Think_Tank/SGML_Resources/Getting_Started_with_SGML/getting_started_with_sgml.html> (May 20, 2000).

UCREL [University Centre for Computer Corpus Research on Language]. 1999. "Corpus Annotation." <http://www.comp.lancs.ac.uk/computing/research/ucrel/annotation.html> (May 20, 2000).

Systematic Dictionary of Corpus Linguistics. <http://donelaitis.vdu.lt/pub-likacijos/SDoCL.htm> (May 20, 2000).

TEI Guidelines for Electronic Text Encoding and Interchange (TEI P3). 2000. <http://www.hti.umich.edu/docs/TEI/> (May 20, 2000).

University of Essex, W3-Corpora Project. 1998. *Corpus Linguistics, Glossary.* <http://clwww.essex.ac.uk/w3c/corpus_ling/content/glossary.html> (May 20, 2000).

Contributors

Douglas Biber is a professor of applied linguistics in the Department of English at Northern Arizona University. He has written extensively on the use of research methods in corpus linguistics to investigate language variation and the characteristics of spoken and written registers. He is coauthor of *Corpus Linguistics: Investigating Language Structure and Use* with Randi Reppen and Susan Conrad.

Stephanie Burdine is a Ph.D. student in linguistics at Rice University. She has conducted various studies in sociolinguistics, language variation, and second language learning using data from primarily spoken French and English corpora.

Victoria Clark is a Ph.D. student in applied linguistics at Northern Arizona University. During study for her M.A. in TESL at NAU, she was involved in the collection of the TOEFL 2000 Corpus of Spoken and Written Academic English funded by the Education Testing Service. Her current focus is writing computer programs for corpus analysis and developing corpus-based language teaching materials.

Mark Davies is an associate professor of Spanish linguistics in the Department of Foreign Languages at Illinois State University. He has created what are to date some of the largest corpora of both historical Spanish and Portuguese and modern Spanish and Portuguese and has used these multimillion-word corpora to research historical change and dialectal and register variation in Spanish and Portuguese.

Susan Hockey is a professor of library and information studies in the School of Library, Archive, and Information Studies at University College, London. Her research centers on markup systems and tools for the analysis of literary and linguistic texts.

Aaron Lawson received his Ph.D. from the Department of Romance Studies at Cornell University in 2000 and is currently a linguistic analyst at TextWise Labs in Syracuse, New York. He has worked in corpus linguistics since 1996 and served as director of Cornell's Modern Languages Corpus project from 1997 to 2000.

Bonnie Malczewski received her B.A. in linguistics from the University of Michigan in 1999. She worked on the Michigan Corpus of Academic Spoken English from January until December of 1999.

Anna Mauranen is a professor of English in the Department of English Philology at the University of Tampere, Finland. She has extensive experience with the Finnish-English Contrastive Corpus and has been director of the Finnish Translation Corpus since 1997 and a consultant for the Michigan Corpus of Academic Spoken English since 1998.

Charles F. Meyer is a professor of applied linguistics at the University of Massachusetts at Boston. He has been involved with corpus-based research since 1983, when he completed his doctoral dissertation on punctuation in the Brown Corpus. He is currently coordinator of the International Corpus of English.

Christina Powell is a digital services librarian for the Humanities Text Initiative unit of the Digital Library Production Service at the University of Michigan.

Randi Reppen is an assistant professor of applied linguistics and the director of the program in intensive English in the Department of English at Northern Arizona University. She has taught courses on corpus linguistics and is a coauthor of *Corpus Linguistics: Investigating Language Structure and Use* with Douglas Biber and Susan Conrad.

Rita C. Simpson is a research associate in the English Language Institute at the University of Michigan. She has managed the Michigan Corpus of Academic Spoken English since its beginning in 1997.

John M. Swales is a professor of linguistics and the director of the English Language Institute at the University of Michigan. He has been codirector of the Michigan Corpus of Academic Spoken English since 1997.

Hongyin Tao is an assistant professor of linguistics and Asian studies in the Department of Asian Studies at Cornell University. He has been involved in the Cambridge-Cornell Corpus of Spoken American English since 1998 and has taught courses on corpus linguistics.

Jenia Walter teaches ESL and other subjects in Sacramento and Placerville, California. In 1999, she received her M.A. in TESL from Northern Arizona University, where she worked as a research assistant collecting and systematizing material for the TOEFL 2000 Corpus of Spoken and Written Academic English funded by the Educational Testing Service.

Subject Index

Corpora (*continued*)
TOEFL-2000 Spoken and Written Academic Language Corpus (T2K-SWAL), 9, 48–56
Corpora and language teaching, 182–84, 191–93, 205–8. *See also* Language learning and teaching
Corpus
complete texts, 166
design and compilation, 10, 17–21, 38, 50–56
of newspaper texts, 28, 58–65
parsed, 8, 17, 21–27
part-of-speech tagged, 8, 17, 21–23, 27, 91
sampling and balance, 17–19, 51, 53
size, 1, 50, 52, 59–60, 65
spoken, 7–8, 18, 48–56, 59
Corpus linguistics, 4, 50, 116, 118, 129, 140, 183
pre-computer era, 7
Corpus-based analysis, 113, 150, 161, 167, 175–76, 192, 207, 211–12

Data-driven learning, 3, 12
Demographic variation, 52–53. *See also* Speaker information
Demonstratives, 188–90
Desear, 66
Detachment markers, 5
Disagreement markers, 12, 198–203, 206, 208–9
Discourse
analysis, 4
management, 146
markers, 11, 24–26, 139, 156, 161
mode, 38, 54
practices, 168, 175
pragmatics, 129–30
reflexivity. *See* Metadiscourse
Document Type Definition (DTD), 35, 81–82

English
British vs. American, 23
national and nonnative varieties, 17, 18–19, 21, 28, 30
Epistemic functions, 11, 129–32, 149
Esperar, 66

Factor analysis, 214–15

Fiction, 18, 59
Fillers, 155–57
Footing, 147, 159
Form-function relations, 130–32, 136–39
French, 12, 179–81, 183–90

Genitives, 85
Genre, 145, 198–99
Get, 106
Grammar
and discourse, 102–3
generative, 116
and usage, 102–3
Role and Reference, 117–18, 141
Guys, 151–52

Hacer, 66–67
Header, 30, 35, 53
Hedging, 4, 168, 173–75
Hey, 152–53
HTML, 40–41, 45, 46, 62, 80, 83, 93
tags, 63

Index, 40, 77, 85
Interactivity, 120, 123, 160, 171–73

Just, 167–68

Keyword comparison, 90
KWIC concordance, 21, 23, 41

Language learning and teaching, 3, 10, 12, 101–2, 196, 222. *See also* Teaching materials; Corpora and language teaching
Language testing, 49, 56
Let, 153–54
Lexical phrases, 12, 195–97, 199, 207–9
Like, 23–27
Literary research, use of computers in, 77, 79, 80
Look, 152

Markedness, 109
Markup, 10, 20, 33, 80–83, 85, 90, 95. *See also* Annotation; SGML; Tagging
Metadiscourse, 11, 135–36, 146, 166–67, 169–76
Multidimensional analysis, 12, 56, 211–12, 214–17, 221
Multimillion-word corpora, 1, 9, 58–75

Author Index

Page numbers for chapters in this book are printed in boldface type.